KEY THINKERS IN CHILDHOOD STUDIES

Carmel Smith and Sheila Greene

First published in Great Britain in 2014 by

Policy Press
University of Bristol
6th Floor
Howard House
Queen's Avenue
Clifton
Bristol BS8 1SD
UK
t: +44 (0)117 331 5020
pp-info@bristol.ac.uk
www.policypress.co.uk

North America office:
Policy Press
c/o The University of Chicago Press
1427 East 60th Street
Chicago, IL 60637, USA
t: +1 773 702 7700
f: +1 773 702 9756
sales@press.uchicago.edu
www.press.uchicago.edu

© Policy Press 2014

British Library Cataloguing in Publication Data
A catalogue record for this book is available from the British Library

Library of Congress Cataloging-in-Publication Data
A catalog record for this book has been requested

ISBN 978 1 44730 807 2 hardcover

The right of Carmel Smith and Sheila Greene to be identified as authors of this work has been asserted by them in accordance with the Copyright, Designs and Patents Act 1988.

The statements and opinions contained within this publication are solely those of the authors and not of the University of Bristol or Policy Press. The University of Bristol and Policy Press disclaim responsibility for any injury to persons or property resulting from any material published in this publication.

Policy Press works to counter discrimination on grounds of gender, race, disability, age and sexuality.

Cover design by Policy Press
Front cover: photograph by Rob Bremner
Printed and bound in Great Britain by CPI Group (UK) Ltd, Croydon, CR0 4YY
Policy Press uses environmentally responsible print partners

MIX
Paper from
responsible sources
FSC® C013604

Contents

About the authors

Carmel Smith is Assistant Registrar and Lecturer in Humanities and Social Care at Carlow College, Ireland, and is a Research Associate at the Children's Research Centre, Trinity College Dublin. She has over 30 years' experience of working with children and young people as a social worker, probation officer and children's counsellor in London, Belfast and Dublin.

Sheila Greene is Emeritus Professor of Childhood Research in the School of Psychology, Trinity College Dublin. She co-founded the Children's Research Centre in 1995 (with Robbie Gilligan) and was its Director from 2004-11. Her publications include *The psychological development of girls and women* (Routledge, [2003] 2014) and *Researching children's experience: Approaches and methods* (with Diane Hogan, SAGE, 2005).

Acknowledgements

Most importantly, we want to express our gratitude to the interviewees for their generosity in sharing their personal stories, professional experiences and perspectives. We hope that they are pleased with the final result.

We would like to acknowledge the support of our respective colleagues in the Department of Humanities at Carlow College and in the School of Psychology at Trinity College Dublin. In particular we would like to acknowledge staff and students, past and present, of the Children's Research Centre at Trinity College Dublin, which has been such an important source of stimulation, support and encouragement for us both.

We are grateful to the Department of Children and Youth Affairs, Ireland for the funding provided for the initial doctoral research on which this book is partly based.

Thanks are due to Ruth Kelly and Paul O'Mahony for help with proof reading.

Our appreciation goes also to the staff who we have worked with at Policy Press, including Isobel Bainton, Rebecca Tomlinson, Laura Vickers and Kathryn King, who have been consistently accommodating and helpful.

We are very pleased that Rob Bremner gave permission for the use of his photograph for the cover.

Finally, Carmel would like to thank Rick, Ciara and Niamh Smith and Sheila would like to thank Paul O'Mahony for being so patient and supportive over the duration of this project.

ONE

Introduction

The focus of this book

This book is about Childhood Studies as seen through the eyes of 22 people who have played important roles in shaping the field. They are all people who have made a substantial contribution to theory and research about childhood and children, and who have helped create a body of work that forms a platform for new ways to engage academically with children and children's issues.

Since the establishment of the academic field that has become known as Childhood Studies, many journal articles, text books and edited collections have been published. This book is meant to complement that existing body of work. It is different from the existing publications in that its focus is on the thoughts and experiences of the people who have created some of the most influential published work in the field, many of whom were centrally involved in bringing Childhood Studies into being. The interviews in this book are aimed at providing insights into this movement and into the thinking of some of its leading proponents.

The book consists of 22 interview texts and two authorial chapters. Interviewees are asked about their personal history in relation to research on children and their involvement with Childhood Studies. They are asked for their views on the past achievements of Childhood Studies, its current status and its likely future. The material gathered is unique in that, although all the participants have published extensively, they have not published their reflections on their own experience as academics and researchers and their own views on the status of the field. The interviews did not follow a standard structure although common themes were addressed. This approach was adopted in order to allow the voice of each individual to be heard and to capture unexpected interests and opinions.

The interviewees were selected on the basis of their contributions to the creation of Childhood Studies and their current engagement with issues and activities relevant to the field. The interviewees were also selected with a view to assembling a comprehensive selection of people from different disciplinary and geographic locations. We know that in terms of our sample of key thinkers we will have failed inevitably to satisfy all readers. Certainly there are parts of the world, countries and disciplines that are not represented. This is unfortunate and is an issue that will be dealt with at more length later in this introduction but it is also, in the end, unavoidable. However there is considerable diversity among the 22 interviewees. The diversity of experience and points of view illustrates strongly the fact that there is not just one agreed definition of Childhood Studies, how it originated, how robust it is at the moment and what the future is likely to bring. In this way the book differs from the usual text book approach where, typically, one story is told, and the inevitable contestation and disagreement that exists in any academic field is not revealed.

What is Childhood Studies?

In the past two decades in many countries, numerous academic programmes, from diploma to doctoral level, have been established with the title 'Childhood Studies' or with cognate titles, such as Children's Studies, Childhood Research, Early Childhood Studies or Child and Youth Research. International conferences have been held under these headings and new departments, research centres and journals, dedicated to the field, have been established. But what is Childhood Studies? There are, as will become clear from these interviews, many possible answers, depending on the specific theoretical orientation of the person answering the question. For the purposes of this book and when approaching the interviewees, the authors used a broad and very basic definition, which made few if any assumptions and which was therefore unrestricting. We defined Childhood Studies simply as the academic field or approach that places children and childhood at the centre of analysis.

It is, in part, the multiplicity of approaches to the field that this book seeks to explore. Some writers and thinkers wish to define Childhood Studies more narrowly than others. In this regard, one evident point of disagreement is the manner of addressing the relationship between children and childhood. Some writers assert that their main interest is in childhood as a structural/discursive category and others that their primary interest is in children and perhaps even the promotion of the rights and welfare of children. Very often, in reality, Childhood Studies incorporates a strong focus on children, as opposed to childhood alone, and therefore pays close attention to children's issues, experiences and rights and to methods suited to exploring and understanding children's lives.

Most authors who identify in any way with or write about Childhood Studies see it as a multidisciplinary, or perhaps even interdisciplinary, field of study that emerged in the late 1980s. Prior to this date the academic study of children was located firmly within disciplines such as sociology, psychology, anthropology and education. It is the case, of course, that other disciplines such as history, law, literature, geography and medicine have things to say of importance about children, childhood and children's issues, but Childhood Studies, as originally constituted, was primarily led by researchers who could be located most appropriately within the social sciences. As it has evolved, the contributing disciplines have expanded and vary according to researcher orientation or programme, some emphasising social science, some including the humanities, some including the study of geography, law and human rights. Some Childhood Studies programmes have as their main goal advancing the understanding of children and childhood, whereas some are explicitly interested in preparing students for work with children. The latter is particularly the case in the early childhood studies programmes that aim to train pre-school educators. A related strand of academic activity has resulted in the growth of postgraduate programmes in child rights in Europe and Latin America, many of which draw upon or refer to theories and principles associated with Childhood Studies (Thorne, 2007).

One of the questions this book seeks to address is whether there is an agreed definition or description of Childhood Studies. Where do the boundaries lie? Are there no boundaries except those formed by a shared focus on children and childhood? The other issue that arises immediately is whether the boundary is formed by identification with a particular approach to studying children and childhood, one that arises from commitment to a shared set of principles framing how children and childhood should be construed. Again this is a highly contested issue. Do all those who identify with an interdisciplinary approach to studying children and childhood share the same set of core principles? Do they share some principles but not others? Indeed, are all of those, whose work aligns with what may be seen as the defining principles of Childhood Studies, committed to interdisciplinary study or do they adopt an approach which is primarily single-discipline based? For many writers interdisciplinarity is an essential feature of Childhood Studies (James, 2010). There are, however, some sociologists and psychologists who express dissatisfaction with how their disciplines have approached children and childhood, but remain firmly embedded in their disciplines and see themselves as belonging to 'the new sociology of childhood' or 'critical developmental psychology', rather than Childhood Studies.

A brief history of the study of children and childhood

The beginning of the systematic study of children is often located in the early observational work of Charles Darwin, who was but one of a number of scholars in the mid-nineteenth century, who were convinced that knowledge about children would inform scientists about human origins and evolutionary processes (Morss, 1990; Prout, 2005). Thus knowledge about children was seen as a route to advancing knowledge about the process of evolution, not as of intrinsic value in understanding children themselves, and not because it would lead to better practices in relation to children. Piaget could be seen as belonging in this tradition since his explicit purpose in studying children was to answer epistemological questions about how we come to know the world. Undoubtedly there are scholars today who study development in children for what it can tell us about 'development' more than for what it tells us about children. The interdisciplinary field of 'developmental science' often makes use of empirical studies of children but maintains a focus on the concept of development and the elucidation of the processes associated with it.

As the study of children took hold it soon became evident that the emerging theory and knowledge in relation to children could be used to structure new practices, whether in the area of education or social welfare and management. Thus for many social and behavioural scientists from the turn of the twentieth century onwards a commitment to a scientific understanding of children's behaviour and competencies and how their lives were shaped was not fuelled solely by a desire for knowledge for its own sake or for a better understanding of children and their life experience, but by a desire to intervene in or even dictate how children's lives *should* be shaped. Child psychology in particular soon acquired considerable confidence in its own methods and conclusions and was widely accepted as the foundational scholarly discipline and evidence base for policy in relation to childcare, child welfare and education (Cairns, 1983).

Developmental psychology (and its related disciplines, child psychology and child development) is generally recognised as having been the dominant and therefore defining academic discourse in relation to children in the twentieth century. From its establishment as an academic discipline at the end of the nineteenth and beginning of the twentieth century (Kessen, 1990) developmental psychology came to both reflect and dictate a new 'scientific' perspective on children and their management. Psychology in general espoused the natural science approach to knowledge, identifying itself as 'the science of behaviour' and its methods as those of the more well-established physical and biological sciences. Thus psychologists aspired to establish the laws of – or, at the very least, the principles of – behaviour. They eschewed the subjective by and large and focused on what could be observed and measured. All told, they adopted the perspective and methods of positivism. For psychologists, positivism entails the belief that human behaviour can best be understood as a natural phenomenon, which is measurable and is itself the product of other observable and measurable processes. Additionally, development was seen as the predictable unfolding of a biologically, and, ultimately, genetically, determined process (Morss, 1990).

In other social science disciplines, such as sociology and anthropology, children were at the margins rather than at the centre of academic interest. They were often subsumed into the family or the household and rarely seen as of interest in their own right. As with psychology, where children entered the discourse the main interest was in how they come to be fitted for life as an adult member of their society. For both sociology and anthropology the assumption was that in order to enter society or culture the child had to be shaped into a suitable form through the process of 'socialisation'. The structural functionalism of Parsons (1964) was very influential and for most of the twentieth century socialisation was the main concept used in relation to children and their function within the social or cultural world. Anne Marie Ambert was one of the first sociologists to comment on the lack of interest in children in her own discipline. She notes that socialisation is not really about children at all but about the process of shaping them into adults and she also famously remarked that 'one does not become a famous household name in sociology by studying children' (1986, 24).

The beginnings of Childhood Studies

From the literature to date it is clear that the beginnings of Childhood Studies is just that, multiple beginnings or strands of thought coming together in different ways, in different locations. The history is written differently depending on the perspective of the writer. Casting more light on this history and its inevitable entanglement with individual biographies and perspectives is one of the aims of this book.

Philippe Aries' book *Centuries of childhood* is often cited as a turning point in prompting a new academic interest in children and childhood. Ironically, for Childhood Studies scholars this was a work from an historian not a social scientist (although there are some historians who would not flinch at being labelled social scientists). Aries' book certainly heralded a new interest on the part of historians in childhood and its historical meanings and manifestations. Historians, previously preoccupied by grand affairs of state, were beginning to uncover, and find interest in, evidence of the daily lives of ordinary people. Cultural and social history acquired a new respectability. The work of writers, such as Aries (1962) and De Mause (1974), which had an influence beyond their discipline, fed into the growing awareness of the historical nature of childhood. Their work questioned the account of childhood as natural and fixed and replaced it with one of multiple representations across time and circumstance. This new awareness was augmented by cross-cultural data from anthropologists and others, again shaking the notion that childhood was a fixed and universal phenomenon (Mead, 1961).

Towards the latter half of the twentieth century, in the spirit of the post-modern suspicion of all taken for granted sources of authority, a critical eye was turned on psychology (and within psychology, on child development), as a hegemonic and potentially harmful discipline. Psychology was ripe for deconstruction as the demolition of old certainties and hitherto unchallenged professional claims on authority became widespread (Greene, 1999). Foucault (1980) pinpointed developmental psychology as one of the significant disciplinary technologies that served to codify knowledge and shape political and public discourse.

In the 1990s in the UK a number of sociologists and anthropologists including Jenks (1982; 1990), James and Prout ([1990] 1997) and Mayall (1994) started to question both the approach to children and childhood which was typical of their own discipline, and the claims of child psychology. Similar movements took place on the continent of Europe where Alanen proposed a new approach to sociological thinking about childhood in 1988 and a group of sociologists formed to develop the 'Childhood as a social phenomenon programme' (Qvortrup et al, 1994; 2009). In the USA sociologists had started writing about children in their real world settings (Thorne, 1987; Corsaro, 1985). These sociologists noted that sociology had neglected children and childhood as a topic of central concern and that, where the discipline did deal with children, the conceptual approach was seriously flawed. In the USA in 1991 Gertrud Lenzer published a paper entitled 'Is there sufficient interest to establish a sociology of children?'. However, while addressing this question to fellow sociologists, she also argued for the value of 'a genuinely interdisciplinary multidisciplinary new field of study' (1991, 8).

In the first chapter of their edited book, *Constructing and reconstructing childhood: Contemporary issues in the sociological study of childhood*, Prout and James outlined 'the key features of the new paradigm' for childhood sociology (James and Prout, 1990). The 'new sociology of childhood' defined itself not only in terms of the inadequacies of sociology but in terms of the damaging claims of the psychology of child development. In a later work, James, Jenks and Prout (1998) accuse psychology and psychoanalysis of preaching the doctrine of 'the naturally developing child', noting that 'it is within this model that we encounter the unholy alliance between the human sciences and human nature. Psychology... firmly colonised childhood in a pact with medicine, education and government agencies' (James et al, 1998, 17). As for Piaget, they conclude that his work 'instilled a deep-seated positivism and rigid empiricism into our contemporary understandings of the child' (1998, 19). The key features of 'the emergent paradigm for...childhood sociology' as proclaimed by Prout and James ([1990] 1997, 8) were: 1. that childhood is understood as a social construction; 2. that childhood is a variable of social analysis; 3. that children's social relationships and cultures are worthy of study in their own right; 4. that children must be seen as active in the construction and determination of their own lives, the lives of those around them and of the societies in which they live; 5. that ethnography is particularly useful methodology for the study of childhood; 6. that childhood is a phenomenon in relation to which the double hermeneutic of the social sciences is acutely present, that is to say, to proclaim a new paradigm of childhood sociology is also to engage in and respond to the process of reconstructing childhood in society.

In the second edition of *Constructing and reconstructing childhood* (published in 1997) James and Prout comment that 'the traditional consignment of childhood to the margins of the social sciences or its primary location within the fields of developmental psychology is beginning to change'. They add that the first edition of the book had 'posed a challenge to what we then characterised as the dominant and dominating conceptual pair of socialisation and development' (p ix). Two key features of the new sociology of childhood were that children were not passive recipients of socialisation but active social actors and agents and that childhood was not a natural given but a social construction, varying in its characteristics across location and time. Since these positions were ones which resonated with scholars outside sociology it was not long before the fledgling discipline became re-labelled, by some but not all of its practitioners, as 'the new social studies of childhood' or 'Childhood Studies' (Christensen and Prout, 2005; Woodhead, 2003).

At an early stage different approaches within the new sociology of childhood were evident. In 1998, James, Jenks and Prout identified four main theoretical positions: the socially constructed child, the tribal child, the minority group child and the social structural child. James and Prout remark that these 'reflect not only different methods and approaches to the [*sic*] childhood studies – some emphasising childhood as a conceptual space, while others engage with children as social actors – but they also represent differing positions with respect to the broader sociological questions of universalism/particularism and structure/agency' (1997, x).

During the same time period psychologists were becoming more vociferous in criticism of their own discipline. Tracing the first rumblings of dissatisfaction of psychologists with the assumptions of mainstream developmental psychology is not easy and indeed there have probably always been dissenters and figures within psychology who either explicitly opposed the approach taken by developmental psychologists or themselves represented an alternative tradition. An historical perspective reveals the fact that developmental psychology was never a unified discipline. Indeed, from early on there were clear divisions between those who were maturationists, those who were Freudians, those who were behaviourists and so forth. Certainly in relation to psychology's adherence to positivism, there were early dissenting voices, some of them very well known. As Kessen (1979) discusses, two such dissenters were William James and John Dewey.

One of the most important sources of dissent came from those psychologists who focused on children's cultural contexts and on how children became members of their cultural community. These psychologists were influenced by the thinking of Vygotsky, who, unlike Piaget, emphasised the social roots of knowledge and the role of the cultural context. Vygotsky wrote at the beginning of the twentieth century although most of this work was not translated until the latter part of the century and his influence was not strong until the 1970s (Vygotsky, 1978). Vygotsky was quite clear about the purpose of child psychology and was stubbornly at odds with the positivist goal adopted by most western child psychologists. He argued that the task of psychology is not to 'reveal the eternal child,' the task is to discover 'the historical child' (Vygotsky, cited by Rogoff, 2003, 10).

By the 1970s there were increasing signs of disaffection with traditional positivist-empiricist approaches and methods in developmental psychology. This was crystallised in the following statement from an eminent developmental psychologist, William Kessen: 'It might be wise for us developmental psychologists to peer into the heart of the positivistic nightmare – that the child is essentially and eternally a cultural invention and that the variety of the child's definition is not the removable error of an incomplete science' (Kessen, 1979, 815).

In the UK, a number of psychologists appeared in print who took a radical, critical perspective on their discipline. They included Richards and Light (1986), Walkerdine (1993), Burman (1994) and Woodhead (1999). In Australia, Bradley (1986) and in New Zealand, Morss (1990) joined the mounting criticism of 'developmentalism' and traditional developmental psychology. Some of these psychologists recognised an alignment between their views and those promulgated by the new sociology, particularly in relation to the plurality of childhoods and the importance of cultural context but also in relation to the dawning interest in children's experience and in seeing children holistically and as persons (Greene, 2006).

   Although the origins of Childhood Studies were in anthropology and sociology, it quickly became clear that scholars from other disciplines identified with the approach to Childhood Studies as set out very explicitly by James and Prout in the UK or exemplified by the work of other pioneers such as Corsaro in the USA and Qvortrup in Scandanavia. As is the case with many new ideas a number of scholars came to similar conclusions at the same time. They were, after all, influenced by the same academic fashions and social movements.

Childhood Studies as an interdisciplinary field

One of the issues explored in this book is interdisciplinarity. For many, one of the defining features of Childhood Studies is that it is interdisciplinary. Some may concede that it is more appropriately classified as multidisciplinary, in that there has been a failure to integrate disciplines and methods to the extent that a truly interdisciplinary enterprise deserves. Both 'interdisciplinary' and 'multidisciplinary' are somewhat vexed terms, with no fully accepted distinctive meanings. In reality they are often used interchangeably. The term 'transdisciplinary' has also been introduced. What does emerge from this dispute about disciplinary mixing and merging is that it is not an easy thing to do. Liu comments that interdisciplinary study is 'the most seriously underthought critical pedagogical and institutional concept in the modern academy' (1989, 743). However there certainly are barriers to interdisciplinarity that have to do with academic structures and their resistance to change as much as the intrinsic difficulty of forming a new coherent discipline out of two or more disparate elements. Nevertheless there are several examples of robust new disciplines in the natural sciences, in technology and in the humanities and social sciences. So, for example, we have new departments and centres of neuroscience, bioinformatics, medieval studies, ethnic studies. It has been argued that the main breakthroughs in science and scholarship in general will occur through interdisciplinary initiatives, yet, at the same time, traditional disciplines are firmly embedded in most universities and tend to resist their own dismantlement and the establishment of potentially threatening new departments and centres. Even those who are committed to and excited by interdisciplinary work might agree with Moran when he says that the very idea of interdisciplinarity can only be understood in a disciplinary context (2010, ix). There are many who see a very firm footing in a single discipline as a necessary foundation before venturing into the uncharted waters of interdisciplinary engagement. Esteem indicators within academe remain firmly single discipline-based. Some interdisciplinary disciplines seemed to have established strong new roots, such as Biochemistry, but some have struggled and may have tenuous purchase, flourishing for a few years and then fading away.

   Whether Childhood Studies is an intrinsically multidisciplinary or interdisciplinary field or whether its core goals can best be advanced through the traditional disciplines is still a matter for discussion. Some question whether the idea of interdisciplinarity is more a matter of rhetoric than reality. Thorne comments that many of the academic programmes in Childhood Studies (and child rights) offer what can best be described as *'pluridisciplinary* knowledge – arrayed for picking and choosing and leaving it to students to try and make sense of the whole' (Thorne, 2007, 148). In a 2010 editorial in *Children's Geographies*, James expresses concern about what she sees as the retreat back into disciplinary bases and remarks on the 'fissions… developing within this commitment to interdisciplinarity' (James, 2010).

In 2005 Prout commented that 'after two decades of extraordinarily creative effort, leading to new theoretical, methodological and empirical insights, the new sociology of childhood is increasingly troubled'. He suggests some solutions mainly based on the dismantling of old unproductive dichotomies. He calls for Childhood Studies to move into a new phase where it relinquishes the oppositions that were so central in defining the new social studies of childhood when it first emerged. One of the key oppositions was to the view of the child as a natural entity. In emphasising the role of culture in the construction of childhoods, the material and the biological have been left out of account. Prout suggests that the 'hybridity' of childhood be fully recognised – a clear call for an inclusive interdisciplinarity. Thorne (2007) calls for mutual dialogue between the new social studies of childhood and the old enemy, child development, in order to end the 'continuing wall of silence' and for an opening of Childhood Studies to the theorising of age and temporality. More recently, Alanen (2012) comments on the continuing structural, cultural and knowledge barriers that 'make cross-disciplinary work onerous and discourage cross-disciplinary work among researchers' (p 421) and argues that 'disciplinarianism and interdisciplinarianism' are both necessary. Childhood scholars, to her mind, should continue to make strong connections with their base disciplines (p 421).

Timing and relevance of this book

One aim of this book is to capture a moment in time. As a distinct field of study Childhood Studies has been in existence for approximately 25–30 years, depending on one's opinion about how and when it became established. Many of the people who were centrally involved in establishing the parameters and core principles associated with Childhood Studies have now retired from academic life or are about to do so. They are in a good position to reflect on how and why Childhood Studies emerged, what has been achieved within the field, what they see as its defining features, whether it has met expectations, what remains to be achieved and whether they are optimistic or pessimistic about the future of Childhood Studies.

From this point of view the following examination of Childhood Studies through the eyes of some of its most important exponents and champions can be seen as having relevance beyond the precincts of Childhood Studies. The appearance of a range of interdisciplinary or 'area' studies has been a characteristic of the academic landscape in recent decades. Within the social sciences the new fields of study have typically taken as their focus a social group or social issue that has been previously neglected or misrepresented by traditional disciplines. Thus we see, in and around the 1970s and 1980s, the emergence of women's and gender studies, ethnic and racial studies, disability studies, black studies and so on. The trajectory of each of these disciplines is different and some inevitably flourish more than others. The rise of Childhood Studies can be and has been explained as a function of its time – the late twentieth century. Its current status and its future trajectory are also subject to the influence of external social and political movements and the internal political environment of the academy. Currently, for example, some scholars assert that what we need is more study of intersectionality, not disciplines focused on one defining social characteristic such as age, gender, race, class and so on (McCall, 2005). Histories of academic structures and priorities reveal that the pursuit of knowledge follows a rocky road fraught with power struggles. The structure of the academy is not set in stone. Will Childhood Studies continue to flourish or is it an idea that has had its time and now will fade away? What determines its ongoing health or decline? These are questions addressed in some of the interviews in this book. Children will always be with us but that does not mean that the interdisciplinary academic study of children and childhood will establish a firm hold in the academy and garner the kind of respect and resources granted to currently more favoured disciplines.

A second major aim of the study was to elicit the kind of opinions and experiences of researchers and scholars that are often hidden from view. The interviews have a personal focus and emphasise personal biographies and personal viewpoints, arguably extremely important determinants of how any field of study is initiated and maintained, but they rarely emerge in print. Most academic publications, even those which are avowedly reflexive, do not give much scope to the individual's views on the nature of their own personal engagement with their chosen field of study or to their personal context – the challenges they confront and the challenges within their discipline. Many, but not all, Childhood Studies researchers use qualitative methods that promote reflexivity or recognise the value of making their own position clear. Nonetheless the data revealed by one to one interviews are often very different in content and tone from the kind of reflexive position statements typically offered in academic publications.

Selection of the interviewees

A primary criterion for the selection of the 22 individuals whose interviews form the basis of this book was that they had made a significant contribution to the field of Childhood Studies, broadly defined. We decided to push the boundary of Childhood Studies a little beyond where it is most commonly drawn in order to be as inclusive as possible in terms of discipline and focus. That said, there are many people reading this book who would draw the boundary in a different way and would make a different selection of interviewees. Certainly the criterion 'having made a significant contribution' is highly subjective and problematic. We did confer with many colleagues as to whom they thought were the key thinkers in Childhood Studies, but the final decisions were our own. As it turned out, only one person whom we approached did not want to be interviewed for the book. There were many others whom we did not approach but whom we would have liked to have included based on their undoubted contribution. In a project such as this, space is obviously a major restriction. We were also concerned to select a mix of people in terms of discipline, theoretical and methodological approach and geographical location.

There is only one interview with a person who was born and raised in a majority world country, Brazil (although several interviewees have lived and worked in majority world countries). This a reflection of the reality that in the making of the new field of Childhood Studies there were very few researchers from outside the minority world. It also reflects the lack on the part of the authors of a capacity to read research conducted outside the English-speaking academy. That said, several English-speaking countries such as Canada, South Africa, Australia and New Zealand are not represented. Again this is largely a matter of space, combined with the reality that the impetus for the new approach to studying children and childhood centred on the UK, the Nordic countries and the USA.

Perhaps another collection of interviews from new voices around the globe is needed?

In the final analysis we have interviews from scholars based in the UK, Denmark, Norway, Brazil, Finland, USA, Malaysia and Ireland. Their disciplinary backgrounds encompass history, psychology, anthropology, sociology, social work, communication studies and more. As the interviews reveal, many started out from an unexpected disciplinary base, have a mixed disciplinary background or resist identification with any one traditional academic discipline.

Elite interviewing

The approach to interviewing that the authors adopted falls most readily into the category of 'research with elite groups'. In his classic text on this subject, Lewis Dexter (1970, republished in 2006) acknowledges the discomfort associated with using the term 'elite', with its connotations of superiority. Nonetheless the term has widespread currency and it makes sense to use the term which is commonly used and generally best understood. Odenhal and Shaw note that while social scientists do acknowledge and write about elites to some extent, they more frequently 'investigate those without influence, over whom power is exercised rather than society's decision makers' (2001, 299). Gillham suggest that participants in research with elite groups are usually experts in positions of authority and influence, by virtue of their expert knowledge and experience (2005). The interviewees in this book fit this definition. They are all without exception current or previous holders of professorial university posts, almost all being holders of Chairs. Additionally they are widely published and have held positions of influence, such as being members of the editorial boards of journals, presidents of professional societies and so on.

We include biographies of all participants to aid the reader in understanding the history and positioning of each interviewee.

The study of academic elites is not as popular as the study of some other categories of elites such as business leaders, politicians, Nobel Prize winners and such like but there have been a few examples (such as Wiles et al, 2006). Stephens (2007) suggests that academics have a number of distinctive characteristics, the most obvious being their willingness to engage articulately and at length on topics that interest them. There is no problem getting them to talk! They are also likely to have a heightened appreciation of research and the potential value of contributing to a research process that catches their imagination.

Wiles et al (2006) suggest a number of approaches that may be considered good practice, such as giving the interviewees the opportunity to edit their own transcripts to provide some reassurance that they have the ultimate say about what might appear in print. In some research with elites, confidentiality may be a major issue but this did not arise in this situation since the interviewees' public recognition and profile is considered one of the main points of interest. Thus all interviewees were made aware from an early stage that a condition of being a participant was to be named. Such exposure has risks attached and we appreciate the openness of all participants, who have agreed to expose their ideas and their personal stories to public gaze. For them to agree to having their interviews made public, it was important to reassure the participants that nothing would be published without their agreement. Typically interviews lasted for about one and a half to two hours. Some interviewees were interviewed twice, having been participants in Carmel Smith's earlier doctoral research, which covered topics overlapping with those covered in the main interviews for this book (Smith, 2011). All interviews were taped and fully transcribed by the interviewer (16 interviews were conducted by Carmel Smith and six by Sheila Greene). Interview transcripts were returned to the interviewees for checking. At this point they could excise, change or add clarifying material. The authors then cut each interview down to about 4,400 words and returned the shortened transcript to the interviewee for further checking and the addition of references, where required. All interviewees also checked and approved the biographical pieces.

All interviews were conducted in a one to one setting where the interviewee was comfortable, typically in their home or in their workplace. Two were conducted via Skype and one by Skype messaging.

Topics covered in the interviews

As stated, the interviews were loosely structured but there was a core list of issues to be addressed, as follows:

- How the interviewee came to conduct academic research with or about children

- Their disciplinary base and views on the interdisciplinary nature of Childhood Studies
- How they explain the emergence of Childhood Studies
- What they see as the core features of Childhood Studies
- What reflexivity means in their practice
- What methods they use and promote
- What they think of the current state of the field of Childhood Studies
- How they see the future of Childhood Studies

Although all the above issues were raised in all interviews, other questions were also raised and the same questions were not addressed to all interviewees. Given the diversity of interviewees this would not have made sense since, for example, some interviewees had spent a lot of time conducting empirical research with children, while others had confined themselves to theory or secondary data analysis. So the questions were adjusted to fit the profile of each participant and to elicit the most interesting responses. Furthermore, if the interviewee raised new topics or issues the interviewer went along with them, thus adopting the method associated with qualitative interviewing, where there is typically a commitment to letting new and possibly surprising material emerge. An effort has been made to capture, as far as possible, the flow and flavour of the discussions that took place. This informal, conversational style provides an alternative to the more formal academic style of most conference papers, books and journal articles in the field. Additionally, in editing the interviews, selections were made in terms of the perceived interest and value of the statements made, not in terms of recording the main message nested in the interviewee's response to every question addressed to them. Thus each edited interview is different, not only in content but in structure. We emphasise that the interview transcripts are therefore not intended to reflect every interviewee's views on the same questions.

A collaborative approach to data generation enabled a high degree of trust and rapport to be established between the authors as interviewers and the interviewees. The generosity of all participants in terms of their time and their engagement with the cutting and editing of the transcribed interviews is much appreciated. In the final chapter of the book we summarise the material covered in the interviews under the following themes: the history of the field of Childhood Studies; researching children and childhood in the field of Childhood Studies (including sections on the biography of the researcher, different methodological approaches, the topic of agency and parallels between women's studies and Childhood Studies); and the status of the current field and possible future directions.

In conclusion

We do not set out in this book to try to answer all the questions that are relevant to Childhood Studies, as it was, as it is and as it might be in the future. We do want to highlight, by means of the reflections of experienced and esteemed figures in this field, some possible answers and ways forward. We also wish to highlight the multiplicities of perspectives that a label can encompass and the complexities involved in making a new academic field and then sustaining it. There has been a number of recent reflections on the field of Childhood Studies such as the papers included in the *Palgrave handbook of Childhood Studies* (2009) and *A history of the sociology of childhood* (Mayall, 2013). It is evidently time for a critical review of the field and it hoped that this text will contribute a rich source of ideas and stimulus for debate.

What resonates, for us, throughout this set of interviews is the interviewees' commitment to scholarship and their commitment to the value, for children and society, of a greater understanding of childhood, childhoods, children and how we choose to think about them.

References

Alanen, L, 1988, Rethinking childhood, *Acta Sociologica* 31, 53–67

Alanen, L, 2012, Disciplinarity, interdisciplinarity and Childhood Studies, *Childhood* 4, 419–22

Ambert, A-M, 1986, Sociology of Sociology: The place of children in North American Sociology, in P Adler, P Adler (eds) *Sociological studies of child development*, Greenwich, CT: JAI Press, 1, 11–31

Aries, P, 1962, *Centuries of childhood: A social history of family life*, New York: Knopf

Borstelmann, LJ, 1983, Children before psychology, in PH Mussen (ed) *Handbook of child psychology*, *vol 1* (3rd edn), New York: Wiley and Sons

Bradley, B, 1986, *Visions of infancy*, Cambridge: Polity Press

Burman, E, 1994, *Deconstructing developmental psychology*, London: Routledge

Cairns, RB, 1983, The emergence of developmental psychology, in PH Mussen (ed) *Handbook of Child Psychology*, *vol 1* (3rd edn), New York: Wiley and Sons

Christensen, P, Prout, A, 2005, Anthropological and sociological perspectives on the study of children, in S Greene, D Hogan (eds) *Researching children's experience: Approaches and methods*, London: SAGE

Corsaro, W, 1985, *Friendship and peer culture in the early years*, Norwood, NJ: Ablex

De Mause, L, 1974, *The history of childhood*, New York: The Psychohistory Press

Dexter, LA, 1970, *Elite and specialized interviewing*, University of Essex: CEPR Press, 2006

Foucault, M, 1980, *Power/Knowledge*, New York: Pantheon

Gillham, B., 2005, *Research interviewing*, Maidenhead: Open University Press

Greene, S, 1999, Child development: Old themes, new directions, in M Woodhead, D Faulkner, K Littleton (eds) *Making sense of social development*, London: Routledge

Greene, S, 2006, Child psychology: Taking account of children at last?, *Irish Journal of Psychology* 27, 8–15

James, A, 2010, Interdisciplinarity – for better or worse, *Children's Geographies* 8, 215–16

James, A, Prout, A (eds), [1990] 1997, *Constructing and reconstructing childhood: Contemporary issues in the sociological study of childhood* (2nd edn), London: Routledge/Falmer

James, A, Jenks, C, Prout, A, 1998, *Theorizing childhood*, Cambridge: Polity Press

Jenks, C, 1982, *The sociology of childhood: Essential readings*, London: Batsford

Jenks, C, 1990, *Childhood*, London: Routledge

Kessen, W, 1979, The American child and other cultural inventions, *American Psychologist* 34, 815–20

Kessen, W, 1990, *The rise and fall of development*, Worcester, MA: Clark University Press

Lenzer, G, 1991, Is there sufficient interest to establish a sociology of children?, *Footnotes of the American Sociological Association* 19, 8

Liu, L, 1989, The power of formalism, *English Literary History* 56, 721–77

McCall, L, 2005, The complexity of intersectionality, *Signs* 30, 1771–800

Mayall, B (ed), 1994, *Children's childhoods: Observed and experienced*, London: Falmer Press

Mayall, B, 2013, *A history of the sociology of childhood*, London: Institute of Education

Mead, M, 1961, *Coming of age in Samoa*, Harmondsworth: Penguin

Moran, J, 2010, *Interdisciplinarity* (2nd edn), London: Routledge

Morss, J, 1990, *The biologising of childhood: Developmental Psychology and the Darwinian myth*, Hove: Lawrence Erlbaum

Odendahl, T, Shaw, AM, 2001, Interviewing elites, in JF Gubrium, J Holstein (eds) *Handbook of interview research: context and method*, London: SAGE

Parsons, T (1964) *The social system*, London: Free Press.

Prout, A, 2005, *The future of childhood: Toward the interdisciplinary study of children*, London: Routledge Falmer

Prout, A, James, A, [1990] 1997, A new paradigm for the sociology of childhood? Provenance, promise and problems, in A James, A Prout (eds) (2nd edn) *Constructing and reconstructing childhood: Contemporary issues in the sociological study of childhood*, London: Falmer Press

Qvortrup, J, Bardy, M, Sgritta, G, Wintersberger, H, 1994, *Childhood matters: Social theory, practice and politics*, Aldershot: Avebury Press

Qvortrup, J, Corsaro, WA, Honig, M-S (eds), 2009, *The Palgrave handbook of Childhood Studies*, London: Palgrave Macmillan

Richards, M, Light, P (eds), 1986, *Children of social worlds*, Cambridge: Polity Press

Rogoff, B., 2003, *The cultural nature of human development*, Oxford: Oxford University Press

Smith, C, 2011, *Qualitative research with children: The perspectives of elite researchers*, PhD thesis, University of Dublin, Ireland

Stephens, N, 2007, Collecting data from elites and ultra elites: Telephone and face-to-face interviews with macroeconomists, *Qualitative Research* 7, 203–16

Thorne, B, 1987, Re-visioning women and social change: Where are the children?, *Gender and Society* 1, 85–109

Thorne, B, 2007, Crafting the interdisciplinary field of Childhood Studies, *Childhood*, 147–52

Vygotsky, L, 1978, *Mind in society*, Cambridge, MA: Harvard University Press

Walkerdine, V, 1993, Beyond developmentalism, *Theory and Psychology* 3, 451–69

Wiles, R, Charles, V, Crow, C, Heath, S, 2006, Researching researchers: Lessons from research ethics, *Qualitative Research* 6, 283–99

Woodhead, M, 1999, Reconstructing developmental psychology: Some first steps, *Children and Society* 13, 3–19

Woodhead, M, 2003, *The case for Childhood Studies*, Dublin: Children's Research Centre, Trinity College Dublin

TWO

Leena Alanen

Leena Alanen is Professor in Early Childhood Education and Docent in the Sociology of Childhood at the University of Jyväskylä, Finland. She has been active in developing Childhood Studies since the 1980s through her research and as a member of the International Sociological Association (ISA) where she was President of the Board of Research Committee 53: Sociology of Childhood (1998–2002), and the European Sociological Association (ESA). Professor Alanen's research interests centre on the social theory of childhood, early education, generational relations and intersectionality. She has been involved in numerous national and international research projects, including *Childhood as a social phenomenon* (1987–92) and *COST A19 children's welfare* (2001–6). Her national projects include *Children as agents of their health and well-being, Regimes of childhood and children's welfare, and Children's welfare and (new) forms of governance.* Professor Alanen's current funded project is *Intergenerational partnerships: emergent forms for promoting children's welfare* (2010–13). Her numerous publications include *Conceptualising child–adult relations* (ed. with Mayall, Routledge Falmer, 2001), 'Generational order' in *The Palgrave handbook of Childhood Studies* (Qvortrup et al, Palgrave, 2009) and *Fields and capitals: Constructing local life* (ed. with Martti Siisiäinen, University of Jyväskylä, 2011). She is an Editor of *Childhood: A Journal of Global Research.*

Sheila Greene So, Leena, could you talk me through how you came to work in this area and about the beginnings of your career?

Leena Alanen It is a long story. I started my university studies in mathematics and statistics and philosophy and only later, after three years, I went, just out of interest, to take a basic sociology course. It was in the time of the student movement. I had friends and colleagues in the student movement and some of them were sociologists.

I remember a get-together with my student colleagues who were ready to make a revolution about anything else, but not on childhood. When I kind of introduced children they did not think there was anything wrong with children and childhood. And I thought, 'Haven't they even read Philippe Aries and his history of childhood, don't they know about it?' Their idea was that childhood should be happy and that they had had a happy childhood, more or less, and so then that can't be an issue. For them, class was an issue, or gender, because we were socialist feminists at that time.

SG What made you think that way about children, do you think?

LA It wasn't until the 1970s that I did my first big project with children and that was the first time I had to deal professionally with children and childhood. This was before that, in the 1960s, seven or eight years before, it came out of my own life story, my own life experience.

SG Because you had had these experiences yourself, moving from country to country and from language to language?

LA Yes. In my early years I lived in Canada and returned to Finland at the age of seven, without knowing any Finnish or anything about life in Finland. My own family was a quite normal middle-class family, a well-educated family. It was not a question of having a bad childhood, it was a 'normal' childhood but the experiences of crossing borders, entering new social worlds as a child made me think that nothing in a child's life is necessarily simple. It may have been simple when we lived in Canada but it certainly wasn't simple to enter the different world of childhood in Finland. This came back to me when I wrote my dissertation, although before that I had already done three projects dealing with children. So it was just a reminder, a flashback of my memories. My student colleagues could not understand what I was talking about, why is it an issue?

SG Did you start looking for theories to support your interest?

LA I did my second master's thesis in education at the end of the 1970s (I had done one in sociology earlier on a completely different topic) and I chose to do an ideology critique of the concept of socialisation, a history of the concept of socialisation from the time of Emile Durkheim and how the concept was shipped to America and after the war came back completely different – very Americanised. So I went through the history of the concept and then, as the Germans say, looked at the Gedankenform. There were a few articles that I found, but not much. I was reading in German on ideology critique so I had the method and I just applied the method to socialisation. I covered the American work and continental sociology such as Weber and Durkheim, but mainly Durkheim. Marx of course, I went through the classics. I had a very nice supervisor for my Master's thesis, she more or less let me study whatever I wanted. She was just happy that I was doing something different to the normal students [laughs]. So that was that. Then it became topical to try to find concepts for grasping what childhood is, how to deal with childhood and children, if socialisation is not good enough. At first, in what became the sociology of childhood it was critique before anything else came up. I remember well that in 1986 I was at the International Sociology Association meeting in India and looked through the very thick book of abstracts to see if there was anything on children or childhood and I think I found Jens Qvortrup, but I didn't meet him there, it was such a huge place. I gave my paper on the critique of socialisation in a family sociology group because that came closest to what I was doing.

SG And what response did you get?

LA I had copies of my paper, 20 or 30, and all of them went, but nobody came to me and said that they had been thinking similar things, but how would they? It was family sociology and very adult-centred, as it still is. Children are something parents have. They are not children who have parents [both laugh]. I was then invited to a conference in Trondheim, the first big conference organised by the Norwegian Centre for Child Research. I never checked why I was asked, maybe Jens found out what I was doing? I was invited to present for a smaller audience, the same stuff on socialisation, and then people came to me and said 'Are you going to publish this and can we publish it?' It was published in the conference proceedings but also in the *Social Studies of Children*, a book series. So that was the first signal that there were people out there who were interested. Someone said to me 'This is something new, something I have never heard before'. But that was 1986 and already there had been the first Nordic seminar in Helsinki and then in 1987 we started the 'Childhood as a social phenomenon' project. In 1986 also I contacted Barrie Thorne, whom I did not know. I saw an announcement in an American sociology journal that the first Cheryl Miller Lecture was going to be given by Professor Barrie Thorne on 'Where are the children?' I sent her a letter – this was the time before emails [both laugh] and I said 'I am doing the same kind of thing and I would so much like to have a copy of your paper'. She replied that it was to be published in *Gender and Society* and that is where I read it.[1]

SG She was influenced by feminism as you were, too.

LA Yes, in my student years I became a Marxist feminist and was also very much in contact with Marxist feminists in Germany. This is also where I got this Gedankenform, this idea about how to relate the forms of thought, the categories and concepts in which we think and how they relate to the wider context. My first contact with feminism, however, was as an activist. I was an activist when I was a student in Helsinki but it was not until later that I read for the first time that feminist studies are in academia, that science can be done here, not just activism. That is where I got the idea of thinking about feminism as a parallel to the situation of childhood. It was a gender issue and a generation issue; and generation was *the* issue in the 'Childhood as a social phenomenon' project. At that time there were not many people thinking about childhood. In the project we were sociologists, and sociology then was in the sad situation that it didn't know how to think about childhood.

SG Right, you just had socialisation.

LA And that was not good enough. There were these other ideas. Jens Qvortrup had already written an article in 1985, and I had read it of course, in which he introduced the generation concept.

That project was enormously successful and productive. It opened our eyes, not just to generation but to all kinds of new concepts derived from generation like generational order, which I related to gender order. First, I took it like a parallel and then I looked at it more closely in terms of what it meant.[2] How does it make sense? It is not a simple parallel, because children become adults, but women rarely become men or men women. So this is a major difference. Academic studies on childhood are not driven by children, they are done by adults, whereas feminist studies are conducted by adults. Anyway it was a huge leap forward and so inspiring.

SG Was that an international project or was it mainly Nordic?

LA There were researchers from 18 countries involved, mainly European. Qvortrup, Sgritta and Wintersberger, all three initially planned the project when they were coordinators for a European project on the family. They were wondering aloud, especially Jens, 'Where are the children?'

SG Another question you asked was 'Where are the children in feminist debates?'

LA Yes that's why I was so interested in Barrie Thorne's lecture, but I think our views were not too similar.

SG So there were differences between your approaches?

LA Yes I think so and it has something to do with the differences between American feminism and European feminism. Ours was much more Marxist and structural. Also it must be something to do with Barrie's approach to doing sociology. Mine was much more structural. Also the 'Childhood as a social phenomenon' project was meant to adopt a structural approach. So it was not about the micro-level, about what children struggle with daily and all that. It was asking 'What is childhood? Childhood is a structural element in society.

SG So your interest is more in childhood than in children?

LA Yes; but there is no childhood without children, of course. There is a link and you have to work out the link.

SG Indeed. So in terms of this new paradigm, have you any other thoughts on how it evolved?

LA Well I personally know best the path that I have taken. But of course I have read about anthropologists and sociologists in the UK organising a series of meetings out of which the 1990 James and Prout book emerged. The book had a much more anthropological orientation and that would explain why there was a micro-level focus on children as social actors and meaning makers, children's experiences, how children think, how competent children are. To see an injustice in not recognising children's many competences was a bit different. There you have to step out of the micro-level and look at the society and the contexts where children are subject to injustice and inequality. People like James and Prout were looking at childhood but they were more influenced by new methodologies and epistemologies like social constructionism, the idea that childhood, too, is socially constructed. I would say that most of the interest was on the phenomenological level because of the anthropologists' influence.

SG You sound sceptical about the usefulness of social constructionism?

LA As the only approach. Obviously they put more weight on the micro-level and on meanings and how children are constructing their own worlds, in which also various categories of adults are implicated; but it seemed to me that they weren't that interested in the further realities of their worlds, the structural arrangements in which all of this happens. In the 1990s in sociology the division into two paradigms, the agency paradigm and the structural paradigm, was clear, but there were attempts to link the two.

Social constructionism, as it was broadened in the research in the 1970s, 1980s and 1990s, became so vague. Constructionists love gerunds. Everything is constructing, building, forming, all ends in *ing*, focusing on processes, but processes on a micro-level, in which children are actually seen as actors. I don't think it needs to be emphasised that those of us working on the structural level did not ignore this, but something was lacking. So I was not that enthusiastic about social constructionism, eventually it explained nothing. Something gets done, yes, but please specify what the processes are, what is actually done? Children construct their families, children construct this and that. What is going on? It becomes an umbrella term but underneath you don't really know what is happening.

SG And what about discourse?

LA It was very much linguistically influenced. The main method was ethnography, but also discourse analysis. Later on, in this new century, there is much more critical discussion and debate about what help social constructionism has been or not. It is high time to leave behind the vague terms. I am too much of a mathematician and I like logic. I would like people to think clearly about their concepts and not only make nice ethnographies and 'thick descriptions'.

SG OK. So that obviously relates back to your early interests?

LA Yes, rigour: I love it. Clear analytical thinking.

SG And you don't think there is enough of it around?

LA No, and I think it has got worse. It is not just in this field, it is the way university training has gone. I do think I got a much better university education in thinking, in methods, and so on than students nowadays get, especially at the Master's level.

SG More was expected of you?

LA At that time there were fewer epistemological grounds for doing your research. You knew that the positivist paradigm was this and there was Marxism and there was phenomenology and so on. Now it is so chaotic, especially for students. Also, they are not required to read the classics. They do not know the history of the concepts which they are using. So they talk about 'constructing' and they think that's science.

SG Could we talk a bit about working with children? I know your primary focus is on childhood, but what influence has your empirical work with children had on your theoretical work?

LA It's difficult to say. In 'Childhood as a social phenomenon' we worked on secondary data. I have, however, used quantitative data, qualitative data, mixed methods, as they say now. It depends on your main problem and for me the main problem has not been on the level of children as social actors; there is much more to work on on the structural side and that's my area.[3] Of course my mathematical and statistical education at the university was in quantitative methods. I never lost confidence in the importance of quantitative statistical methods, only it has to be problem-led. You need to have all kinds of methods, but I think that most of my work has been theoretical. I have done three or four empirical studies myself. Of course I also supervise Master's students and doctoral students doing empirical studies.

SG So you would supervise quantitative work?

LA Yes, but most of the students that choose to do Childhood Studies are not interested in quantitative methods [both laugh].

SG But this is a big issue for the field, isn't it? Is Childhood Studies incompatible with quantitative research?

LA There comes a time for all kinds of methods. It depends on where you are working and how. The latest article I am working on is on social work practice and in that area of work there is much more use of interviews and qualitative data but also documentary data analysis. It depends on the problem. University training in any discipline, especially at Master's level, should ensure that students should have a basic understanding of all the basic methods, to be able to be critical when reading scientific articles.

SG So as a journal editor and supervisor, what do you think about the quality of qualitative research?

LA There is much to be done to improve it and my feeling is, as an editor of *Childhood*, that we get more and more of the same, and there is very little progress to be seen: new data, new children, new country, new topic, but more or less a similar kind of method and way of thinking. There might be many factors behind that. Maybe certain kinds of researchers like to send their manuscripts to *Childhood*? Also I see here in the Early Childhood Education Department, of the Master's students, as well as the doctoral students, those who do Childhood Studies seem to have the idea that there is only one paradigm, the ethnographic paradigm, for looking at how children construct the world.

Isn't it interesting that it is very often students in the more applied sciences who become interested in doing childhood research? Very few psychologists in my university are interested in Childhood Studies. Students in applied fields – social workers, those in child welfare – have an obligation to work in children's best interests. The early childhood education students also are interested in working with children in a new way. I can see the enlightenment in their faces when drawn into Childhood Studies, sometimes so over-interested that they are not critical any more. They start seeing children as wonderful children, heroic children, building a new world and for themselves there is no going back to the objectifying gaze of psychology; but then they may also go over the edge.

SG Do you think that the detachment from core disciplines is a problem for the field?

LA Yes that is exactly what I think. You can't be interdisciplinary without a strong base in a discipline.[4] People in Childhood Studies need to have a connection to their home disciplines as well as working with people coming from other disciplines. Childhood Studies seems to be going in the direction where we all form our own circles and work only with other childhood researchers. As if that were enough. There seems to be very little progress, in fact one can see stagnation, theoretically, methodologically.

You have to be connected with the basic debates of science, you have to connect to where social science is heading. You have to bring those debates into Childhood Studies and bring Childhood Studies into those debates, and I think that is not happening enough.

SG Do you have any reflections on communicating with children and reflexivity before we go on to the future of the discipline?

LA That is the most difficult question for me given the focus of my research. Bourdieu has this notion of reflexivity, that doing research with people, especially if you personally meet them, means you have a relation to them, you are positioned there, so that what you are and what you learn from meeting them depends on what your relation to them is or becomes. Earlier, when doing my own empirical studies I did not realise that, but I realise now that I was doing a kind of reflexive sociology of my own life experience as a child. Your own life story, especially if you have moved around a lot in the world, may give you a lot of empirical data.

SG Do you think you should be very explicit about that as a researcher? Were you trained to do that?

LA No, but Bourdieu does train you. We were not talking about reflexivity at all when I was a student. We were trained to be objective, systematic and so on, but of course kind to those people we were interviewing, and ethical. Most ideas about reflexivity in the research process do not go as far as Bourdieu in being explicit about the data being based on your power relationship with whoever is in the field where you are.

SG And would you encourage your students to be reflexive in this way?

LA Yes. Just last week one of my doctoral students defended her dissertation; she wrote her life story into the dissertation. She uses Bourdieu's method to analyse, as a sociologist, her own life story and thereby generates an explanation for what this dissertation is about and why – a study on women in their mid-life living in a small locality. In research with children power relations are of course very important. Power is about the relationship, it is not something you can 'have'. If you mis-recognise the relationship, the research results are contaminated by that misrecognition. It goes much further than being ethical or the 'least adult' and that kind of thing.

SG Anything else you would like to mention about research with children?

LA I am myself so much of a theory person that I don't have too much more to say on that. I am not necessarily proud of being a theory person. I don't want to be only a theory person, but I do think that there is a lack of clear rigorous analytical thinking.

SG But I gather from your writing that you get frustrated with theory that is just up in the air and has nothing to do with the material condition of children?

LA A theory is a process, you don't just have theories and then apply them. That's the way I was taught of course, there's Piaget's theory, there's Parsons' theory and so on, and you read them and then try to apply them. Now I am quite excited about Bourdieu's thinking about what theory is, theory as process. A theory is a set of concepts that you use as tools for thinking.

I am a professor in an early childhood education department and, among the professors, the only sociologist, the others being in developmental psychology and in pedagogy. Our aim is to try to collaborate so that we get all these areas to link, but obviously there needs to be some shared ontological ground to succeed in this. It is much easier for me to work with psychologists and educationalists who have an interest in Vygotsky, for example, because his brand of psychology is relational. They deal with individuals in their real life relations, and sociologists deal with many more levels, so it is hard work to bring them together. It is a huge project and it will take 10, 20 or 30 years and lots of people. I think sociologists of childhood are in a good position to do this because in many other areas, in practice areas like social work or education, you have to consider children as psychological and biological beings, who have bodies and brains and you cannot afford to focus on the social world surrounding them, not just the immediate environment but all these institutional levels, up to the capitalist structure of the global world. In the end childhood and every little child is connected to all of this, is a part of it. It is a very complicated network of relations, on many levels.

SG So you see the field as quite static – you seem a bit disappointed by that?

LA Yes I am a bit disappointed to see that things are not happening quickly enough, but maybe I am not realistic. In 30 years quite remarkable things have happened in our scientific knowledge and ways of dealing with children and childhood. So maybe it is unrealistic to believe that things will happen quickly, but I would hope that children would be more central to sociology. The discipline is still very adult-centred.

In a 1986 article Anne-Marie Ambert said that you don't become a household name in sociology by studying children and that is still the case. If you are a sociologist studying children and childhood people say, 'OK', as if they know what it is about. Children and childhood seem so marginal when you consider class, global capitalism, the welfare state, the World Bank and so on, as agents, compared to children. They hear one or two or three presentations on children as social actors and they have had it, that's enough. That is the problem: we present childhood without social structures and sociology is after all about social structures; there would be no sociology if we dealt only with individual social actors in their individual settings.

SG But there are sociologists, like you and Qvortrup, who focus on structures. Are you listened to within mainstream sociology?

LA Not really. We don't get invited to present papers in general sociology meetings, we organise our own meetings. And if we are part of larger conferences we have our own stream, so we very often find all our nice colleagues there and we talk with each other.

I think Jens is now retired and I will also retire soon. Is there nobody else 'doing structures'? But of course there are people we don't know about, we can't read everything, in different languages and so on. But I am very annoyed that the common understanding of the sociology of childhood is so much based on the 1990s 'paradigm'. We need a much broader research agenda in Childhood Studies, including of course the notion of children as social actors.

SG Do you think it is time to abandon the 1990s paradigm and find a new one?

LA There is no need to abandon it because that is one level, seeing children as social actors in their immediate social environment is important. If the analysis remains on that level, however, all the other levels are left unexamined or just referred to but not rigorously analysed.[5] Mediations between levels are needed. Psychology is important. Psychology has to develop as well and you can't just drop it, even if there are still only a few, if any, conceptual bridges between the psychology of childhood and the sociology of childhood.

SG So you think that if the field is to develop there need to be new breakthroughs in terms of theory and analysis and obviously you would like to see more people attending to issues around structure.

LA But structural matters are not very interesting to people. All this 1970s and 1980s post-modernism, deconstructionism, all these new epistemologies said goodbye to structures. But what are they doing? They are looking at structures, discursive structures, linguistic structures. Structuralism, however, has a bad name. Where I think there is some green light coming, is in this idea of relationality, which is emerging in a number of disciplines, from the natural sciences to philosophy. So we do have relational psychology, relational economics; brain research is relational by its nature. Even modern physics is relational. This idea of relationality gets stronger. Vygotsky's activity theory is relational, so I see a connection there with my psychology colleagues. We need to build up a community.

SG To wrap up is there anything else you would like to say?

LA I think everything has come up, probably in a quite confusing way because I am not used to talking about these issues in English, not even in Finnish. I have just started to write about some of these topics, for instance encouraging my colleagues to think seriously about their ontologies, what sense they give to social reality. So I would like Childhood Studies to be more philosophical, and maybe that is the same as being more analytical, more rigorous.

References

[1] Thorne, B, 1987, Revisioning women and social change: Where are the children?, *Gender and Society* 1, 85–109

[2] Alanen, L, 1994, Gender and generation: Feminism and the 'child question', in J Qvortrup, M Bardy, GB Sgritta, H Wintersberger (eds) *Childhood matters: Social theory, practice and politics*, Aldershot: Avebury

[3] Alanen, L, Mayall, B (eds), 2001, *Conceptualising child–adult relations*, London: Falmer Press

[4] Alanen, L, 2012, Disciplinarity, interdisciplinarity and Childhood Studies, *Childhood* 19, 419–22

[5] Alanen, L, 2009, Generational order, in J Qvortrup, WA Corsaro, M-S Honig (eds), *The Palgrave handbook of Childhood Studies*, London: Palgrave MacMillan

THREE

Priscilla Alderson

Priscilla Alderson is Professor Emerita of Childhood Studies in the Social Science Research Unit, Institute of Education, University of London. Professor Alderson has worked in research since 1984 and has over 300 publications in areas such as children's rights, ethics and health as well as in broader social and economic contexts. Her recent publications include Alderson and Morrow, *The ethics of research with children and young people: A practical handbook* (SAGE, 2011) and chapters in key Childhood Studies texts: 'Younger children's individual participation in all matters affecting the child' in *A handbook of children and young people's participation* (Percy-Smith and Thomas, Routledge, 2010) and 'Children as researchers: Participation rights and research methods' in *Research with children: Perspectives and practices* (Christensen and James, Routledge, 2000; 2008). Professor Alderson's latest book is *Childhoods real and imagined: An introduction to critical realism and Childhood Studies, vol 1* (2013), published by Routledge.

Carmel Smith Priscilla, would you start by saying a bit about your background and training – a potted history of your research career to date?

Priscilla Alderson My training is that when I left school I trained and worked as a school teacher. Then, when I had my children, I was very involved in hospitals with them and because of that I got involved in a pressure group to let parents into hospitals. I was on a medical ethics committee looking at research with children, the ethics more than the practice; that was in 1980. Through that – there were all these famous people, I was the token mother – somebody said to me one day: 'We are looking at parent's consent to medical research, no-one has researched parent's consent to treatment, it is all based on the idea of the adult patient consenting for themselves, and I think somebody should do research in it, in sociology as a PhD, and it should be you.' I was an English teacher so I thought it was a joke, actually. Anyway, eventually I got an ESRC grant, access to two children's heart surgery units and did my PhD. I went to Goldsmiths College (University of London) and did a crash course in sociology for a year, part of a Masters in sociological theory and quite a bit on qualitative theory. Goldsmiths is a very theoretical place, so I was very lucky to be there. My PhD was a very unconventional one as it was a mixture of philosophy, ethics, cardiology and sociology. I was fortunate because I began with David Silverman as my supervisor, then moved to Caroline Ramazanoglu, a well-known feminist sociologist, Vic Seidler, a philosopher and I also had a cardiologist supervising me so between them I had a rather amazing experience. Once I finished my PhD I immediately went back to work in a charity but Margaret Stacey, my external examiner, said to me, 'Be a sociologist, write a book, get a grant.' Ann Oakley later phoned me and asked me to come here. That was in 1990. So it was actually people saying: 'Here's a door open, come through it,' which lots of women need, don't they?

CS An unusual route?

PA That parent's consent research led on to children's consent and I was so lucky, I got a Leverhulme Grant which is *so* hard to get. It's amazing really, I was such a novice. I had no training at all in practical interview techniques – nothing. But before that, because I was in these voluntary organisations and pressure groups, I had learned loads of things. I had learned how to lecture, how to write and lots of useful stuff like that and that was really how I learned to do my first research in a hospital. A friend and I were furious because in the ward where our babies were born we were only allowed to pick them up every four hours, we couldn't touch them – they were taken off into another room. So in 1978 as members of the local Community Health Council, with this friend, who was a midwife, and we were both pregnant, we did a survey of mothers' views and although at first the midwives rejected our report, within five months they had changed that place. So that was my first research project and it was long before I had done any sociology or a PhD, but it worked; it was probably the most effective piece of research I have ever done. Everything in that hospital changed and, better still, six months later we went back with a new Sister showing us round saying: 'We do this, we do that, we do the other' and she had no idea that they were our ideas and we didn't tell her because the triumph [for people] is when they think they are their own ideas [laughs]. So I have always been interested in research that will change the world or at least increase people's understanding and tolerance – not tolerance of bad practices though [laughs]!

CS So in terms of writing and presenting research, particularly qualitative research, what can researchers do to try and maximise its impact?

PA I think research should stand the test of critical policy makers. I think it is terribly important to write for practitioners and policy makers, as far as possible, in their terms and not in 'sociologese'. It is also important to try to show why your analysis stands up – with examples, with references and with adequate quotes from your data. In all my studies I need to write up a whole set of different papers for doctors, for nurses, for parents, for policy makers – each with particular readers in mind.

CS You have published some very important work on ethics and have also written well-known books on ethics in research and consulting with children and young people. What informs the way you engage with children and position children in research?

PA Well, I like to think of it as a human–human relationship and to question any age stereotyping in our manner, our assumptions or the topics covered. I think that I probably don't approach them as a child but a person – well, I hope I do, that's my aim really. I think that happened when I was doing the children and consent research. It was 1989 to 1991 and I was astonished...I had never imagined that these young children – eight-, nine-, ten-year-olds – could talk with such courage or with such complexity.

I think some people are quite critical of me, thinking that I am not interested in power; but I am very interested in power – I am not pretending it is not there. Also, of course, lots of times children want you to be an adult and you can't force them out of this. They get confused, they maybe are not used to talking to strange adults and that's fine because then you adapt to what they want, being led by them as far as you can. Power is such an enormous problem particularly when you are doing intimate interviews and you've got this tugging to and fro: you want to get all the data that you can out of people like a pump, but you don't want to milk them and intrude and go too far and mis-time things. It is also important to respond well when people say the most extraordinary things.

CS What it is that enables children to say extraordinary things, for no other reason than that they want to tell you? What is the quality of the researcher that enables that?

PA I think it goes back to power...coercive and oppressive power, but there is also power of energy and of potency and of agency...Children have got to know that you are confident, and are not going to fall apart in front of them – that is probably why they keep so quiet, they don't want to upset their parents. You also have to have patience, tact and loads of other ordinary everyday personal qualities.

CS There are some people within the field of Childhood Studies who believe that we should be studying childhood rather than children. Micro/macro is perhaps a bit too crude as a way to portray it, but there does seem to be this division. Is there room for both?

PA Well, the social constructionist people tend to do agency and weak structures and the macro people tend to do strong structures but weak agency. I have written in response to people, such as Jens Qvortrup, who argue for childhood and not children. I have said, as with feminism, there is a lot going on but feminism couldn't possibly be understood without knowing how women perceived and experienced it. Similarly, childhood cannot be understood without understanding how children perceive and experience it...as well as all the things that are done to them and how adults perceive...I don't think you can split it apart like that.

CS Why do you, Priscilla, think that we haven't drawn more on feminism to recognise all of those things so as to help us to progress in Childhood Studies?

PA I think it is quite deeply psychological. Most childhood researchers are women, aren't they? Most of them would say that they are feminists and I think they feel a deep split between their feminism and their loyalty to themselves and childhood. One thing I have read recently is that feminists have very ambivalent attitudes towards the body because the body can separate them off, be a nuisance – leaky and interrupt their careers and their public life. The body is private, intimate, often shameful, linked up with the emotions and identified with the woman as opposed to the rational man. That makes it difficult for women to think about childhood bodies whether they recognise it or not. I mean, the book, *Contested bodies*[1] isn't much about bodies, and actually bodies are not contested. Bodies go on existing and they are functioning, that is not the topic of the book, which is things like teenage pregnancy, alcoholism, HIV/Aids and obesity. Now these are social behaviours, which are contested, but they are not physical bodies and yet the title slips between behaviours and attitudes, and loses ontology – the reality of the body.

Another thing about feminists, a lot of us have managed our careers as well as having children and it has been a toss-up sometimes, with great difficulties, so that we are supposed to suspend our underlying attitudes to children, our great love and involvement, and be slightly detached people – that is another complication. Our work is intensely emotional and yet we are supposed to conceal and disguise a lot of that – in the mainstream view of things. The third thing is that feminism, by definition, has a simple indisputable aim: men and women should be equal – Childhood Studies doesn't have such an aim. Equality between adults and children is enormously difficult, complicated and confusing – it is not a simple thing. Ann Oakley and Leena Alanan have both commented on the hostility of feminists towards childhood.

CS Turning now to the field of Childhood Studies, would you say something about your understanding of the evolution of ideas leading up to the 'new paradigm'?

PA Well a lot of my understanding of this is based on the recent history written by Berry Mayall.[2] There seems to be the 'macro' people, such as Jens Qvortrup and other Europeans, and the 'micro' social constructionist people. It is important for me to say that throughout the 1980s I was just beginning to be a sociologist and doing a PhD. For the next 15 years I was so busy fundraising, rushing round getting research data and analysis and writing, that I didn't have much time to think about theory. However, I have been very lucky because in 2009 I had the chance of taking early retirement and it has been absolutely fantastic! I still do some part-time work here, but it has meant that I can really study theory and sociology and go to all those interesting meetings you haven't got time to go to when you are working full-time.

Roy Bhaskar works here, he came here around 2008 with a huge international reputation. He has developed this philosophy of social science that reconciles interpretivism and empiricism and the 'macro' and the 'micro' in, I think, the most exciting and amazing ways. He started 40 years ago and he has had loads of flak because his books are very dense; hard, hard work to read. Since then quite a few people have written rather simpler versions. Then there is Margaret Archer at Warwick who has been a critical realist for years and she does structure and agency in the most exciting way. You have really got to have both...and the interaction between them...you can't really understand agency without structures. For instance, if you are a real agent and you make choices, if these choices really matter, they are structural, they are religious, traditional, cultural, economic, political – they are deeply complicated things and that is what makes you a real deliberating agent. Without those structures you would just be an amoeba floating around. Margaret Archer's work, she interviewed 20 adults, is about how they mediate structure/agency through internal conversations and they draw on their culture and structures and work out what really matters to them in these conversations as agents. She has done it with adults and that is just waiting to be done in Childhood Studies. There are so many exciting and worthwhile things for us to do.

One of my students in 2010 finished doing a critical realist PhD in Tanzania in two slum schools in Dar es Salaam on corporal punishment and children's rights. Now, to do that you really have to have an idea of bodies and suffering, physical reality (which the social constructionists and the macro people aren't very good at) and you must have an idea of universal human rights. Freedom from torture is a universal human right, it is not cultural relativism, you cannot...of course, you interpret rights and practise them in different ways around the world but there is the key real right which the social constructionists and anthropologists and a lot of geographers find...well, a difficult idea. In critical realism, things are real: your body is real, the right to freedom from torture is real, torture is real, it is not just all in the mind, it is not just a social construction and it is not just a whole set of statistics either. I could go on for hours about this but I won't [laughs].

CS Roy Bhasker has clearly been very influential in your thinking?

PA He has written 'pure' critical realism books and he is now editing a whole set of 'applied' ones on climate change, disability, economics and all sorts of things and he asked me to do the one on childhood.

CS What is the book called?

PA It is called *Childhoods real and imagined*.[3] It is about children and childhood around the world and how childhood is a social construction but also a structure, a very strong real structure as well and children, of course, are all real entities too. The aim was to bring together how children are missing in nearly all the adult literature: housing, crime, the credit crunch, banking...you name it. I wanted to point out how they're missing, but how they are actually central and how they are often going to be much more affected than we are by economic debt and by ecological debt and how those things all work together. I couldn't pack it all into one book so volume two is going to be more about that.

CS So it is interdisciplinary?

PA Yes, critical realism is about bringing the disciplines back together again.

One of the chapters is mainly about the soul and the self because unless we think really deeply about our beliefs about the human self, the human person, we can't understand babies, children, childhood, needs, citizenship, well-being, anything. Yet most people don't seem to define human nature or even think about it and some say, 'Oh, that's philosophy' or 'I'm a sociologist, I don't look at human nature.'

The chapter on the soul and self...which is partly a review of a book by a philosopher and a psychologist on 2,500 years of thought on this, they say the idea of soul went out when science came in, and the idea of self is going out now through becoming so fragmented and split. Lots of post-modernists think we don't have a self, we just have slices of momentary existence and the self is split between neuroscience and you name it...Then they say that what we consistently have is bodies – well that's back to Descartes isn't it? So I have hung on to the idea of the self with a bit of spiritual in it. It is not about religion, but we are not just material beings, and the way to understand that is to draw the disciplinary thinking together again but, of course, they have split up partly for financial reasons. Everybody has to belong to a new sub-speciality that has unique claims to knowledge and funding and a unique department...and it has split apart so many complicated concepts like childhood, for example. Childhood really is split, lost, into economics, biology and all sorts of things. Childhood Studies is so interdisciplinary, thank goodness, but we could be more so.

CS   Having written your book, what is your thinking about the future of Childhood Studies?

PA I have been wondering where Childhood Studies is going. One original aim was to bring children into mainstream sociology, as feminism has done for women. Instead, we seem to be locking them further away into subspecialties of research about children and young people. Mainstream social science continues to be largely adult-centric and to ignore children, while childhood researchers often seem remote from the 'adult' world, such as when rights and citizenship are seen as interpersonal, and not primarily legal and political concerns.

Another problem, shared with all social sciences, is the great rift between empirical and positivist researchers who aim to deal with facts, and interpretive ones who hardly believe in facts. How can anyone take social research reports about children seriously, when the researchers themselves criticise one another's basic theories and methods? Indeed, the founding tenets of each side seem to be defined by their mutual opposition.

CS Can you say more about that?

PA Well, in my new book I have identified seven things that positivists do and seven things the interpretivists do and they are diametrically opposite.

Positivists tend to assume that data, such as babies' brain scans or different measures of poverty, can be: One, objective, self-evident facts separated from values; Two, understood apart from their social context and as separate variables; Three, seen as independent and pristine: whoever observes, records, reports or reads about them sees the same fact; Four, seen as having essential inherent qualities; Five, seen as having a stable lasting reality out there in the world that can remain unchanged when transferred across time and space. Two further points are that: Six, positivist social research, modelled on the natural sciences, can therefore, discover general laws, replicable findings and reliable predictions; Seven, this confidence encourages assumptions that 'evidence based' findings can support self-evident conclusions about causes and effects in social life and provide effective solutions to public and private problems.

There are, of course, a lot of good things in all of this and there are some truths in it as well, but there are problems. Shall I talk about the seven tenets of interpretivists now?

CS Please do.

PA Number one, interpretivism cautiously treats phenomena as if they are constructed by subjective human perceptions and values and negotiated interactions. Two, they are within specific contexts and cultures. Three, phenomena are contingent and depend on our individual social selves and perceptions. Four, it is as if phenomena have few or no essential inherent qualities. Five, it is as if phenomena have no independent lasting truth or reality of their own that could transfer in fact across time and space. They do not exist 'out there in the world' but only through the social institutions and cultures that give them meaning. Six, interpretivism recognises unpredictable human agency which can be intellectually, morally and pragmatically liberating when it deconstructs ideas of fixed realities seemingly determined by biology, history, economics or religion – this is very much true for childhood. Seven, connections between research data, conclusions, recommendations and later policy making are questioned, they are not self-evident as for the positivists. They are questioned as tenuous constructions instead of being assumed to be self-evident conclusions.

Social empiricists can seem naive about complex social data and how we are able to know about them. Interpretivists can seem vague and remote from reality and policy making. Childhood Studies is riven between these two positions like 'Solomon's baby' and people are not really engaging in how to resolve the differences.

CS So how can these two positions be drawn together? How can this be taken forward?

PA One way forward could be through critical realism as in Roy Bhaskar's work.[4,5] Bhaskar points out the error running through both positivist and interpretivist approaches – nearly all the time they are committing the *epistemic fallacy* whereby we don't accept that things actually really exist and we reduce them into our thinking. Childhood is a good example; it's an idea basically isn't it? The positivists reduce things into their statistical and multivariate analysis as if real mother/child relationships have no relation whatsoever. Neuroscientists reduce consciousness into a brain scan; that is the epistemic fallacy. So positivists do it as well as interpretivists – we all do it. What we have got to do, through this four stage way of approaching the world, is to step back and think…you're you before I saw you and after I leave you, you are still you. The ocean is still the ocean and it is not just there when we are looking at it and it is not just our perception. That applies to a lot of social things as well, such as poverty and shame – they have many different aspects but they have a core reality that we actually recognise; children recognise terribly early about shame, don't they?

The other thing, it is so simple, is the difference between the *transitive* and the *intransitive*. You are the intransitive Carmel, you exist. My perception of you is transitive, it's partial, it's changeable, it probably misunderstands a lot of you. Children in a playground are intransitive; they exist before we see them and after we leave them. They are separate from and cannot be reduced into, our subjective transitive perceptions. However, our shifting perceptions, as interpretivists recognise, are also vital in our understanding and our partial reshaping of realities such as childhood. Intransitive realities and transitive perceptions interact, but do not reduce into one another. They are two quite different things. One is the positivist approach, in a way, and the other is the interpretivist; you can have both of them and you can respect both of them, they don't have to be reduced one into the other.

CS They are both important?

PA Yes, very important. Critical realism builds on the strengths in each position, while overcoming their weaknesses. If researchers deny an enduring being/reality, they cannot validate their work by the accuracy of their reports about that original reality. They then tend to burrow further into the epistemic fallacy, searching for validation in their own theories, or in their methods such as perfect randomisation or statistical analysis.

Critical realism accepts the possibility of naturalism, that there can be a unity (though not uniformity) of methods in the natural and social sciences, because they are more alike than is usually believed. Natural science does not simply research things, and social science does not simply research ideas. They each deal with both. Newton and Darwin moved beyond empirical observations of things in order to propose imaginative abstract ideas: gravity and evolution can never be seen or proved, except in their visible effects and plausible explanations. Social science also deals with both things (real children, values, relationships) and ideas (about how we understand things). Like Newton and Darwin, social scientists need to move beyond describing observed events to analysing *natural necessity* in *deeper causal reality*, powerful influences, such as in the structures of generation, class or economics. Like evolution, these explain and influence events but do not wholly determine them.

This is because closed systems, which have a single overwhelming force, almost never occur. Instead, in open systems, two or more causal powers compete. Bird flight defies gravity, but does not disprove it. A disadvantaged but successful child overcomes adverse social systems but does not disprove their general power. In open natural and social systems, powers are determining (influential) but rarely determinist (wholly controlling). Once complex uncertainties in natural science are accepted, they can be more accepted in the social sciences too, when they aim to understand and to change the world.

CS So this is an inclusive interdisciplinary approach wherein positivist approaches and interpretivist approaches have their place, they don't have to be in opposition or reduced one into the other?

PA Yes, a very important place. Also, everyone can have their place, everyone can feel really included and complementary, they don't have to be there only if the others aren't. It is so simple yet many people aren't thinking like that.

CS These are the types of discussions which will be important if Childhood Studies is to grow and prosper as a diverse but coherent field. Before we finish, Priscilla, is there anything else you would like to say to students and those currently working in the field?

PA Well, I hope my work helps people to clarify their theories and therefore, their research methods and therefore, their aims. I have written quite a lot on whether social research should be value free or not and a lot of people still think that it should be value free, in the sense of neutral, and that morals aren't integral to it, whereas critical realism says that the whole thing is drenched in morality and ethics — not just the methods which I have previously written about. Now I am writing about the ethics of the whole of research. So I hope the few brief points I have covered in this interview will encourage people to explore many further ideas in critical realism, and its potential practical contributions to Childhood Studies.

References

[1] Hörschelmann, K, Colls, R (eds), 2010, *Contested bodies of childhood and youth*, Basingstoke: Palgrave Macmillan

[2] Mayall, B, 2013, *A history of Childhood Studies*, London: Institute of Education

[3] Alderson, P, 2013, *Childhoods real and imagined: An introduction to critical realism and Childhood Studies, Vol 1*, London: Routledge

[4] Bhaskar, R, 1998, *The possibility of naturalism* (3rd edn), London: Routledge

[5] Bhaskar, R, 2008, *Dialectic: The pulse of freedom* (2nd edn), London: Routledge

FOUR

Erica Burman

Erica Burman is Professor of Education at Manchester University and is also a group analyst. She has written extensively about the gendering of childhood, critiques of developmental psychology and the ways the child is mobilised within problematic North–South relations in global discourses of development, as well as about making methodological interventions, highlighting the critical potential of discourse analysis. She has also written about power relations and difference in psychotherapy, in which models of childhood connect with fantasy and memory, and minoritisation and racialisation in service provision. Professor Burman has published extensively over the course of the last 25 years on a broad range of topics including *Deconstructing developmental psychology* (Routledge, 1994, 2008) and within key childhood, psychology and education journals. See www.discourseunit.com for further information.

Carmel Smith Will you start, Erica, by saying something about your training and background, a 'potted history' of your career?

Erica Burman Well I trained as a developmental psychologist – I actually studied developmental psychology and the other half of my degree was cognitive studies, artificial intelligence, at a time when artificial intelligence and developmental psychology were almost the same, the information processing metaphor was coming into developmental psychology. So the trajectory from where I started to where I am now is really one of the kind of issues posed by thinking about the relationship between developmental psychology, child development, individual development, human development and the concept of development; it is really about working out something about the relationship of each of those together. Really, however, it was my doctoral work – I took Piaget's ideas about age and I was interested in using his clinical method or critical method and seeing what emerged. The research engagement was very much both a methodological adventure and a conceptual one at the same time. That was my first real – or proper – experience of researching in schools, I interviewed children, aged four to eight, that sort of age, and I was really being struck by all the other things that are around children in the school system. I had to broaden my question because I was faced by all the questions and complexities of power relationships between adults and children, including my role as a researcher. At that time there was no real framework for conceptualising those except through the feminist literature on research that I began to engage with at the same time.

CS I am interested in what you say about Piaget because there are a lot of people, particularly in the sociology of childhood, who cite Piaget as symbolising almost everything they believe to be wrong with developmental psychology.

EB Well, I do think that there is a lot in the sociology of childhood critique of developmental psychology as a model of the deficit child and their focus on the child in process rather than a competent social actor. But really I think that this is a question about ahistorical and acultural readings of the reception of Piaget. I mean, the Piagetian group hated the way in which their work was taken up in the Anglophone contexts. So you can do a kind of historiography of the reception of certain ideas and their transformation across the Atlantic or across the Channel and that really does make quite a difference. In a general sense, however, when I think of the use of the ideas, I am with the sociologists of childhood, except that they tend to flounder on questions of developmental limits.

CS So you have got a psychology background, you trained as a developmental psychologist...

EB And I am also a group analyst and psychotherapist.

CS Will you now say something about how you understand the 'new paradigm' of the social studies of childhood which has subsequently evolved into Childhood Studies?

EB What the term 'new paradigm' primarily means to me says a great deal about my own disciplinary trajectories. So 'new paradigm' refers to a set of epistemological and conceptual and ethical debates that occurred in psychology from debates arising in the social and human and sciences from the 1970s, in psychology they kind of arrived in the 1980s, and were called 'the crisis', especially in social psychology. There was a methodological and ethical crisis that brought about a lot of questioning of what psychology is and does, and particularly, in terms of its model of the human being and questions about the ethics and politics of research. It was primarily a humanist movement, followed by the more anti-humanist elements of the post-structuralist turn, but both of those have been very, very important in my own formation as someone very involved in, being inspired by, and enabled by critical methodological and conceptual debates outside psychology to bring them into psychology. In that sense, what you are calling the 'new paradigm' around Childhood Studies, or the rise of Childhood Studies, is simply one aspect of that for me, so I suppose that I wouldn't situate myself entirely within the new social studies of childhood, or Childhood Studies, although I would certainly want to be in it too. That raises questions about where psychology fits in to Childhood Studies and I have been following, as much as I can, discussions about disciplinary stakes and discussions about disciplines in Childhood Studies over the last few years. In a way I think it is a question I have been grappling with for quite a long time precisely because of the perception and image of developmental psychology in Childhood Studies from the very beginning, from those very earliest meetings. I am sure Allison James will remember in the 1980s and 1990s [Erica Burman was aware that Allison James was being interviewed later that day] that when I pitched up at one of these meetings they kind of said: 'What are you doing here?' when I said I taught psychology. As Barrie Thorne also wrote, I think the suspicion and trenchant critique of the function of developmental psychology in so many policy and practice contexts is quite correct, but that is something to do with the reception of the theory and, of course, the hard work of some psychologists to make psychology the kind of discipline that it is now. It is written into the history of psychology, the psychology of testing, surveillance, control, classification, segregation, regulation, all those Foucauldian arguments; and that is a lot of what psychology has become in bourgeois democracies, neocapitalist and very much a tool of neoliberalism now. So these critiques around psychologisation that are coming out of critical psychology of various kinds are very, very important and particularly relevant, actually, for Childhood Studies. One key point I would want to make is, and I think that Barrie Thorne and others are certainly aware of this in the things I have read during the last few years, that the kind of psychology that is the dominant psychology is only one of the psychologies that could be drawn upon and mobilised as a resource and there are very significant reasons why that is the case. So it is up to all of us to work together to find helpful other resources. I don't think you can privilege or scapegoat psychology as the monster that needs to be ejected or repudiated from the disciplinary debates within Childhood Studies. That is not to say that I certainly wouldn't want to privilege it, but as I said earlier, what I see time and time again in the debates about Childhood Studies is people moving around, searching for different sets of conceptual frameworks, tools, the next new set of ideas that comes up across the human and social sciences. We all do it and then, every so often, they come up against something about childhood that requires some critical psychological understanding of capacity, limits, or whatever, and they are nested in all those debates about needs and rights and limits. So I think psychologists have to be part of those discussions but it matters, as with which kind of anthropology, which kind of sociology; they are all highly contested disciplines and it would be naive to think otherwise. I don't think psychology is particularly more problematic than any of the other disciplines but, in general, perhaps in the general reception and political ethos of Childhood Studies, it appears so.

In my own work, of course, primarily my target is criticising psychology so, for me, that is the main thing I think about, but that's because I am a critical developmental psychologist, not a critical anthropologist or sociologist. There is a big issue about the kind of psychology that has come to be dominant which is Anglo-US psychology allied to particular political frameworks, pragmatist in the US, empiricist in the UK, and allied to a particular model of knowledge that follows from that and a particular political-economic vision that cashes out in terms of models of the individual and their relationship to societal processes and practices, of which images of childhood, or specific children and childhoods are just an exemplar of that. So it is not surprising, really, that those attract a large amount of critique quite correctly; but there are other psychologies that also, for significant reasons about the dominance of...the globalisation of northern European, and particularly Anglo-US cultures, are marginalised although that is not to romanticise them either. A lot of the divisions across disciplines that seem very intractable and profound here in twentieth and twenty-first century Britain, if you go to somewhere like Brazil, South Africa, you go to other contexts and they matter far less and it is much more about what people do together. Yes, I think we have got some work to do and it is more hopeful, actually, than we imagine because it is really about how people forge the links. On the other hand, I wouldn't just say: 'Oh well, Piaget is bad and Vygotsky is good and let's all go to Reggio Emilia.' Obviously there are a lot of reflections about the naivety of those kinds of views too. In the summer [2012] I went to a conference on Marxism and Psychology and there were lots of people there who were working on the history and reception of Vygotskian ideas, looking at which Vygotsky gets taken up and which gets ignored, particularly his model of the subject and emotions. His initial work was on the psychology of art and aesthetics, it was also quite psycho-analytic, and with interesting possibilities around re-theorising understandings of the personality and also understandings of ability and disability in a social relational way from the outset.[1] You have got two different currents in the reception of Vygotsky because the Soviet rehabilitation of Vygotsky is one that has been too socially determinist, while the western take-up has been as a cognitivist, educational instructionist. In a way, there is quite a lot of work to do in harmonising the kinds of ideas that are being fruitful in psychology around rethinking ideas about childhood and their relationships with the frameworks that are circulating elsewhere to show that we are not just simply jumping ship to another discipline to say, 'Oh, this one's better.' On the other hand, when I say 'harmonise', that doesn't mean that I think that there can be easy, harmonious relationships across the disciplines; if there were, that would be a shame because I think that the tensions and the ways in which we rub each other up the wrong way around concepts, methods, models is actually really, really necessary and helpful. I don't believe it is a good idea to have a grand narrative about children and childhood – that would be a very unhelpful thing to do because it would immediately become oppressive and coercive and normalising. For me, the arena of field of Childhood Studies, or whatever we want to call it, is necessarily going to be quite patchy and disparate and what I find very interesting is the way in which we can have very helpful and inspiring conversations with people who work in massively different areas that directly transform some of my own teaching and research practices.

CS What do you see as the current challenges and tensions in this broad field of Childhood Studies?

EB Well one can always be a victim of one's own success so the explosion of interest in children and childhood…I know some people would disagree…yet at some level children are always talked about, or childhood is, yet real children are ignored and overlooked and it is *which* children become the focus of attention and which ones are overlooked that are the very key questions. I know that last time we spoke I talked about how, as you move around the world, the debates about childhood vary according to the political contexts and the US not having ratified the Convention, and so on. At least, however, the official rhetoric around childhood…again, one could say that it has increased massively, but I suspect that is a historical question to check because I think that people have always talked a lot about children. Whether that has made any difference and in what ways, is another matter. Now, as a field, Childhood Studies is certainly much more institutionalised than it was 10, 20, certainly 30 years ago and, broadly speaking, I think that is a fantastic thing. One of the things, however, as someone who is both in and out of it and always concerned about what is going on in people's investments in particular kinds of children and childhood – and they are always particular because there is no general child or childhood – is to have to continuously interrogate how those boundaries are drawn, not only about who is included and excluded, but what function that concern about childhood is playing for others. When I teach about the psychology of childhood, that is the title of the course I inherited, I say that it is not only about the children's psychology, it is about the psychology that surrounds the notion of child and childhood so it is everybody else's ideas, relationships, fantasies, investments, and so on, in children and childhood. There is a danger if we only focus on what is going on inside, or the perimeter, of the discipline, that we ignore that key issue. I think we have to, therefore, do that work of stepping back and looking and plot what is going on in Childhood Studies and which topics. People are doing that work looking at the shift of categories of concern within UNICEF, within the ILO looking at which kinds of children seem to suddenly catch the public national and international imaginations: the girl victim of sexual abuse, for example. There is also the need to think about what function that fulfils as an index of general concern for everyone, which actually goes back to William Kessen's really early articles about the hardwired child as the bedrock of certainty in an uncertain world where we can't trust our procedures and we don't trust any authority so we kind of think at least it's there, in there somewhere, already. This is a very prescient insight that has been echoed subsequently by so many people in different varieties of forms, whether its Vanessa Pupavac, or other political theorists and feminists also looking at those contested relationships between models of individuals' security and protection, whether it's child protection or protecting women against violence right through to national security, international security – they all connect up.[2] The international political economy of discourses about childhood, I think, connect up in some very real and direct ways with broader discussions about security and insecurity around conflict resolution around invasion and occupation. If you think about the ways in which discussions about girls' education functions in Pakistan and Afghanistan

– sometimes very cynically, sometimes very emotively. I don't care whether you call Childhood Studies interdisciplinary, cross-disciplinary, multidisciplinary, and I know there are differences between those and I think it is probably all of those and, I hope, more than that and necessarily so. I think it is naive, stupid and unhelpful to think that one dissolves disciplines, everyone is formed by their own particular histories and backgrounds, whatever they are, which might not be uniquely individually discipline-specific anyway, but we use what we have learned and I think this has something to do with this question about theory and which theories and models we use. There are fashions across the social and human sciences and Childhood Studies kind of trawls through those in the same way as everyone else does, whether it is actor network theory, Deleuze and Guattari – Deleuze in particular (I remain agnostic about which ones, because I think theory is what you use to help you think), whether it is in a therapeutic situation or any other, it is something that enables you to think and helps you to think more useful thoughts and it is always going to be partial about what it can do for you so we always have to find other theories too.

CS Erica I am aware that you have written a lot in the international development literature and I am aware for this book that we are, for various reasons, still mainly focusing on those from dominant English speaking countries. Will you say something about how you see Childhood Studies moving forward and how we can further incorporate the ideas and perspectives from majority world contexts?

EB Well that's a tricky question that sparks off a range of associations for me. I mean, at a personal level, I would say I have learned a great deal, but different things, from different kinds of conversations with childhood related researchers in different contexts: the northern European, the Norwegian childhood researchers, many of whom are psychologists [both laugh] and feminists who bring that kind of activity theory, the Vygotskian, a particular reading of Vygotsky, into the studies of children's everyday lives.[3] Methodologically, conceptually they are very, very interesting and insufficiently known about here in this country, especially in psychology [laughs]. But, on the other hand, the disjunction between the debates about childhood in rich countries and those of children in poorer countries, and poor children in rich countries too, whatever terms we use – south or majority, they are all inadequate too – those discussions, in terms of international development, have been the ones that have enabled me personally and the critiques of development in the broadest economic sense, national and international development, they are the ones that have been most helpful for me to understand the limits of and problems with psychology as a discipline and its contribution and participation in those systems and also to understand more about what is at stake in ideas about children and childhoods. It is not only happening through children and childhoods, but that is a particular expression of those things. I think if you talk to some of the international childhood people they will say what great disjunctions there are in models of childhood and preoccupations about childhood in different parts of the world. If you are working around…you are not allowed to talk about child soldiers any more but the children who have been involved in militarised conflict situations in many diverse ways, questions about children's competencies aren't so much at issue – it's a lot of other things. Questions about children's agency and some of what is at stake in those kinds of arguments also…the character of the discussion and the issues are just very different in different places and people work pragmatically, tactically and strategically and that's sometimes played out in the discourses around rights versus culture or needs or whatever. I suppose one has to find the right level of conceptualisation for the particular task at hand. I was interested to read, I finally got hold of a book – it is a discourse analysis of the UNCRC [UN Convention on the Rights of the Child] – and the various drafting processes.[4] It was so interesting to read that some of the supposedly hot topics that western countries assumed that particularly African countries wouldn't be prepared to talk about, they effectively foreclosed that discussion it was around early marriage and FGM [female genital mutilation] and that sort of thing, that actually the African countries then introduced their own Charter in 1990 around precisely those issues. So those broader discussions of international relations and politics will always be played out in relation to children and childhoods because everyone wants to be seen to be being nice to children [both laugh]. There is a key reason why the UNCRC got through and was ratified by more countries faster and quicker with more participants than any other Convention and we have to think about and remember that in relation to what we think that that Convention can do because it fudged, necessarily, as all these Conventions do, lots of issues, foreclosed lots of them and people have their own stakes in it and that is always going to be the case for models of children and childhood and I think, in Childhood Studies, we're (I say we) we might end up, as with Women's Studies, at times celebrating the demise of our own discipline if it means that we get more adequate models of positions and conditions. In Women's Studies it was important to name our marginalised position and then well, the good reasons why we weren't talking about Women's Studies any more and moved into sexuality studies, gender studies, queer perhaps, was that we were in danger of creating another kind of abstraction, ideal type, prototype, normalising orthodoxy that was exclusionary in its own ways. I think some of the international childhood researchers are very concerned about the models of childhood that get re-inscribed as normative and prototypical. At the moment I think there are quite lively debates about that going on and I am certainly not saying that we shouldn't have Childhood Studies [laughs].

CS Will you say a bit more about the parallels between ideas about the demise of Childhood Studies in relation to equivalent discussions that took place in Women's Studies?

EB In the ways that the category 'woman' came to be challenged for instituting or justifying certain normalisations and corresponding exclusions around who is qualified as the prototypical woman, so too there is a danger that this would/could happen with 'child/children'. Here, methodologically and conceptually, all the debates about intersectionality that have come to preoccupy gender/feminist theory and research are very relevant – not only to help generate consideration of *which* children we are thinking about/working on or with, but *how* that very category is structured, inflected and configured in relation to other axes such as class, 'race', gender, sexuality, culture, religion, dis/ability and geographical location.[5] The other related issue is about the work done by the concept of childhood, how it always – given dominant meanings – invites a particular abstraction from social contexts and relations that means we should always be suspicious of the work done by this notion.

CS Can I also ask you to say a bit more about the concept of 'agency'. In the literature there are very different usages of the term 'agency', what do you understand by 'agency'?

EB Well, it speaks to me of a set of political and sociological debates that in some ways I hope…I know the terms 'structure' and 'agency' are very important, but I feel more aligned to models of subjectivity and relationships and practices that necessarily see these things as relative and interconnected. That doesn't mean it's relativist but no-one has absolute agency, no-one is entirely structurally determined – no individual, no social category – so we are always talking about relative constraints, and freedom and rights are also relative because we are interconnected and relational beings. It is very important, for all kinds of reasons, to have quite a sophisticated analysis of these issues for children and Childhood Studies not only because of the ways in which children are dominated structurally but because of the ways their attachments and relationships to others will always mean that they both figure and function in relation to others in complicated ways and that they actively know that and contribute to that. There are some very interesting psychological, philosophical, sociological, anthropological and geographical theories that, I think, help us to begin to think about those questions in quite useful ways, but one can't have a single answer because I think that you have to ask the question, 'Well, who is asking this question about structure and agency and for what purpose and therefore, what kind of answer might it be appropriate to try and formulate?'

CS Before we end, Erica, is there anything you would like to say to students coming into the field, particularly those who are interested in critical developmental psychology and who want to take international perspectives and work with other disciplines. Your work has been very important and influential in providing another voice in psychology and an important voice for students. What could they take from your work?

EB Well, I am very flattered and honoured to hear that, really. I feel very conscious of the arbitrariness of my particular routes and trajectories and in that sense I don't think there is anything very absolute I would want to say. Just as with my engagement with discursive approaches, the route I came into that work informed the particular ways I do that work, but given that, there are so many other possible routes. When I have taught about discursive approaches, this is generally, and mainly but not only to psychology students, I have found myself trying to give a map of the general diversity of uses of the term 'discourse' and then something of my own trajectory in and through that, but it is certainly not the only way. I think my particular history in and through developmental psychology is a very specific one, at a very particular time and place, and that illuminates particular things about the shape and the distribution of the discipline, particularly in Europe and the US, but also politically at a very particular historical period that will not be repeated and is different now. So I feel that I am continuously learning and that the issues and debates and modes of possibilities, conceptual, methodological and political possibilities around these discussions, are shifting all the time. If people find my narration of those particular debates helpful as offering some kind of landmarks and reference points, particularly through the history of some of the kind of politics of psychology and childhood stuff, then I am very pleased, but I wouldn't expect it to map on to current and future debates projectively of course, although I think sometimes having some historical understanding can be helpful to make sense of what is going on.

References

[1] González Rey, F, 2011, A re-examination of defining moments in Vygotsky's work and their implications for his continuing legacy, *Mind, Culture and Activity* 18, 257–75

[2] Pupavac, V, 2002, The international children's rights regime, in D Candler (ed) *Rethinking human rights: Critical approaches to international politics* (pp 57–75), London: Palgrave

[3] Andenaes, A, 2012, The task of taking care of children: Methodological perspectives and empirical implications, *Child and Family Social Work*, doi: 10.1111/j.1365-2206.2012.00897

[4] Holzscheiter, A, 2010, *Children's rights in international politics: The transformative power of discourse*, London: Palgrave

[5] Crenshaw, K, 1991, Mapping the margins: Intersectionality, identity politics and violence against women of color, *Stanford Law Review* 43, 6, 1241–99

FIVE

Pia Christensen

In January 2013 Pia Christensen was appointed as Professor of Anthropology and Childhood Studies at the University of Leeds, UK. Prior to that she was Professor and Director of Research at the Institute of Education at the University of Warwick between 2005 and 2012. Professor Christensen's research focuses on children and young people's agency in everyday life through the lens of ethnography. She has undertaken and published extensive ethnographic work with children, both in Denmark and the UK, over the last 25 years. Professor Christensen's numerous publications include *Children in the city: Home, neighbourhood and community* (edited with O'Brien) (RoutledgeFalmer, 2003) and (edited with James) *Research with children: Perspectives and practices* (Routledge, 2000; 2008) which has become a key text for those working and undertaking courses on research with children. She is currently working on a major direc year ESRC-funded project, 'New Urbanisms, New Citizens: Children and Young People's Everyday Life and Participation in Sustainable Communities' (NUNC) http://newcitizens.wordpress.com/.

Carmel Smith Pia, will you say something about your background and the evolution of ideas leading to the 'new paradigm' for the study of children and childhood? I am particularly interested in your perspectives and experiences because you have worked in both Denmark and the UK.

Pia Christensen I can say a little bit about my background and way into it as a Danish scholar. It started while I was doing my Magister in Denmark, which is similar in many respects to a Masters by Research in the UK. As part of your graduation you have to give a public speech. I had previously been involved in a study where I interviewed children and young people in families where a family member, a parent, had had a stroke and I was surprised about how little work had been done on children's and young people's perspectives. This was in the late 1980s and it was in 1991 that I gave the public speech for my Magister, which I named 'To be as a child'. At that time I was trying to think about how the study of children had been undertaken in anthropology. My presentation was basically a critique of Margaret Mead's approach and others, where it was very psychologically and psychoanalytically informed, particularly in American studies, Ruth Benedict and studies like that. I was trying to say that there was something we have not seen and that is the world from the child's perspective, hence why it was called 'To be as a child'. It was dedicated to my son who is called Tobias (in Danish pronounced 'To-be-as'). When I was preparing the talk, my supervisor said: 'Pia, this is psychology' and I was worried thinking: 'How can I stand up on Monday at 2 pm and talk about psychology when this is actually a degree in anthropology?' So I was really scared. I talked with a good friend who was also an anthropologist and she was also very sceptical because it was completely new to begin to think about: 'Can we do this, can we look at it from children's perspectives?' One of the very few things available at that time was the work of Charlotte Hardman who had been talking about the child's perspective so that was where I found a little bit of an opening. I had not discovered Alan Prout and Allison James at that point; this is 1990/1991, so I hadn't discovered their work when I gave the talk. So I took a taxi in the night from my friend who was, as I said, very sceptical (she knew my supervisor) but I still felt there was something to be said and that I should be doing this because of the perspectives I had seen and heard from the children and young people. I asked the taxi driver whether he thought there would be a train at that late hour to where I was staying in preparation for this talk. The taxi driver began to calculate aloud, 'Yes, half-an-hour ago I passed the station and there were people there and some were waiting for a bus but maybe…' So he was doing this back and forth consideration about whether there would be a train or not ending up with a conclusion. So I thought, 'I am going to ask him this question.' I tried to translate what I was going to do on Monday at 2 pm and I said: 'You can understand that if I am going to be an anthropologist and if I then talk and everybody sees it as psychology, what am I going to do?' I was terrified. He said to me, 'You go up and you speak with conviction just like you are doing to me now and then you will be all right. Just believe in what you say.' I did that, Carmel, on the Monday I thought: 'I am going to convince them.' My second supervisor, who was sitting on the panel observing and listening to this public speech and who was at the highest level in the Copenhagen Institute of Anthropology at that time, said to me afterwards, I can't remember the exact words, 'Pia, it was like a ride through the literature with this progressive thinking.' In the meantime, I went to England where I met Alan Prout and Allison James and when I returned to Denmark I said: 'I know there is a field' because they were talking about the same things that I was talking about. I had come to it from my little experience, if you like.

From there, during the preparation and early stages of my PhD I met Jens Qvortrup. He talked to me about people in England like Berry Mayall, Alan Prout, Allison James so I came with that introduction through Jens Qvortrup. At the same time, at home, I was applying for funding for my PhD. Again, the advice I received was to do it quickly, to apply for funding for two years and to get it done. My supervisor told me, 'I am not going to hinder you; you want to do this on children but do this quick and get on to the real anthropology.' Another one said to me, 'I could never study children but I know that you can because of the way you are as a person.' I was thinking [laughs], 'Does she mean I am a little bit childish or does she mean that I just have this kind of way or openness or whatever?' but everybody was sceptical about the field as, at the time, studying children in their own right was not seen as a serious topic of study. When I went to the UK, it confirmed that there was a field there, I met with

Allison James who helped me in my thinking about the child as an agent and as a social actor, and how I could get that angle into my PhD. Basically I framed my PhD to look at what children are *doing*, so I was looking at actions of help, not of care, because I wanted to focus on children's agency (rather than any affective or emotional connotations to 'caring') in relation to everyday illness episodes, everyday accidents and so on.[1] From there on I realised that my colleagues were in the UK. In Denmark at that time PhD students were encouraged to spend at least six months overseas to study. I came to the UK for half a year and ended up staying for eight years – that is my joke because that is basically what happened!

CS So where were you based when you originally came to the UK?

PC Brunel University. I placed myself in London because there were lots of meetings there at that time. Alan Prout and Berry Mayall had a series of seminars where childhood researchers came together. That is probably…when people say now that it is all falling apart and so on, I can imagine that it might be the UK researchers saying that because at that time people really came together and it was very intense and exciting; people like Chris Jenks, Martin Woodhead, Allison James and all of those names and a few Americans, like Barrie Thorne, Myra Bluebond-Langner and Bill Corsaro. I had a very close relationship with Allison and that is why I later moved to Hull to work with her. Allison also became my supervisor and I finished my PhD from Hull.

CS So what year did you first come to London?

PC 1992 was the year when I started my PhD and I gave my first presentation at a sociology conference in the UK. The work I had undertaken was pioneering in Denmark at the time and part of that was luck in the sense that I met some of the key thinkers in the field and they might have seen something in me, I don't know, but I became part of those discussions very early on. At the same time, I appreciated Jens's [Qvortrup] work, who was the quantitative person in Denmark, but in terms of my approach, as an anthropologist and ethnographer, the closest one was actually Allison [James]. So I found an academic home and a great sense of colleagueship with the thinking of people in the UK!

CS It also sounds like an exciting time and whenever there is that big shift of ideas and accompanying excitement it can never last forever. Do you think maybe that's why people are now feeling a bit shaky about where the field is going because those heady days couldn't last forever?

PC I think maybe that's right but I also think that there has been disappointment because there has been a repetition of studies saying the same thing, understanding the child as a social actor in a particular way and in not a very sophisticated way.

Most of the work has been continually showing children as active participants in their everyday lives. Fair enough, but what then? We need something more.

What it has meant for me personally is that I have collaborated with the colleagues that I have found, some within Childhood Studies, and I have done a lot of interdisciplinary work. For many years I have done a lot of pioneering work in terms of working with other disciplines within medicine and health[2] and lately, with geographers because I am excited about what comes out of these collaborations. It has been hard work but I don't think the field is dying at all. I feel that there is still so much to learn and so much to do. I have recently presented the latest work that I have been doing (on new communities, children as citizens, children's mobility, children's participation and these kinds of themes) to an audience of anthropologists, other social scientists and architects. It has been fantastically inspiring as one of their missions, in the lecture series I am involved in, is to get social scientists and architects to speak to each other because that is needed in the design of new cities. I get a lot of inspiration from that because people are often very interested in my work. I was invited recently and one of the organisers said: 'You are one of my heroes!' – so I still feel that there is so much to be done. It shows that childhood research can contribute to many other fields.

There has also been a split in people's way of collaborating within the field, there have been some lines drawn, which, I think, has been problematic. For example, do we take a quantitative approach or do we do ethnography? The response from some, to even writing in an ethnographic style, is 'We don't need it, it is all this detail, it is nonsense…', and so on. The person to whom I have compared myself, and whose work I see as being most similar to mine, is Bill Corsaro. All my work is based on ethnography. I also think that there has been too much qualitative work that has not gone into the necessary depth. I am proud of my work, particularly when I hear that others have read it and really like it, but I set myself high standards in order to get the necessary depth and insight because I truly want to understand children and young people's perspectives as best as I can.[3]

CS In terms of the current state of the field what research should we be doing in terms of looking to the future?

PC I am now going to Leeds [to a new appointment] to work with people in inclusive education and disability – these are not areas in which I am a specialist, but I am already thinking about links and bridges, how can my particular perspective be shared and how alike is our theoretical thinking and so on? I am excited about that and, for me, interdisciplinary work is the appreciation of mixed methods. I have worked internationally with the Institute of Public Health in Denmark, with medical people and with quantitative researchers. I have done it now in a series of projects; in the latest work on children's mobility I combined ethnography with GPS and mobile phone technology and therefore worked with people who were more technically qualified.[4] In my latest study it has been fantastic to work with geographers, Peter Kraftl and John Horton. I find the methodological innovations very interesting. It is a big ESRC project, so part of the project was about getting some training – that was the first thing – so my colleagues went out on observations in these communities and came back with field notes. I was reading these and I said, 'No people?' There were no people in these field notes! Wonderful descriptions and maps of the community, very good observations about the environments, about the built environment, housing and streets and whatever, but not a person! So I said to them: 'Were there no people?' and they said: 'Yes, there were,' and we have had so many laughs since that first time when they think about me saying, 'Were there no people there?' So it was about training and then combining my expertise on looking at the human, looking at the social, looking at the actors in the field with their expert knowledge about the environment and how to describe it. I remember years ago when I did a study with Allison and Jennifer (Jenny Hockey in Hull) on farming communities and farming families, I really wanted to describe the natural and built environment …but I could see just how little I had learned during my anthropology degree about how to describe an environment. Not only that, but describing it in English! That was the time I got to know about semi-detached and detached houses [laughter] and what particular stones are called, what kind of bricks were used and what is particular about the rural landscape of East Yorkshire. You could say that I am now getting a lot of that from geographers, so we can do fantastic work, very in-depth, because we can show the breadth of our studies. It has brought this way of thinking about planning, thinking about the site, describing the built environment, making maps in different ways. We then have my insight into human and social interaction and children and young people's perspectives so that we can combine those into building very good policy material, and when we communicate with planners we can talk with weight.

CS Pia, do you study children, childhood or both? I ask that because this has been one of the tensions in the field of Childhood Studies.

PC First of all, as an anthropologist I am coming from where you ask in anthropology, 'What is a human?' That is the basic question and for me it is, 'What is a child?' I am studying children. In terms of childhood, I argued a long time ago in 1994 when I came to a conference and Allison James, Alan Prout and Chris Jenks were sitting at the table talking and I went up to them and said: 'I just want to tell you that I have discovered that childhood does not exist.'

CS Wow! What response did you get?

PC It took me a couple of years to persuade them, and I did in the end, but they were very dismissive in the beginning, naturally, and it also took me a while to formulate my argument which is basically that childhood is an empirical concept; it means that some societies, some cultures, operate with the notion of childhood. For me, I am studying, for lack of a better word, children. I don't study childhood.

It might be, for example, if I am studying in England there would be a notion about what childhood is and I would be studying that but 'childhood' is not an analytical concept, which is the way it has sometimes been treated. Where I find it makes most sense for me is to talk about it in terms of children's life-course; then it is referring to a particular part of our life-course, where some would say this is childhood. For me, I study children and young people in a particular time and place.

CS And would you see Childhood Studies as incorporating both those who see themselves as primarily studying childhood as a social category and those whose focus is more on children? Because some people seem to think that they do both and some are very clearly one or other. Is there room for everybody in Childhood Studies?

PC Yes there is. That is because I believe very strongly that to dismiss a whole approach (like ethnography for example) doesn't make sense, it is a little bit ridiculous to think like that. I am interested in knowledge and understanding, and learning which I think has been very important for me in my work, I like to learn and I enjoy learning, knowing more and understanding better. That is my endeavour! For example, I remember I learned a lot from hearing how Jens talked about statistics from a childhood perspective. One example I have used many times in my undergraduate teaching is to illustrate that we need statistics to think about how many marriages are dissolved today and we can then take the next step and ask 'How many children are experiencing divorce?' Which of course shows that there are a huge number of children. From there you can then show the different perspectives of children within families and how the experience of divorce actually may be a very different one for different children. We need both qualitative and quantitative approaches to understand fully. For me, putting those two things together is 'Wow!' Statistics help us to show the distribution and how many children are affected. The qualitative studies, the ones that can begin to understand how some children are very resourceful and some are not, that some experience divorce and actually come through it and live a good life while others, within the same family, feel damaged by it. We need that as well to understand such social phenomena or whatever we want to call it. That is why I think we need both.

CS Pia will you say something about what you understand by the term 'agency'? It is a term that is used a lot in the literature. Will you say what you mean when you use the term 'children's agency'?

PC When I did my PhD I focused on help and actions. What I have been interested in is children's self care, various aspects of self care have been part of my work, risk management and so on. At that time I was very interested in self care and how children came to do that and also about how they help other people. So it is like helping and caring for oneself and others. I didn't want to focus on the psychological, the caring, affectionate, emotional child, I wanted to look at the very practical aspects because they are, and were at the time, invisible – the idea that the child was doing some actions that may or may not be helping, may or may not be self-caring, and so on. At that time my notion about agency was very much about the action and about the practice. Lots of my work has been influenced by US colleagues such as Tom Weisner talking about daily routines from an eco-cultural perspective and in the UK, David Morgan's work on family practices. So I had looked at some work within families but very much on practices as a pattern, as a sustained routine, every day. I would say that today my notion about agency is very much influenced by Alan Prout's recent work in terms of thinking about agency as an 'effect', as something that is produced, it is not that we have agency, but it is about, for example, the alliances we make with people and things, and how agency is produced through these or not. So when I teach here [University of Warwick] in two week's time, I am teaching on child agency and children as social actors as a whole session, what I will be showing them is two things.[5] First of all I start with the 'social actor' and 'agency' as thought of by Giddens, as an individual capacity. For me, the study with children very quickly showed me… my very first published paper is about this where I talk about collective agency. I asked the children, 'Who takes the medicine?' and they said, 'I do.' I thought this was interesting and wondered what it was about in terms of trying to understand agency. How can the child say that when it actually looks like there is very little agency? Most people would say there is very little agency, children are simply *given* medicine? However, the children said: 'I do.' Then I carefully looked at how the mum takes the spoon, puts the medicine on the spoon, gives it to the child and the child takes the medicine. The little child who isn't able to hold the spoon would be given it by the mum but who is swallowing the medicine? [Gentle laugh] If you begin to see actions as a number of small actions pieced together then there is agency in all these processes: holding the spoon, putting the medicine on, moving the spoon away from the bottle up to the mouth and swallowing it and the 'biggest' thing children can do, like my own child at that time, is to refuse to take the medicine! Yes, as any frustrated mum, I remember going back to the doctor and the doctor saying, 'That child has too much willpower and if you don't get that medicine…' and I was saying, 'But I can't get him to take the medicine, there must be something wrong with the medicine' and he said, 'You just have to do it'. We know that we thank goodness when the child takes the medicine! So the child saying: 'I take the medicine' is an essential part of this whole process – you can't just give it to the child. So that is how I learned to see small, small things in terms of agency.

CS That is a lovely example, Pia.

PC When you look at what young children do – at that time the children I was studying were about six or seven years old and 11-, 12- and 13-year-olds. But the six- and seven-year-olds…this is what my first paper was about when I talk about the social construction of health. I talk about an example of an episode where two boys are standing in a playground digging and shovelling and creating wonderful water and sand canals. At some point one of the boys hits his foot with the shovel and begins to cry. Another child, there are three, takes the boy who got hurt into the adults because that is what you do in this After School Centre – when somebody gets hurt, you take them to the adults and the adults look after them. One boy is still standing in the playground and he keeps digging. The boy who had hurt himself is sitting on a settee. The staff and I are standing at the window looking out and they say, 'He is a bit ignorant, look at him he is so occupied he is just not interested in thinking about helping anybody and he is a bit like that…' Then I went outside and said to the boy, 'What are you doing?' He said, 'I am looking after this and circled around with his shovel.' So what is it that's happening? I then began to look at what do children do and you actually discover that if you are a young child and you leave the spot then there is no play anymore because somebody else comes and takes over. That is the collective learning, that you need to guard things – 'this is my bicycle', 'this is my seat', 'I sat there', 'this is my playground', 'it's my shovel', 'I had it first' and so on. There is always lots of that going on. So he was doing a very important job.

CS Minding it for all of them?

PC Yes, because the adults put the child with the plaster on the settee and said, 'Sit there until you feel better' and then they disappeared to do other things. Who is sitting with that child? Does the child sit on their own? No, other children will be there and talking to him or her and also saying, 'Do you feel better now?' and 'Are you going to come out and play with us again?' They do the aftercare and then take the child back out. If the boy had not guarded the playground the play could not continue to exist so he is guarding the game so that the two children who had gone in to the adults could go back out and continue to play afterwards. So this is not a child who is ignorant of another child being hurt, he is actually looking after something which was important for them all.

CS Pia, what about the future direction of the field – you sound really hopeful?

PC I think it is about being inclusive. I think it is about realising that we have something to bring to other disciplines and I think we should be doing that with whatever method we are using – it doesn't matter really. For me it has been enriching. I think we need to think about the languages in which we publish. For example at some point the development of Childhood Studies in the Nordic countries took place within the Nordic countries and there was less of a participation in the wider dialogue. This has shifted and become much stronger in recent years, but there are still areas where the dialogue is not happening because of language barriers. Our work is being translated and there are large markets and interest in this field around the world. For me, I still feel that there is so much we can still bring but we need to base it in quality work and, for me that means to base it in a good, rich ethnography.

References

[1] Christensen, P, 1993, The social construction of help among Danish children: The intentional act and the actual content, *Sociology of Health and Illness*, 15, 4, Blackwell: Oxford

[2] Christensen P, 1998, Difference and similarity: How children are constituted in illness and its treatment, in I Hutchby, J Moran-Ellis (eds) *Children and social competence: Arenas of action*, London: Falmer Press

[3] Christensen P, 2004, Children's participation in ethnographic research: Issues of power and representation, *Children and Society*, 18, 165–76

[4] Christensen, P, Mikkelsen, MK, Sick Nielsen, T, Harder, H, 2011, Children, mobility and space: Using GPS and mobile phone technologies in ethnographic research, *Journal of Mixed Methods Research*, 19, 5, 227–16

[5] Prout, A, 2005, *The future of childhood*, London: RoutledgeFalmer

SIX

Daniel Thomas Cook

Daniel Cook is Associate Professor of Childhood Studies and Sociology at Rutgers University, Camden, New Jersey, USA. Professor Cook studies youth and childhood and commercial life from a cultural-interpretive perspective. His research focuses on the rise of children as consumers in the United States, presently and historically. In particular, he explores the various ways in which moral tensions between 'the child' and 'the market' play themselves out in various sites of children's consumer culture, such as advertising, food, rituals, clothing and media. Professor Cook has written a number of articles and book chapters on consumer society, childhood, leisure and urban culture including *The commodification of childhood* (Duke University Press, 2004). He has co-edited (with Wall) *Children and armed conflict* (Palgrave Macmillan, 2011) and is sole editor of *Symbolic childhood* (Peter Lang, 2002) and *The lived experiences of public consumption* (Palgrave Macmillan, 2008). He is the founder of the Sociology of Consumers and Consumption Section of the American Sociological Association and engages frequently with the media on issues to do with consumption, particularly related to children. His forthcoming book, *The moral project of the child consumer* will be published by New York University Press. Professor Cook is an editor of *Childhood: A Journal of Global Child Research* (SAGE).

Sheila Greene Let's start with a very general question about how you got into the whole area of research on children and childhood.

Daniel Cook Well, it might be quite a long answer. What happened was that I was in between degrees: I had finished a Master's degree and was thinking about going on for my doctorate and I started working in a publishing company that produced trade publications, mainly for the fashion industry, but other kinds of industries as well. So it was for vendors and things like that and I was a proof reader. One of the magazines that this company published was *Kids' Fashions* because they had trade clothing conventions for people to buy and sell among themselves.

So I had to read *Kids' Fashions* three times a month for twelve months. I recalled some vague notion, somewhere along the line, that I had encountered, that children had been dressed as adults at some time in the past. Of course, it was Philippe Ariès, but I didn't know it at the time. I was looking at these fashion images of kids and they looked very adult-like, even sexualised, and I thought how it would be interesting to see if this is happening now – a reversion to adultification through clothing. If I ever go back to graduate school, I thought to myself, I think I want to do this.

So when I returned to graduate school I moved into the study that became my dissertation and then ultimately my book on the history of the children's clothing industry and the rise of the child consumer. So that's how I got into the literature on the history of childhood and began to read what was at that time very new work from James, Jenks, Qvortrup, Prout and others.

SG Had you had much coverage of children in your first degree?

DC No, my first degree was in Communications. I am sure that there was some mention of family and things like that, but I don't ever recall us specifically thinking about, talking about or certainly theorising children and childhood.

SG So you found the new theorising fitted the bill for you?

DC Yes, I think so in many ways, but it had and still has a strange relation to the child consumer. I began to work in earnest on that project in 1991, 1992. Someone told me 'You have to read Philippe Ariès and you have to read Viviana Zelizer' and that was the A to Z of my knowledge. When I went looking for other kinds of ideas, however, I came across not simply the quote–unquote 'new paradigm' and the anthropological approach, but also other people who began to talk about the child as a figure, or as a symbol…the cultural representation of childhood. As well, I certainly had advisors around who themselves did not have training in childhood per se, but who were open to the idea of allowing me to look at the phenomenon in this way. I think the other influence, if we are going to look at something that I did read, even prior to all of this, in the early 1980s, was Myra Bluebond-Langner's *The private worlds of dying children*.[1] So I think that was probably somewhere in my head and stayed there, in the sense that I recalled how she treated and talked about children.

SG Your first book, *The commodification of childhood*[2] got a lot of attention?

DC It sure seems like it. I feel good about how people have reacted to it.

SG You have continued to explore those issues about the commodification and commercialisation of childhood?[3]

DC Yes I have continued to explore them. I have to say, however, that I have a very particular definition of commodification that I think most people slide over because I think that there is this received understanding of what 'commodification' means, which people often interpret as implying a passive child subject. So, like anyone, you lose control of your message; but my questions have been more broadly about children's personhood, how children are seen and see themselves in relation to the economic sphere. So it is about commodification and commercialisation; although those terms can have presumptions behind them that I do not share.

I am interested in children and how they are situated in economies of various kinds, but the single nail that I keep pounding and probably will continue to pound for the rest of my career is the need not to see a separation between economy and childhood, whatsoever. I think one of the conceptual difficulties that comes out of all of the things that the people who have been writing about childhood, in many different ways over the decades, is still the apparent need to qualify or think of the economic sphere as a special sphere that separates or disqualifies children in some ways, treating children as an appendix to it. Conceptually, theoretically and practically, children and childhood need to be included in to the mix of economic action and meaning. I'd say David Buckingham and I are close to each other in this view, generally.

SG OK. Can we come back to that later? Maybe if we go back to how you saw the emergence of this new paradigm and what you saw as the reasons for its emergence

DC Well, the key people in making it come about were Allison James, Chris Jenks, Alan Prout, Jens Qvortrup, Leena Alanen, Barrie Thorne. I don't want to keep naming them because I will leave people out. There are a number who have been overlooked a bit, like Norm Denzin, who was Myra's advisor, and his book, *Childhood socialization*; Paula Fass and her historical work; many people of course bring up Charlotte Hardman; Briggs, the anthropologist; some people go back to Margaret Mead in different ways; and then some of the psychologists who were culturally or contextually oriented. My sense of the reasons for the emergence of the new paradigm was that it clearly arises out of the social and civil rights movements of the 1960s and I think it arises from a good number of people thinking about identity politics, thinking about who has been represented, and who has and hasn't had a voice. I remember taking a lot of gender and women's studies courses in the 1980s when it was still pretty new and I had read people like Shulamith Firestone and her discourse about 'down with childhood', and the way, as she put it, children chained women to the home.

So out of that kind of thinking, out of the beginnings of a loosening of the distinction between the biological child and the social construct of the child and childhood, coupled with progressive liberatory politics, emerged a number of people in the UK, in Scandinavia, Northern Europe and the US, who in their different ways, began to develop these ideas. What happens when we put the concept of the child in the centre of our enquiry? There was a good deal of those kinds of convergences. Clearly something was happening, particularly in the European context, because, after all, the UNCRC [UN Convention on the Rights of the Child] came out in 1989 and people had been drafting it for years before. So that kind of international politics was also an influence. So, it was a generational and a political and a gender kind of convergence.

SG Do you think that the US has a very different take on children's rights?

DC Americans generally take the 'rights' discourse as individualised, conflictual and as a zero-sum dynamic, especially when it comes to children. If children acquire rights from the state, it is feared that the state will then intervene in parenting, but if one is poor and especially non-white in our society, the state is sitting there in your living room already.

Academically, my sense is that here there is much more of a feminist, gender studies approach to childhood in the US which is different from the state or international approach that emerged in Europe and was tied to the Convention. Barrie Thorne explicitly made that connection between Childhood Studies and women's studies in an important article in 1987.[4] Ann Oakley also made that kind of connection early on. Then there are people like Berry Mayall and Leena Alanen who take these connections in the direction of theorising 'generationing'. One could go on and on, but, when I try to teach on this, those are the people I go back to because they identified a lot of issues that continue to return.

SG Do you see yourself as a sociologist?

DC I used to say 'no' [both laugh] and then I got into an interdisciplinary space and realised that my perspective and my blinders actually have been informed by sociology, but I don't identify with sociology per se. I feel that I am a cultural–social interpretivist scholar. It seems like, from the US American side, though not exclusively because it might also be a British angle, histories of childhood emerged separately from the new paradigm. Many in American sociology today study children, but many do not take children or childhood into the question, the problem to be engaged; most simply do research which involves or implicates children.

SG In terms of your own experience of empirical research, what kind of theoretical approach would you use as a framework?

DC I guess I would have to say cultural–interpretivist–interactionist – drawing on Geertz, Goffman, Gregory Bateson, Denzin, Simmel, Durkheim, Marx, Weber and the like for a foundation – to assist in seeking out various ways that people express and craft meaning or how meaning, and thus power, is imputed in social situations.

SG The way you have come to do your work is not actually through empirical research with children?

DC Yes that is correct. I came to this work through understanding that this thing called a 'child' could be approached as an interactional sphere, as something which not only includes children, but also adults and institutions and institutional actors, like industries, which shape and contest and mould. So it (the 'child') becomes a kind of quasi-shared idea that gets moved around and itself has exchange value.[5] So when I am talking about the commodification of childhood, I am not necessarily talking about the commodification of individual, biographical children, or that children are becoming more materialistic and things like that. That clearly may be happening and people may want to investigate that, but what I talked about in relation to the commodification of childhood was that childhood itself – that is, the very movement through the early life course – came to be an opportunity to impute and realise exchange value in the economic sphere. Of course, along with economic exchange value arise other kinds of values – symbolic, moral and the like.

I do not think one has to interview or speak with contemporaneous children to engage in Childhood Studies; what one does have to do is to be aware of the kinds of selectivity one is engaging in and account for the inclusions and exclusions which follow.

SG What would you be telling your students about research methods?

DC I encourage an approach which is problem-driven and question-driven. I keep returning to the students and asking them 'What do you want to know?' That gets lost all the time as students try to place themselves in the literature and take on other people's questions and other people's issues. So there is always this back and forth. I would say the other thing that I tend to discuss with students is reflexivity and their own sense of normativity about children, about childhood and about the very particular context in which they want to look at children and childhood, whether it be the commercial–economic sphere, whether it be the home sphere, whether it be a gender or public space. To encourage them to be continually aware that they cannot understand a child or children ever in a pure sense, no matter how elegant a measuring instrument or how finely crafted an argument. This goes beyond ethnographic research; this is why historical and discursive or other kinds of research on children and childhood are necessary. There is a childhood studies that extends further than children's voices, but it can never be indifferent to the absence or erasure of those voices. That's how I teach it and that's how I look at it. Every depiction of a child imputes some notion of childhood.

What I find again and again – and it is not just students but all of us – is that there is a tendency, because the moral discourse is strong and all the surrounding cultural elements reinforce it, to want to get back to some 'true' child. What I say to those with this impulse is: 'When you go home and hug your child or your sister or brother or you get mushy about a child whom you see on the TV, it's OK to have that kind of view. We all have it. That is not, however, what we are doing here in this class and this programme. That is not childhood *studies.*' Like these horrific murders in Newtown,[6] it *is* worse that it involves young children than if it had happened at, say, a yoga studio with adults, but the struggle is to be aware of the impulse and to step out of that frame from time to time. There is a difference between everyday life and the analytic, research, investigatory mode. Sometimes it is brutal to see childhood as a social construction in such a strong way.

SG So that kind of reflexivity is very important to you?

DC Yes, it is inseparable from our work as scholars. What I also realise is that a lot of these views arose from coming into this new programme, where graduate students would sit around the table and look at you and say, 'What is Childhood Studies?' [laughs], and I would think 'The hell if I know. I mean I have a set of texts here, we have got a set of problems.' What emerged for me in the first couple of years in this programme and what has focused me more is that the very idea of the child as construct – where it supposedly can go in any direction and be any kind of thing – really comes from a very privileged position.[7] It is the privileged position of those who do this kind of research because we are standing apart a bit and approach people in their everyday, lived, grounded situations with that kind of lens. Whereas the people themselves, whether it be children or parents or gatekeepers or civil servants or politicians, might have very legitimate reasons not to problematise the notion of the child.

SG You have an interest in personhood?

DC One of the interesting dimensions of personhood, interesting to me, is what I might call interactional personhood. How adults and children or children and children treat each other in interactional spheres. That was part of the insight that I got from a lot of the materials I read for the children's clothing industry history that I did. Some of the reviews I received about the research expressed surprise that children were being spoken to and treated as knowing consumers, as knowing participants, in the clothing shops in the 1920s, 1930s and 1940s by merchants and parents alike. What often gets missed in many studies of children and childhood history are the ways in which the retail, economic sphere can itself be a place where children (and others) arise as persons – where children's perspectives, children's voices, have come to be acknowledged, understood, recognised in ways that it took academics 40 or 50 years longer to get to.

SG Rutgers is unusual in the States in that you have a Childhood Studies doctorate. How do you define Childhood Studies from that perspective, for your programme?

DC Clearly the new paradigm is significant, but it not the only way to understand child studies. For example, there is a great deal of work in children's literature, and on children in literature, children and reading, philosophy, psychology, communication and, of course, history. As well, there are different ways of thinking and approaching research and argumentation – the humanities way of making arguments vs. the social research approach which, despite eschewing science in the positivist sense, can still be evidenced-based in a particular way as in systematic comparison and use of some forms of control. There can be forms of control in historical work. One looks for biases in the materials. One looks at the nature of the documents that you are using and the perspectives which underlie their production. Karen Sánchez-Eppler and Robin Bernstein have offered some of the more innovative ways to think and write about 'the child' and access the child's view and place in historical work, often through its absence.

In our programme, what Cook says Childhood Studies is, is not necessarily what the whole programme says it is, we have to be clear about that [laughs]. And that is good. The way I approach it and what I tell them – because I teach one of the required introductory courses for the doctoral students – is that, although the new paradigm is broad and wide-ranging, it is not the only way to think about the question of the child. So, it is a wide frame I am giving them. In the long run I think the most fruitful generative gift I can offer students is to refrain from foreclosing on the problem of 'the child' and of childhood. Not only asking 'What is the child?' but posing '*When* is a child?' – that is, under what conditions do biological human beings come to be defined as having characteristics, exhibit behaviour or are burdened with expectations associated with shared notions of children? Having them explore that question, posing the question and re-posing it to them in the context of their interests, their projects, to me is an important way to avoid ossifying what is a very dynamic field at the moment.

SG It sound like critical thinking is very important to you? The reflective approach you take is central.

DC For me Childhood Studies does not have a content; it is a perspective, an approach. One can take the Childhood Studies lens and look at any realm of life. It does not always have to nominally include children – mostly it does – but one can look at 'adult institutions' like law, politics and the like and find aspects of childhood encoded within them. What I try to get across is that it isn't the focus on this child or children or social context that is important, it is about an epistemological break or change.

SG Do you think that your approach has policy and practice relevance?

DC I try to get across the idea that the practical implications matter because in any of these spheres of life, whether it be law, policy, schooling or other kinds of institutions, notions of children and childhood are completely encoded within their structures and also encoded in the way these ideas are taken up and put to use on an everyday basis. Being able to understand what the conflicts are, what the confusions are and why people are talking past each other might be assisted with this sort of perspective on children and childhood. So that is my sense of the practicality of the approach. Otherwise if you accept the institutional definitions you are prolonging them. And we have had thirty or forty years in this country of people saying they want to do well by children and they want to do well by education, and things have got increasingly worse for us. So there has to be something more than good intentions; there has to be something more than liking children and wanting to be around children.

SG Very interesting. Do you see Childhood Studies as a field or a whole lot of disparate things which people have pulled together?

DC No, it is certainly not integrated, but I do think that there is something intriguing about this problematising of children and childhood and some people do it more radically than others. It is not truly an integrated field, but I am not sure that too many others are. When you get into any academic field, even in the hard sciences, and you talk to the practitioners, they are still arguing about where the boundaries are and what's in and what's out. This one taps into people's moral and emotional imaginations and lives across a wide spectrum of contexts very differently than if someone is questioning, 'What really is Chemistry?'

SG In the 1980s and 1990s when things were getting going, there was a lot of excitement in the field, do you see the future as exciting?

DC I think there is a tremendous amount of activity and excitement. A lot of people continually get turned on again to these ideas and I see it when teaching introductory courses for undergraduates. You can see a light go on – the bulb over the head. There is something different. They somehow have a new posture toward children and childhood. There is also clearly, and there always has been, an incredibly strong advocacy element to this, always in a strange relationship with what I have just said. To advocate probably means that you have very particular views about children or childhood and/or the politics of them; that has always been an interesting tension and an interesting dynamic. I think the other element that brings people to this thing called Childhood Studies, even when they have very disparate ideas about what is going on, has to do with the moral positioning about children and childhood. The normative, moral aspects of childhood remain strong, even for those who might problematise it. People speak on behalf of children even when they say children should be able to speak on their own. I think in that way there is still a reproduction of paternalism or, at least, of power relations that is unavoidable. It is yet one more tension with which to grapple and I am not sure how it gets resolved. Ultimately those who do ethnographic or face-to-face research are saying 'I want them to speak but they are not going to speak unless I am there to give them the context to speak'…So I am always the adult in the relationship. If I try to make the children co-researchers it is still my project. I am not going to let them write the whole thing [laughs]…for all kinds of reasons. They don't have the cultural capital. Don't get me wrong, I think people are trying to do a lot of interesting stuff around that. I see it, however, as set of pretty strong tensions that don't get resolved but don't stay static; it is a kind of dialectic in the field, a back and forth, which is driving thinking in the field.

I think my students often want to crack me over the head. Every time they want to come down on something, some definition and feel secure, I try to show them that there is another way of seeing. If we just stayed in the comfortable space we wouldn't go anywhere. For me it is about purposeful, reflexive engagement and knowing that you are going down that path and doing it in a directed and purposeful manner.

I want to highlight one more thing in relation to the future, which seems to be so different from what I have been saying because it relates more to a topic. Besides my wish that commercialism and consumption and all of these elements of the economic world be thought of as not only integrated into notions about contemporary children and childhood, but also actually constitutive of them in many ways…Besides that, about which I could go on about forever [laughs], what is emergent, and which has a lot to do with what I have been talking about, is the continual examination of what we might call Global South or majority world childhoods, non-western childhoods, whatever the term one might use. I hope to continue to see different scholars' voices, different kinds of children's voices, different kinds of children's experiences come to the fore that inform and challenge current ways of thinking, including my own.

As well, the area of children's sexualities – of sexual identity, sexual orientation, sexual rights and sexualisation – will continue to grow in importance and will need to be addressed in novel ways by academics, policy makers and others alike. Sexuality speaks the presumed boundaries between childhood and adulthood, challenges that boundary, and thus touches upon power relations in multiple ways. Scholars and students need to move beyond the simplistic views of the market 'sexualisation' – which is one area where few are willing to recognise children's agency.

SG Do you feel optimistic about the future and that there is plenty of grist for the mill for years to come?

DC I think so. I think that one can already see phases. Being an editor of the journal *Childhood* one gets the sense of some things that have come through, but even before that there became a point at which one arrived at a sense in which we do not need any more work demonstrating to us that children have voice and agency. Collectively it is a great insight, it has been an insight for many years and it has been shown in many contexts. But, how can we stand on that without taking it for granted, and do something else? Go somewhere else with it? So I do think that just recently there has been a welcome questioning of the pureness of the child's voice. I am very happy that people like Allison James and Spyros Spyrou and Sirkka Komulainen are addressing this issue. I use these three writers with the graduate students to say, 'Look, if we are going to see children as socially embedded beings, we are also going to have to see that they also have faces to lose and keep, selves to present, and that they have views that come out of their selective and biased experiences. Yes, it's a child's voice but it is not a golden road to truth. It is fraught like anything else, just fraught differently.' I think we are moving past that phase and there are continually going to be new openings and I think that includes historical work, too.

References and note

[1] Bluebond-Langner, M, 1979, *The private worlds of dying children*, Princeton, NJ: Princeton University Press

[2] Cook, DT, 2004, *The commodification of childhood*, Durham, NC: Duke University Press

[3] Cook, DT, 2008, The missing child in consumption theory, *Journal of Consumer Culture* 8, 219–43

[4] Thorne, B, 1987, Re-visioning women and social change. Where are the children? *Gender and Society*, 1, 85–109

[5] Cook, DT (ed), 2002 *Symbolic childhood*, New York: Peter Lang

[6] Newtown, CT, USA where 20 children and six adults were massacred by a lone gunman on 14 December 2012.

[7] Cook, DT, 2009, When is a child not a child, and other conceptual hazards of Childhood Studies, *Childhood* 16, 5–10

SEVEN

William A. Corsaro

Professor William Corsaro was the Robert H Shaffer Endowed Chair and is currently Professor Emeritus in the Department of Sociology at Indiana University, Bloomington, USA. He was a Fulbright Senior Research Fellow in Bologna, Italy between 1983–4 and a Fulbright Senior Specialist Fellow in Trondheim, Norway in 2003. Professor Corsaro has taught at the University of Bologna, Italy and has lectured at several Western European universities. His work is widely cited in North American and European literature and he is internationally recognised as one of the pioneering US scholars in the field of Childhood Studies. Professor Corsaro's primary research interests are the sociology of childhood, the sociology of education, cross cultural perspectives in relation to children's worlds and peer cultures and early childhood education. His extensive publications over the last 30 years include *Friendship and peer culture in the early years* (Ablex, 1985); *We're friends right?: Inside kids' culture* (Joseph Henry Press, 2003); co-editor (with Qvortrup and Honig) *The Palgrave handbook of Childhood Studies* (Palgrave, 2009). The fourth edition of Professor Corsaro's landmark book, *The sociology of childhood*, was published by Pine Forge Press in 2011.

Carmel Smith To start, Bill, will you give me a potted history of how you got to where you are now in your career?

Bill Corsaro Well, I come from a working-class background and I was the first in my family to go to university. I didn't get much guidance, so I had no idea about university and what made sense and I ended up at an engineering school at Purdue University. It was pretty clear after I had been there a short time [laughs] that I wasn't cut out to be an engineer. I subsequently transferred to Bloomington where I fell in love with sociology, basically, and social psychology, but primarily this perspective of symbolic interactionism and pragmatic philosophy: George Herbert Mead and these sorts of people. I really fell in love with the department. They had an honours track and I got in these honours seminars and there were some people who were very influential in my career, professors whom I met there, who later, when I returned there, were my colleagues and who very much supported me.

   Then it was time to go to graduate school and North Carolina, which was a very good place, offered me a full fellowship which I had the whole time I was there. North Carolina was a little bit of a shock because the Social Psychology there was dominated by two or three people who were Skinnerians [both laugh] so it was just the opposite of symbolic interactionism. Leonard Cottrell, who was actually a student of George Herbert Mead, had been in the Chicago school and had published a lot in the Chicago school and he basically took me under his wing. Glen Elder, who is very well known as a life-course researcher, also very much supported me, but it was difficult at North Carolina because there was no qualitative research going on at all – none.

I got very interested in linguistics and read all the Chomsky stuff and the early work on language acquisition by Roger Brown and all these people. I decided to do a dissertation that had to do with children's language use and I was very much supported by Leonard Cottrell. I decided that to really understand children's interaction with each other and with adults I needed to audio-tape and video-tape and he had this money left over from the Russell Sage Foundation and went out and bought me these big, at that time, reel-to-reel video tape recorders and cameras and I basically studied some children of my fellow graduate students in a laboratory. The dissertation primarily turned out to be about how adults talk to children and was the basis of my very first publications on adult language styles with children and tied a lot to Cicourel's work and other work in social linguistics. That was in 1974 and it was the very first qualitative dissertation in the history of the Sociology Department at North Carolina.

When I finished the dissertation Leonard Cottrell and Glen Elder thought that it might be best, even though I had a job offer from Indiana, to consider a post-doc. I already had this whole idea of wanting to study children's interaction and then the idea was to do it in a preschool and Glen Elder had connections to this wonderful preschool, which was sort of a lab preschool, in Berkeley. I was a little bit hesitant about asking, but I had actually worked for the Chair at Indiana as a teaching assistant, so I asked him and he said, 'Well, we want you to get tenure and what's best for you to get tenure is best for us.' I think it was his wisdom knowing that if I was going to do an ethnographic study and have a career it was going to be difficult doing that with a full teaching load. So this then was other people really paving ways for me and helping me make decisions that turned out to be very important. I went to Berkeley, I got in this Child Study Centre and this was the beginning of my ethnographic career and I kind of learned on the seat of my pants how to do ethnography. When I met the teachers they were surprised that I presented myself as wanting their help and their ideas about how I should go about entering the school because this was an observational study and the idea of video-taping and so on. I took their advice and stayed in – this is spelled out in my first book (*Friendship and peer culture in the early years*, 1985) – I stayed in this observation area. What I saw, and this wasn't so surprising given my dissertation, was that adults are very directive when talking to children, they ask a lot of questions and they are very active in engaging children in interaction, but a lot of times children aren't all that interested. I decided that I would develop this 'reactive strategy' which has had quite an influence in the field.

CS Very much so.

BC I would go into an area where the kids were and sit down and wait and let them react to me – I tell this story in the book. I was beginning to question this idea that it was just children learning from each other, there were already things that had made me start to think, 'Hey, they have got something like a peer culture.' At this time in sociology peer culture was for adolescents, nobody ever said even pre-adolescents had peer culture let alone preschool children. The video data really empowered the idea of peer culture because there was so much more going on than I really knew even being right there watching it and trying to write it.

Then the big shift was to take this work comparatively and to go to Italy. I chose Italy for a lot of reasons, some personal, but primarily I wanted to see if I would see peer culture in another country that wasn't that different from the United States and they had one of the most progressive preschool systems in the world at that time, and still do, in many ways. I worked in the north where basically the Reggio Emilia system…I worked in Bologna and Modena but it is all influenced by Reggio. I had some connections there and I wanted to learn Italian – my father spoke some Italian, my mother was not of Italian heritage. So I had to start from scratch and not being fluent in Italian. I used the same reactive method; getting accepted there was much easier because I was seen again as this incompetent adult, who was clearly different from the teachers. I then went to Modena and did the seven-year study, when I followed kids into elementary school. The research shifted a little bit there to involving more interviewing of the teachers and more on transitions. Then I came up with this idea of 'priming events' which extended the 'interpretive reproduction' notion to how children are prepared to make transitions in their lives and how that is a collective process that's done with adults and with each other and that there are things that can smooth these transitions and there are ways that can make them more difficult (spelled out in Corsaro and Molinari, 2005).[1] So, that is a kind of overview of the research.

CS Tell me, then, how you made links with what became known as the 'new paradigm', the key thinkers?

BC Well, this book (*Friendship and peer culture in the early years*) was published in 1985 long before…I mean, Chris Jenks was writing some general theoretical stuff on childhood but it was not empirically based. There was no-one else outside of Piaget, Vygotsky and other people…there wasn't much there. Childhood socialisation almost didn't exist in sociology. This guy Denzin wrote a book called *Childhood socialization* in 1977, he was actually at the same school in Berkeley where I was but after that book he never did anything else on children again, whereas I have never left children. A lot of ethnographers don't stay on a particular topic in the United States, so I was always the child guy and then the Italian child guy [laughs]. The biggest influence on me, outside the United States was here in Norway. There was a guy named Sigrid Berentzen and he was a student of Barthes at Bergen and then he went to the United States, after he did this childhood stuff, and studied with Goffman and collected data on inner-city African American youth. I knew Sigrid quite well but he didn't really publish, he published a thing on children in English but it came out after my book. His, as far as I know, was the first ethnography of preschool children. My book came out in 1985 and then Barrie Thorne's book came out in 1993. The first edition of my *The Sociology of childhood* was in 1997 and that was just about the same time as James and Prout although there wasn't much cross-referencing. Their book is purely theoretical, whereas my *Sociology of childhood* is very empirically based, it is theoretical but it covers a broad range and it also covers social problems with children and so on.[2] It was written as a textbook but very much empirically based on the peer culture parts of it. They put the peer culture stuff as 'the tribal child', they very much wanted to make a cut and differentiate themselves from anything that came before in psychology and sociology that had this notion of the child as a becoming. They wanted it to centre on childhood and that was good, but they did pretty much overlook what I was doing. I don't think there is a reference at all to me in their book; there might be one about one of my early articles, but that's it. They didn't in any way consider the 'interpretive reproduction' notion, it wasn't spelled out at the time in the *Sociology of childhood*, but the main ideas were there in *Friendship and peer culture in the early years*, published in 1985…a lot of people were referencing this book in the United States at the time and some in Scandinavia, but not in Britain.

The bigger influence on me was Jens Qvortrup and his structural approach so I tried to put together, now Leena Alanen says I conflated…[laughing], but it was a way of putting the two together, and the 'orb web model' does that in a way. Jens I see also as…he is very theoretical, but he is really a demographer and brings a lot of demographic and other kinds of empirical data to his arguments, and he is historical, he is a kind of historical demographer. He had directed all these social indicator studies in these different countries, so I was a little more influenced by him. I got to know Jens, mainly through Sigrid who was my connection to Norway until Sigrid died, very young, back in 1996. The seven-year study I did in Italy was supposed to have a Norwegian component to it but I never got to do the Norwegian part because Sigrid passed away.

Then I got very much caught up in…anybody who was writing in that area. I always had a lot of interaction with Barrie Thorne. Then there were a lot of people that were working more with adolescents and pre-adolescents, like my colleague Donna Eder and I did a well-known article on peer culture in the *Annual Review of Sociology*[3] but she is more interested in gender, as is Barrie. This was always something that was brought to me with my work, 'What about gender, what gender differences are you seeing?' 'How would you apply theories related to gender?' The truth of the matter is that for three- and four-year-olds and, to some extent, five-year-olds I didn't see a lot going on. There wasn't that much gender separation. It just wasn't there and people thought it should be. You do see gender separation at the age of five and especially at six and so on, but that was not the age group I was working with. So I didn't talk enough about gender to make some people happy because that was the hot thing in sociology.

The network was beginning to develop in the United States. There was not yet a section in the American Sociological Association (ASA) and these sections were really important in the ASA and have a big influence on the field in research. There was nothing on children, there was nothing on adolescents or youth, there was nothing on socialisation, there was no section on any of those things. Gertrud Lenzer who was the first one to actually teach courses, although she has never done much research, was the first Chair of the Section of Sociology of Children in the American Sociological Association and I was the second but then I immediately saw that we weren't going to survive if we just stuck to children. I said that we should call it 'Children and Youth', which we then did, and the trend has been away from children and more towards studies on youth – it has become a bigger umbrella. At first there were more qualitative people than quantitative, now it's probably more quantitative, but we have the Section and it's a good Section.

On the other hand, in Britain things really took off, in Britain and Scandinavia, and networks began to form. Leena Alanen and Berry Mayall came together. Then James, Jenks and Prout came together a little bit with Jens but mostly they stayed…well, Pia Christensen who worked with Jens then working with Alan Prout and Allison James and there was communication and there were conferences and more involvement and things began to develop. Allison and, to some extent, Alan Prout did more empirical work. Chris Jenks doesn't really do that much empirical work, it is more theoretical and it kind of stays at a high theoretical level. I think it is interesting – I guess later when we get to where I see the field going, I am having some problems with this kind of more abstract theorising or wanting to tie theories of childhood to certain philosophers, like Bourdieu; Prout in his last book was doing a lot of the French philosophers. I don't know if that's the way to go. I will be quite frank, I am not well versed in philosophy, in reading social philosophers, I don't quote Foucault all the time, I haven't read all that. So is my resistance because I don't know it so well or because I really don't know if that is going to get us somewhere? I do think there is a lot to this inter-generational approach. Michael Honig is somebody you would know, of course he was in *The Palgrave handbook of Childhood Studies* (2009), but Michael hasn't published that much in English – I don't read German. I know Leena Alanen… but I am not all that impressed with Mannheim and I don't know where that goes, but I do think the inter-generational aspect is important. The work I am doing right now [research in Trondheim, Norway] is quite inter-generational because this whole civic society and celebration on 17 May is a very inter-generational thing. So I do think that that is a very good approach and I have never taken a position that adults aren't important, but still my main focus is on, 'What are the lives of children like?'

Now, let me say something about the multidisciplinary…I don't see much interdisciplinarity in childhood, what I see is multidisciplinary and I see many different people coming from different fields and different angles and I think our book (*Palgrave handbook of Childhood Studies*, 2009) relates to that. We didn't get as many people who are doing things in developing countries as we wanted. We did get a couple of geographers in there. Then there is all this new work, I talk about this in the latest edition of my book, in technology and the new media and how that has affected children's lives and how there we are seeing…I mean the whole notion of texting was created by children of a certain age, of a certain generation. To me that's all about childhood, so that is where exciting things are going on. Those people are coming from communication departments they are not typical developmental psychologists or sociologists. A lot of them are from Britain and data is being collected in Japan and other kinds of places. There's this book by Mizuko Ito, I don't know if you know this book, *Geeking out*, it is mainly older children but it is very, very interesting.[4] We have got some people from sociology; in the United States, though, there is less and less on young children from sociology. Then a lot of people from education, or practitioners or social workers, especially in Britain you'll see people, if you look at those who contribute to the Journal *Childhood* now, a large percentage of people are coming from Britain. To me, however, it is multi-disciplinary, there is not much that is interdisciplinary going on, in the sense of somebody from psychology working with somebody from geography, but you are seeing people reading each other's work from these disciplines, referring to it, publishing in journals that are broader than their particular discipline and I think that is a good thing but I don't think it is interdisciplinary, I think it is more multi.

CS And do you think, staying on that, that we can call it a distinct field? Is Childhood Studies a distinct field?

BC I think it's a distinct field: in that the focus, the centre of analysis, what Barrie at one point called the conceptual field, is children themselves and childhood. Then there is this debate: is it children or childhood?

CS Which some see as fundamental?

BC To me that has always been beside the point, I think it is both – it is children living their childhoods in a collective way. To me, I am fine if you just want to say childhood because childhood is…well it should be and it would seem like it would be…it is the collective activities of children during this period of their lives.

Now at a more macro level, out of Jens's viewpoint, I think what's really interesting demographically in the United States, and now in Europe, is how children's lives are going to be affected both as immigrants and as natives dealing with changes in their societies that immigrants are going to provide. So take Norway right now, Norway is making up their whole mind about, 'We want assimilation, we don't want assimilation' or 'We like multiculturalism but we don't like some of the practices of these people, they go against our notion of human rights.' So how do you balance these things out? Norway has this very wonderful welfare state compared to the United States but in terms of immigration law they are much more conservative than the United States. If you are born in the

United States you are a citizen immediately. Here you often have to wait until you are 18 before you can even apply to be a citizen.

CS Really?

BC There are exceptions to this but often you have to wait. On the other hand, Norway takes much better care of immigrants who have access to a very generous welfare state. In the United States we don't have a very generous welfare state so many of our immigrants are living in poverty, living in very poor situations, very difficult situations, many of them end up in prisons or in crime, their education is very limited especially given that they speak a different language and so on. So to me this is a wide open area for Childhood Studies, the whole issue of migration and immigration, what's good for children and how it affects their lives and is it even good for a child in certain developing countries for their family to migrate? Would they be better off staying where they are if we could deal with the corruption and other things that may be going on in their countries? On the other hand, you are going to have more immigration, especially in countries like Italy, where the fertility rates are very low, they actually need more children. This, to me, if I could continue my career in Italy, for example, this is what I would be studying. I am doing a little bit of it here [in Norway] but I don't think it's going to go much beyond this article I am working on, or maybe a book down the line, but I see this as something we need more of. I also think that we need more about the issue of globalisation, and how globalisation is related to immigration, and there, again, I think Cindi Katz's book is a really important book in Childhood Studies yet a lot of people aren't aware of this book.[5] It really showed how global factors had an enormous effect on children's everyday lives in the Sudan and, again, because it was longitudinal, on how their lives were affected when they became young adults. So, to me, that's an area where I would get excited and I would hope we would have students.

CS During this last part of the interview, given your profile and experience as an ethnographer, I must ask you about qualitative research. You have already covered some of this, but tell me about your experience of qualitative research and your theoretical framework.

BC Mostly I was self-taught and I have to say that I did have the support of this man to whom I dedicated the 1985 book, Leonard Cottrell, who got this equipment for me, which was very important, and who gave me moral support. The same can be said of the person who was the chair of my dissertation, Glen Elder. He was not a qualitative researcher but he gave me the kind of moral support and recognition I needed, and it turned out, as I said, that I was the first person in North Carolina to do a qualitative dissertation. I am sure that there have been more since, but still not very many [laughs]. In a way I was pretty much self-taught. Some of it, to a certain extent, was luck, but it was using the ethnographic imagination, we talk about the sociological imagination, but the ethnographic imagination in the sense that you listen and learn and make decisions in a careful, rigorous way. On the other hand, I think qualitative research should be rigorous.

CS Please say more about rigour in qualitative research.

BC This label that it is soft…rigour is…wasn't Michelangelo pretty rigorous and he wasn't a physicist? The idea that only hard sciences are rigorous, you can be very rigorous in qualitative research. You are rigorous in qualitative ethnography by documenting what you do, the decisions you make. I don't think we should throw out criteria like reliability, validity, generalisability, we should look at these criteria and apply them to the nature of qualitative research. This idea that I wanted an interactive episode or a unit of collection, not everybody agrees with me about this, I think was important in my work. This notion that I wanted representative sampling of the group that I was studying, in addition to theoretical sampling, I think is important. Then, with validity, you have this rich data, make the most use of it, immerse yourself in it; force yourself. The generalisability issue, can you generalise from qualitative research? Well, you can if you do a series of studies that build upon one another. I went from 20 kids to hundreds and hundreds of kids, studies that allowed me to see again and again the same kinds of patterns and routines, or interesting variations culturally, that then allow me to generalise a lot more or to compare my findings to other ethnographic studies, or even quantitative studies that bear on the same kinds of issues. Now, there is the challenge, these post-modern people that go on about this crisis in representation, there is the challenge of how you represent the voices of those you study and we do that best by engaging them in our research the best that we can. This idea of research with, rather than on, children I think is important. I think I have got better at that. At the same time, I think it should be rigorous, we can't think we can just go in there willy-nilly or call everything ethnographies. Some people do ten interviews and they say its ethnography – it's not; or they observe for a very short period of time – that's not ethnography. That is where, as I said, I do get worried about people getting support to have the time to do this kind of rigorous, long-term, intensive kind of research.

I, also, don't believe that it's necessary to constantly fight the battle between interpretive science and positivistic science. I don't see them, necessarily, in opposition. They make different assumptions about how to go about doing research, especially what's the best way to do it, and in the social sciences I think the interpretive way is the best way, but to have battles with these people is, I think, unproductive and certainly they are making contributions. At the same time, you have to stand up for what you believe in and you can't…people say, 'Well, why can't we do multi-method things?' Well, a lot of times you can't because these people take a positivistic approach, they want to take your interpretive approach and they want to turn it in to what they want it to be, something else, and I don't want it to be something else. That doesn't mean you can't do multi-method research but you have to stay truthful to your assumptions.

References

[1] Corsaro, W, Molinari, L, 2005, *I compagni: Italian children's transition from preschool to elementary school*, New York: Teachers College Press

[2] Corsaro, W, 2011, *The sociology of childhood* (4th edn), Thousand Oaks, CA: Pine Forge Press

[3] Corsaro, W, Eder, D, 1990, Children's peer cultures, *Annual Review of Sociology* 16, 197–220

[4] Ito, M, 2010, *Hanging out, messing around, and geeking out: Kids living and learning with new media*, Cambridge, MA: Massachusetts Institute of Technology Press

[5] Katz, C, 2004, *Growing up global: Economic restructuring and children's everyday lives*, Minneapolis, MN: University of Minnesota Press

EIGHT

Judith Ennew

We note with sadness and regret the untimely death of Judith Ennew on 4th October 2013 in Kuala Lumpur.

Judith Ennew was awarded a PhD in social anthropology in 1978 from the University of Cambridge, UK. From 1979 she was an activist and researcher in the human rights of children, initially specialising in child workers, 'street children' and child sexual exploitation. A recent focus was on statelessness, working towards giving people who live, but do not exist in any records, an identity through a supra-national civil registration system. Dr Ennew published extensively throughout her career but is possibly best known for her book, *The sexual exploitation of children*, published by Polity Press in 1986. She worked as an academic as well as a consultant and adviser to organisations such as Anti-Slavery International, the International Labour Organization, Plan International, Save the Children, UNICEF, WHO and World Vision, working in Latin America, Africa, South and South-East Asia and Eastern Europe on children's rights issues. As an activist, she was involved in various programmes to strengthen capacity in rights-based research with children, especially among grass-roots workers, through the non-governmental organisation, Knowing Children.

Carmel Smith Judith, will you start by saying something about yourself and your career to date – a potted history?

Judith Ennew I was born in 1944 in the middle of an air raid (which some might say explains a lot). My family were London Welsh (I'm very proud of the fact that my grandfather and his older brother started the London Welsh Choir). In my family I am the only child of my generation, and the first person to get past elementary school. I won a scholarship (11+) to a direct grant girls school and was encouraged to do well academically both at school and at home. This personal detail partly explains why I am not particularly interested in gender or 'wimmin'. That has never been an issue with me – class and ethnicity shaped me. So my teenage rebellion was to leave school, having walked out in mid A-level exams, get pregnant and be a teenaged unmarried mother – not deliberate, but the best thing that ever happened to me. It was totally outrageous to be a happy unmarried mother in 1963 – 'single parents' had not been invented then.

CS Do you think your early experiences gave you an insight/empathy with children and young people?

JE No, I think my early experiences give me an ability to relate to people, of any age or gender, who are scared, powerless, puzzled and don't know where the next meal is coming from. I am, in principle, not interested in children and young people any more than in women as a group. I am interested in human rights.

Skip past being a housewife in suburbia and a host of jobs (barmaid, cleaner, then finally beauty consultant). At the age of 25 I went to teacher training college as a mature student with the intention of being a primary school teacher. There I was influenced by 'The Plowden Report'[1] and Jackson and Marsden's, *Education and the working class*.[2] The scales fell from my eyes and I realised that my issues with life were class issues and not my fault for being 'too emotional'. I also discovered the social sciences. I had a great sociology lecturer (from the first wave of Leicester University sociologists) and by a social anthropologist who inspired me, as well as a fantastically good philosophy lecturer. I also gained a good grounding in child psychology. I am sorry if all this seems self-indulgent but I hope it begins to explain why I don't have a career, but I do have a vocation.

CS Not at all self-indulgent, it makes sense. Knowing why people came to work in the field seems really important in order to understand their subsequent work.

JE I then went to Cambridge for the fourth year of my BEd, still expecting to be a primary school teacher. I ended up doing a PhD in social anthropology on trade unions in the oil industry of the Outer Hebrides, Scotland. This is where I realised the ethnicity stuff. For the first time, after an English education in 'history', I discovered that I am a Celt and learned about the internal colonialism of the United Kingdom – better called the Disunited Queendom these days!

CS What happened during your time at Cambridge that led to you playing such a pivotal role in the field of Childhood Studies?

JE I actually deliberately avoided courses on family, women and children at all times. I fell in with a lot of what might be called Marxist epistemologists from different disciplines. It was the early 1970s, it was okay to be Marxist and the Communist Party of Great Britain was very open. I am still a Marxist in the sense that this provides the best explanation of the way the world works. I discovered and revelled in Althuser, Lacan, Foucault – and these are all still major influences. I had to read them all in French in those days. My main influence was Paul Q Hirst and the group that gathered round him and Barry Hindess (Leicester University sociology again). Whatever I have written or 'presented' from 1972 onwards, you will always find a reference to Marx/Althuser/Lacan/Foucault, if you look for it.

CS Tell me about the journey from your time at Cambridge to where you are now.

JE I had discovered human rights, through meeting Jeremy Swift and Steve Jones (then causing a revolution in the Anti-Slavery Society [Now Anti-Slavery

International, ASI] – the oldest human-rights' organisation in the world) at a conference on indigenous peoples. I worked with the ASI as a consultant from 1972, was employed by them in the mid-1980s (while still being an academic) and ended up on their board for a while in the 1990s.

I made a major decision in the 1970s to combine activism with academic life – social anthropology was also an influence here. It seemed like colonialism… remember this was the period of new nations being 'given their freedom' at a tremendous rate. The decision was based on a commitment to what was then called the 'Third World' – under-developed by what was then called the 'First World' (or 'The West' – there's a great book to be written on the construction of this…). I could see people going off to work in the Third World as a career decision and they were not always rigorous thinkers. I committed myself to trying to combine getting my hands really dirty in activism and using academic rigour as best I could.

CS So that explains how you came to be based in Thailand and Malaysia?

JE Eventually – but after 93 other countries. I finished my PhD in 1978 and I learned about human rights and the UN by practical work for the Anti-Slavery (ASI) in the 1970s (that is, not as an academic). Annus Mirabilis was 1979, the UN International Year of the Child (although it was actually run mostly by NGOs). Anti-Slavery asked me to do a piece of research (funded by the Ford Foundation) on child work, to be a contribution to the International Year of the Child as a kind of rebuttal of the ILO [International Labour Organization] contributions, which were all based on national statistics of the 'formal' labour market.

So I chose to go to Jamaica – where ethnicity met racism and I grew up. It was a wonderful place. Marley was still alive, everyone and everything was 'jumping' – and I met my first street children. I also started the research approach that is now 'enshrined' in 'The Right to be Properly Researched' in relation to children's opinions and experiences (never children's 'voices'…ugh!). I decided to work through finding out what children tell you when they are not asked direct questions, to see how work fitted in to the rest of their lives.

CS Tell me why you find the idea of children's voices problematic.

JE When people talk about 'collecting children's voices' – what are they doing? Surgically removing their vocal cords? In today's mistaken political and academic context children have 'voices', but only adults have opinions. Until it is recognised that children have valid opinions and are not just decorative additions to political life, their human rights will continue to be violated – often by the very people who think they are helping.

CS I am intrigued by your comments about the violation of children's human rights often by those who think they are helping. Does that include those working in Childhood Studies?

JE People working in Childhood Studies rarely have any idea about children's rights. They make the crassest mistakes in discussing the UNCRC [United Nations Convention on the Rights of the Child] and have no idea about human rights. Similarly human rights academics and practitioners tend to be ignorant of children's rights (I have known some who think the UNCRC is a UNICEF welfare charter) and those who specialise in children's rights are quite isolated. All social scientists could do with a proper background in human rights and knowledge of the UN system (including knowing about the League of Nations – and going back to Tom Paine...). I made/make it a point from 1980s onwards that, whatever courses I lectured on, there was one lecture on the UN and human rights.

In 1984, when I came 'back' to the UK from Peru (where I pursued the street and working children issue after Jamaica), I had become involved in two important field-based activities. First, the group of people who were pushing the drafting of the UNCRC and influential figures such as Nigel Cantwell. Second, children's participation as political 'protagonists' (does not translate well from the Spanish *protagonismo*) through the work of MANTHOC – associated with liberation theology – where the influence of people such as Alejandro Cussianovich were very important.

Then in the mid-1980s I was working in King's College Research Centre (alongside Anti-Slavery work and consultancies) and I had free use of a seminar room. I knew about 12 people doing social-ish research with children, but they mostly did not know each other, so I thought that we might have fun meeting for a day to discuss the methods we used. Three weeks later there were about 80 at the party and we took over a conference room. That was the 'Ethnography of Childhood Workshop' in 1986 and it went on for two to three days. There was no time to raise funds, so I was in debt to Kings for at least a year. Pamela Reynolds happened to be in the UK at the time and I can remember Jean La Fontaine being there. I think Alan Prout and Allison James were both part of it, Jo Boyden, and Benno Glauser were there and Carolyn Steedman was at the first and third. Ginny Morrow (then my PhD student) was a major supporter and organiser as was Brian Milne (at that time my second husband) who has been involved in all my plots and plans from 1984 onwards although he only attended the second, third and fifth workshops in subsequent years.

CS This is the workshop that so many people refer to as being the first time they realised other people were doing the same sort of work?

JE Yes. There was a wonderful follow up in Canada the next year. It came back to Cambridge in 1988, in Newnham. That was the first time anyone from the

'Childhood as a Social Phenomenon' project, such as Jens Qvortrup, came. That project had started relatively recently. I was part of it and it was very well represented at the third workshop, which was also the first time that Alan and Allison began to gather together the new Sociology of Childhood 'paradigm'. They recruited many at that meeting. I was never intended by them to be part of it, which I was not upset about – we remain good friends. Then Pamela Reynolds set up the Fourth Ethnography of Childhood Workshop in Zimbabwe. The next one was due to be in Delhi, but the local organiser died suddenly, so they petered out until Roxana Waterson and I did another (Asia-oriented) workshop in NUS [National University of Singapore] in July 2006.

CS How do you feel personally knowing that you were responsible for bringing together what turned out to be such an influential group of people?

JE Just one step on the road – happenstance. I'm glad people 'found' each other. I had fun, but for me the deeper understanding of my work, and the things that I am proud of being involved in, came later.

CS Can you say more about that deeper understanding and the things you are particularly proud of?

JE My line when people ask me what I do is to say that I am an activist and academic, in that order, and that I work in human rights, which happens mostly to be children's rights. This means mostly children's wrongs; there is no money in children's rights, only in children's wrongs, that is, 'exploitation'. What I focus on now, as my mind and body fade, is to pass on as much as I can of the lessons I have learned to young people who can make models appropriate to the South. The staff of 'Knowing Children' are all 18–26 years old, and we facilitate a children's organisation for reporting on children's rights in Malaysia, 'The Mousedeer Organisation for Children's Rights', which was officially launched last Saturday [7th December 2012]! The key to 'Knowing Children' is that it is about better data for children in policies and programmes based on their right to be properly researched with no quantative/qualitative distinction. I have never been part of the academic tendency in social sciences to make that distinction. Nor am I advocating 'mixed methods' – the term I use is 'triangulation'. In my activist work, statistics (themselves cultural products) are required to make governments and other power brokers sit up and take notice/action.

CS So how would you summarise where you are now?

JE I work in statelessness in this corner of the world with the Karen, Rohingya, Chin and other minority groups. I also work to try to destroy dominant ideas of nationality globally. My influences here are Hobsbawm[3] and Benedict Anderson.[4] Children are a way in to this, but the 'This Is Who I Am' programme of 'Knowing

Children' is equally 'do-able' with adults. The key idea is to give people, who live but do not exist in any records, an identity through a supra-national civil registration system. We are thinking big.

CS Can I now just take you back to the 1980s and ask you about the UNICEF CEDC [children in especially difficult circumstances] process, the work on sexual exploitation and how you joined the 'Childhood as a Social Phenomenon' project.

JE During the early 1980s, UNICEF was involved in the 'Child Survival Revolution', basically oriented in the health of children less than five years old. This had a lot to do with why UNICEF was not interested in (indeed against) the drafting/development of the UNCRC. There was something of an uprising within UNICEF against this, by field directors, mostly inspired by Tarzie Vittachi, trying to re-orient UNICEF towards older children and social issues. The key argument was, okay you vaccinate and feed them and then, when they are six, they become healthy child workers, street children and child soldiers.

Between 1984 and 1985 (when I was working for Anti-Slaves as their Child Labour Officer) UNICEF Executive Board set up a series of consultancies to write papers on these groups of children. Anti-Slaves was given the consultancy for working children; so I did the one on child labour, then one of the two on street children, and finally the one they could not find anyone else to do – on child prostitution. I said that I didn't know a thing about it but UNICEF said, 'Nor does anyone else, so you might as well try'.

CS So UNICEF was focusing on child health and survival issues rather than quality of life issues?

JE The idea of 'quality of life' for children was not born then outside academic circles. UNICEF only worked on MCH [maternal and child health], the GOBI-FFF approach (growth charts, oral rehydration therapy, breast feeding, immunisation, fertility control, food supplements, female education). The basic goal was to reduce under-five mortality worldwide. The debates were between UNICEF and WHO (which wanted to do this health stuff); within UNICEF, and between UNICEF/the US government and the emerging movement for children's rights.

CS Where did you position yourself in those debates?

JE I was with Tarzi Vittachi and the human rights guys. As children's rights were raising the barrier for childhood to 18 years, UNICEF (as the 'lead organisation' – the only one – for childhood within the UN system) had to raise it too.

CS How did you begin to understand child prostitution theoretically as well as personally? I ask about theory because from what you have said you wouldn't have seen it as child rescuing?

JE Labour market theory – not gender first. You will have guessed…children as agents, boys as well as girls – rescue is not the issue. The report I did on this for UNICEF was repressed when all the others were released, apparently because they thought that this issue might be bad for their image. So I rewrote it as a book [*The sexual exploitation of children*], which was published by Polity Press in 1986 – and is probably the academic(ish) book for which I was and am best known. Note that this happened at the same time as the first Ethnography of Childhood Workshop…guess which I found most important?

CS The more I listen to you the more I understand how human rights are at the core of everything you do and are interested in. When I hear some of the current arguments in Childhood Studies I am reminded of some of those that happened in Women's Studies when, I felt, we lost sight at times of the economic underpinnings and wasted a lot of time. That is sometimes my fear for Childhood Studies.

JE Ha! A fellow believer.

In terms of 'Childhood as a Social Phenomenon', just to finish the period 1986–93, I got in to it by accident – as usual. On the day I arrived in the University of Essex for a temporary job there was an invitation on my desk, which had originally been sent to Peter Townsend I think, to an inaugural meeting of the 'Childhood as a Social Phenomenon' project. This was to take place after an international conference 'Growing into a Modern World' at the Norwegian Centre for Child Research (Trondheim, Norway, 6–9 June 1987). So began a glorious five years of meetings organised by the European Centre in Vienna taking place in different places in Europe and Canada. I worked with wonderful colleagues, had great fun and huge debates with some of them. The main links academically were with Jens Qvortrup, Helmut Wintersberger, (the late) Lea Shamgar-Handelman and (the also late) Angelo Saporiti. For me the key issue was not the idea that childhood was a social phenomenon – obvious to an anthropologist from the start – but the development, by Angelo Saporiti, Giovanni Sgritta and An-Magritt Jensen, of children-centred statistics. That blew my mind. This was also the beginning of 26 years of association with NOSEB (Norwegian Centre for Child Research) and, through 'Childhood as a Social Phenomenon', with Scandinavia/Nordic countries; although I already had links with Norway because of the oil stuff, with Denmark because of the Caribbean stuff and with Sweden because of the child sexual exploitation stuff and children's rights.

In 1992 (or 1993) there was another conference organised by NOSEB, after which I was invited on to the boards of both Childwatch International and *Childhood*. Sharon Stephens was a leading light in both. If you want to know more about her influence read the introduction Ginny Morrow and I wrote for a special issue of *Childhood* in 2002 after Sharon's death.[5] For a long time after she died, my reaction to any new idea I had would be, 'I must talk to Sharon about this'.

In 1993 an informal group developed in response to the first three country reports to the Committee on the Rights of the Child. We rather grandly referred to it as 'The London Process' because it met in the offices of Save the Children UK. Out of that process came two of the best experiences of my life: The Childwatch International Monitoring Children's Rights Project and the research process now known as 'The Right to be Properly Researched' (RPR). This has nothing to do with Childhood Studies and everything to do with studying children. I also undertook major work in...if I can remember them all, Senegal, Zimbabwe, Nicaragua, Kenya, Tanzania, Turkey, Palestine, India, Nepal, Venezuela, Vietnam, Thailand, South Africa, Indonesia ...I once counted 95 countries that I have visited in my life – all but two of them for work.

CS You are one of the few people whose work can be said to be truly international and that gives it an edge and a depth that is not possible for those of us coming from minority world contexts with little knowledge or experience of the great big majority world out there? I have read the 'The Right to be Properly Researched' material and in the light of that what do you think about the children's research output from the field of Childhood Studies in recent decades and what should we be focusing on now?

JE Some of it is very good – but barely reaches beyond the Straits of Gibraltar. They need to get their hands dirty in the Global South (can't get my head around minority/majority); and they must stop challenging the UN Convention on the Rights of the Child [UNCRC] as 'not culturally relevant' when they are ignorant of children's rights.

The focus is their choice; but (back to epistemology) their choice is limited by the structures that position them. That is why I am cosied up in the South, where there are more children, and specifically in the part of the world that is home to the majority of the world's children. That is why 'Knowing Children' is registered here – to develop models that work here, are relevant here and not imposed from the North. At the same time, I retired completely from academic life over 18 months ago, although I still do the occasional plenary/keynote in Conferences. The best scholars I have ever met were in Africa – I mean *in* Africa – in the 1990s. Although trained in the North they are committed to the South. With African universities often closed, under-funded and starving for books, they got to discuss the real issues (similar to some of the 'underground' seminars in Eastern Europe before 1989).

CS The other thing you have done, which I find really interesting, is to focus on employing young people in your organisation. Do we need to rethink scholarship?

I interviewed someone the other day who said that in a recession we should cut out the 'middle man' and go straight to the children?

JE That's it exactly and it is not just children – 'The Right to be Properly Researched' [RPR] works with adults, especially those who have had no 'voice' – stateless people, for example. If they learn how to do their own research, then they are empowered (forget teaching them to fish). Another of my influences was Paolo Friere – I'm a 'child of the '60s'. The main point about RPR, however, is that we are systematic enough, and reach big enough samples, to produce good statistics (and teach children how to interpret/analyse them). There is no chance of influencing policy unless you have good, powerful numbers.

CS And that then explains your rejection of any notion of a quantitative/ qualitative distinction?

JE Exactly again! Pictures and cute sayings don't change the world. Nor does research with the few children of the North.

CS What about the current state of the field? Does it need to be really shaken up in order to find a new energy?

JE One of my Argentinean colleagues in the YMCA once said something to me that I repeat as often as possible, about the South and North: *Nosotros vivimos – tu viviste!* Loose translation: 'Here [in the South] we are still living – you [in the North] used to be alive!' Capitalism needs to be shaken up. In earlier economic times, scholars could have influence (although they also could be executed or imprisoned for challenging the dominant social paradigm). Now I think scholars are, in general, too hidden in their little university holes trying to survive in an uncertain world. On the other hand, I went to a Conference at Rutgers University in the US not so long ago and was really impressed by the presentations of MA and PhD students. Marx did say the revolution would begin in the US…

CS And what about the future? You are very clear as to why 'Knowing Children' is constituted as it is. What else would you like to see happen on a more global level? Is it time that Childhood Studies moved towards seeing children's rights as part of an integrated struggle for human rights?

JE The vision of 'Knowing Children' is that all policies and programmes for children will be determined by rights-based scientific data – worldwide. If anything, I would like to see better research with children with disabilities (we are piloting some), greater understanding of and commitment to the human rights of children, and links between child research and peace research. I don't mean solving conflicts, I mean exploring peace as an option when interests are at variance – in families, neighbourhoods, across religious divides and between 'nations'.

We need to separate children as an oppressed group for the same reason that we have a UNCRC. They need additional human rights to provision (families, healthcare, nutrition, education and so forth) and protection (from all the nasty things that adults do). Yes, they are part of the human–rights' struggle, but to be equal you have to sometimes treat groups differently. You cannot give the same education to all children (some of them are deaf, some cannot see…), but you have to have *very good reasons* for treating people differently in order that they can be equal.

CS What advice would you offer to new people coming to work in the field of children/childhood? As one of the early and key thinkers leading to the 'new paradigm' for children and childhood, what has all your years of experience taught you?

JE Don't think welfare – think rights!

References
[1] 'The Plowden Report', Central Advisory Council for Education (England) into Primary Education in England (1967) *Children and their primary schools,* London: HMSO, www.educationengland.org.uk/dcouments/Plowden
[2] Jackson, B, Marsden, D, 1962, *Education and the working class*, London: Routledge
[3] Hobsbawm, E, 2012, *Nations and nationalism since 1780* (2nd edn), Cambridge: Cambridge University Press
[4] Anderson, B, 2006, *Imagined communities: The origin and spread of nationalism* (2nd edn with additional material), London: Verso
[5] Ennew, J, Morrow, V, 2002, Releasing the energy: Celebrating the inspiration of Sharon Stephens, *Childhood* 9, 1, 5–17

NINE

Ivar Frønes

Ivar Frønes is Professor of Sociology at the University of Oslo, Norway, and senior researcher at the Norwegian Centre for Child Behavioural Development. His work and international experience covers a variety of areas, with an emphasis on life course analysis; children, youth and family sociology; well-being and social exclusion. Professor Frønes is a member of the Board of the International Society for Child Indicators, and on the editorial board of *American Journal of Orthopsychiatry* and *Child Indicator Research*. He is the founder of the journal *Childhood* and among the group that initiated Childwatch International. His numerous publications cover various perspectives on childhood as illustrated by publications such as, *Among Peers* (1995); Status zero youth in the welfare society (2007); On theories of dialogue, self and society: Redefining socialisation and the acquisition of meaning in light of the intersubjective matrix (2007); Theorising indicators. On indicators, signs and trends (2007) and Childhood: Leisure, culture and peers (2009). In Scandinavia Professor Frønes has published books on digital divides, modern childhood, marginalisation and risk, cultural trends and a variety of subjects related to childhood, youth and life course development. At present he is working on projects on life course, childhood and marginalisation.

Carmel Smith To start, Ivar, perhaps you could give a potted history of where you began, to where you are now in Childhood Studies and in your career?

Ivar Frønes I think where I started is important because I am from a working-class background and the idea was to become an engineer [both laugh]; that is what you do if you are reasonably clever in school and you have a working-class background, you become an engineer. Then I realised I wanted to become a psychologist and then a sociologist; I think the reason for that was partly political. This was the late 1960s, so sociology was part of the social and political revolutions that were effectively taking place at that time. I was also a folk singer and was involved in 'rock and roll' and all that kind of stuff. I realised that that was a very tough career and that I was not good enough, and I am very happy with that [laughs], and I decided to become a sociologist. I had been involved very much with young people and subcultures, so I thought the sociology of youth was a natural place to start. If you have been on the stage for a little bit you have a feeling for contexts, and I had the idea that this could be useful both as a social worker and as a sociologist. So I started to work in youth clubs with teenagers and began working with the sociology of young people and subcultures. I remember when I was in my twenties I gave lectures in lots of places in Norway on the sociology of youth, very few people in sociology were involved in that field. It is interesting that the sociology of childhood and the sociology of youth were different in the sense that adolescents were always understood as subjects, in fact as very innovative subjects; in the traditional understanding of childhood, as you can see, for example, with Mannheim, childhood is a period when cultures are transferred from the older generation to the younger.[1] Related to youth, however, Mannheim changed perspective: the young people were subjects confronting the society and the older generations. This interaction constituted what he called a 'historical generation'. He didn't use the phrase 'cohort' that came especially with Ryder and Elder. So the understanding of teenagers was very different from the understanding of children. So I came into sociology and the sociology of socialisation of children through being a social worker. I also have psychology and anthropology as what are termed 'supporting disciplines' in the traditional German inspired system known as Magistergrad. My subsequent doctoral thesis focused on the position of peers in the socialisation process.

CS Sounds very rounded: sociology, psychology and anthropology?

IF Yes. It was focused on the sociology of young people and socialisation but I was also fascinated by psychology. Of course, when you are young you are fascinated by Freud [laughs]. I read Freud but I also read Lacan which was not that common in the mid-1970s. Later on I focused on theories of cognitive and moral development, and of course, Vygotsky and what is termed 'theories of activity'. Activity is a broader concept in English than in the Scandinavian languages but it is not completely identical to 'Tätigkeitstheorie'.

The anthropological perspective is interesting because anthropological studies illustrate that childhoods vary and are interwoven with general cultural and social patterns. The work of Margaret Mead, Ruth Benedict and Eric Erikson (in *Childhood and Society* where he merged psycho-analysis and anthropology)[2] all underlined the relationship between childhood and societies.

CS Tell me about how you brought these disciplines to your study of childhood.

IF I have always been involved with practitioners: with teachers, social workers, pre-school teachers, psychiatrists and clinical psychologists. I have also always been interested in Darwin and evolutionary psychology; I have even been to the Galapagos Islands. Modern evolutionary thinking is very interesting from a childhood perspective as it provides a framework for the understanding of genetic factors in children's development. Partly because of the terrible Romanian orphanages, we now know a lot about the sensitivity of the phases of childhood and how deprivation may influence the development of the brain.

CS Are you referring to Rutter's work and the longitudinal study with Romanian adoptees undertaken by Rutter and his team in London in the 1990s?

IF Yes, he was involved in one of the first articles on Romanian orphans in the mid-1990s and we also have American studies on deprivation indicating that some kids have lost up to two 'intelligent years', at the age of six. This, of course, is very important if you are interested in social inequality and the diversity of lives of children, not only the general category of childhood. I suppose partly because of my background I try to keep both the life course developmental perspective and the childhood perspective. The problem is to integrate them, but if you lack one of the perspectives you will simply lose track of what is going on. I remember that there were some discussions in Norway where somebody was asked about the effects of biological factors or genetic factors, and they answered, 'We are not working with that.' That is okay from one perspective but if you want to explain behaviour problems you have to bring in genetic profiles. Genes are of course interacting not only with social conditions on the micro level, but with the wider societal framework. In Norway 1,000 years ago the Viking kings were looking for tall teenage boys with lack of impulse control, who became heroes; but those guys now are living in a very different context, in the educational knowledge economy. If you want to understand aggression and the behaviours that are related to traditional criminal behaviour, then you have to bring in genetic factors, but in interaction with social, economic and cultural contexts. One illustration; ADHD has biological roots, but is also rooted in the knowledge/educational society. Some of the scientists working with genes simply lost the perspective of social context and explained everything by genes. That was the debate in the 1970s, starting with the book by Wilson on sociobiology, but evolutionary psychology today is quite different from the sociobiology of the 1970s. In accordance with new perspectives on biology the recent decades have also seen a constitution of a 'new' infant and child; the child as an active subject. Just to give you one illustration, in the famous book by Berger and Luckmann, *The social construction of reality* (1966), there is a section on socialisation and they say something like, the society and the parents try to socialise the child but the little animal fights back.[3] Now we know that this is completely silly, the little animal socialises itself. It doesn't fight back; neither is it a tabula rasa. Even a newborn baby is actively shaping its own socialisation. If you want to understand not only childhood but also the children that are passing through childhood, you have to have this perspective – children are active developing subjects interacting with social, cultural and economic frameworks.

CS Tell me, Ivar, from your recollection, how did the ideas come together to such a point that there was a declaration of a 'new paradigm'? Can you recall some of that period and what you remember about it?

IF For me, an essential part of the new paradigm was the understanding of children as subjects and their right to a voice. I think it was, as you say in English, it was 'in the air'. If you look at the countercultures from the 1960s and the young people fighting for, in psychological terms, self-realisation, the idea was not only that you had a political right to a voice; self-expression was also about identity. This was always at the core of youth studies, for me it was natural to expand this perspective to the understanding of children. The old authoritarian regimes were falling everywhere: at the school, at the workplace, in the family. There is also, of course, a relationship between feminist thinking and the sociology of childhood. In addition, there was a legal development in this period: children were becoming individuals, not only members of the family. The Convention on the Rights of the Child came into force in 1990 but there were few studies where children were given a voice. In sociological theories of socialisation children are not subjects, they are simply being socialised. In anthropology it was different. Some ethnographical studies were giving children at least some kind of voice in the late 1950s and early 1960s. I know that some anthropologists feel that the 'new' paradigm was not new to them. In the sociology of socialisation, however, children had not been given a voice; in the understanding of socialisation children were objectified. So it was a political paradigm, it was a normative paradigm, it was a moral paradigm and it was a sociological paradigm. The child had always been a subject of developmental theories, as with Piaget and Kohlberg, but their focus was on development, not on children's experiences and perspectives as such. The sociology of childhood emphasises children's lives as children, not development, and not the relationship between your position as a child and your position later in life. For me the dominant focus on children as children and not on development and life course became a problem; children's lives and the development of modern inequality can only be understood in the perspective of life course development. The focus on children's lives as children, however, brought a lot of research on children's perspectives on their own lives. It was also based on a perspective that I knew from my experience as a social worker, that when you talk to kids you get different answers to when you talk to their parents or teachers.

CS So Ivar, given the range of disciplines that you draw on in your work how did you consider that that range had been included? Did you feel that the range in terms of disciplinary representation, was right for the time or did you have some misgivings that some of these perspectives weren't included?

IF The sociology of childhood was of course mostly a sociological endeavour, lacking interdisciplinary perspectives, and mostly qualitative. As I see it, we need interdisciplinarity; that is, the combining of different perspectives and methods. We have to grasp childhood as children's lives, as children's daily lives at different age levels, but also as life course, how children pass through childhood. There are a variety of childhoods and perspectives when you see childhood through children's eyes. The diversity, however, is even more dramatic when you look at childhoods from a life course perspective, the variety of developmental and life course paths though which children pass through childhood. This is extremely important if you are concerned about inequality and the integration into adult life.

The UN Convention on Children's Rights underlines children's right to a voice, but what is striking with the Convention is that it puts emphasis on development. I can't exactly remember how they phrase it, but a child has the right to develop its potentials to the fullest. There is a current trend to focus on well-being – and well-being is a complex concept. Well-being came into modern politics from economics partly because the concept of standard of living and the old utility perspectives were too narrow. Well-being points in the direction of quality of life as well as towards both good health and self-realisation. If you look at Amartya Sen's understanding of well-being he is putting an emphasis on the opportunity structures and development, freedom and rights, as well as on the life at the present.[4] Rights imply a good life as a child, but also that you are not blocked from development because of class, caste or gender.

CS I want to ask you about qualitative approaches to research and the proliferation of methods focusing on gaining access to children's voices in Childhood Studies.

IF I think what we need is what I call mixed methods or multi-methods because in many cases you cannot secure validity in qualitative research. You can see in some students' Masters' thesis that they too often draw general conclusions based on a few qualitative interviews. I have always found the combination of longitudinal quantitative data and qualitative data fruitful. In the Scandinavian countries we have the whole population on registers. I have a data set consisting of every person born in Norway since 1946. Then you can connect kids to their parents and, in some cases, to their grandparents. I can follow groups of children, and see how certain social background factors and life course events influence their life course. But we need qualitative methods to go into the factual social dynamics; the mechanisms of the processes. The good thing with a multi-method perspective is that when you combine methods you can really utilise the strength of each method. What people often do if they use only one method is that they broaden or 'dilute' the method, and then they are weakening their perspective. If you are interviewing 20 kids and you want to generalise, perhaps you expand your sample while shortening the conversation with each child. It is much more fruitful to get an overview by big surveys or registers, and use the qualitative measures to acquire depth in your understanding. The multi-method approach sharpens each method.

There have been developments in quantitative methods in the last decade, pushed by the new longitudinal data sets. This opens up the potential for new developments in demography, through matching and simulation. I would argue that in sociology we have put too little emphasis on selection; that children are actively seeking and constructing contexts, they are not just influenced by contexts. The understanding of children as subjects entails a focus on processes of selection; children construct their lives. This of course brings us over to genetics and the interplay of social and genetic factors. In the near future it will be impossible to put forward assumptions about the effects of social factors without bringing in the interplay with genetic factors. The influence of genes seems not to be weakened over the life course; in many cases they will be strengthened. Genes also raise new questions of what is just and fair: sociological criticisms of educational systems seem to define meritocracy, everything is based on talent and efforts, as equality. It is unfair to base salaries on inherited cultural capital, but is it fair to base them on genetic capital? Michael Young (he coined the concept in his science fiction thesis) had a much more elaborate perspective.

CS Ivar, I also want to ask you about reflexivity which emerged as a highly contentious topic during my doctoral research. Will you say something about how you understand the concept and why you consider reflexivity to be important?

IF It is a very complex concept and its roots are in different languages. Reflexivity is the ability to be able to grasp different perspectives on the same subject or topic. If you use Habermas as the point of departure, reflexivity is based on a dialogue between different perspectives, which then takes us back to Piaget and decentration, which means that you have to be able to grasp the *perspective of the other*. Reflexivity is about the constitution of the other as a subject. This recognition, in a Hegelian sense, is a prerequisite for reflexivity. If we keep that dialogue idea, for me reflexivity will be to provide different perspectives and the recognition of the other as subject, the relation to the other has to be constituted in the 'I and Thou' sense of Buber. This is at the core of the multicultural and individualistic society. That's why I think it is so important to have an interdisciplinary perspective on childhood. Reflexivity also has evolutionary roots. Children are born as, effectively, subjects that take things in all the time; reflexivity is an inborn disposition, as is the capacity to constitute the other as a subject. You may get religious when you study evolution. I have never understood why religious people do not understand that. God even plays a bit of dice to get things going. Babies have inborn capacities for autonomy as well as for decentration, they are struggling to achieve both, as illustrated by psychologists like Winnicott. Kids are even born with a capacity for a dialogue and of course they are socialising themselves, under conditions over which they have little control. So for me, being reflexive is being able to apply different perspectives, being reflexive is an internal dialogue fuelled, of course, by participation in external dialogues, as with Habermas, an open-minded free dialogue between subjects that recognise each other as subjects.

CS Before we end I would like you to say something about where you see the current tensions, dilemmas, challenges for the field of Childhood Studies as we know it. Do you think there is a distinct field and, if so, what are the possible directions for the future?

IF For me, the challenges are related to interdisciplinarity, reflexivity and being useful for groups of children and societal development. The democratic way of being useful is to provide support for reflexivity. Science must not be remote from real lives and practitioners. We need elaborated analytical perspectives, but if you are presenting some ideas and theories for teachers and they say, 'this is completely silly' or 'obvious and uninteresting' then you really have to rethink it. You may be right but you have to rethink your model so that people understand what you are talking about. The purpose is to contribute to reflexivity, not to distribute 'the truth'.

Childhood is a structural framework laying the premises for children's lives. I am, for the time being, working with life-course analysis because for me, this is the best way to understand children's lives, as related to family, social class, background, ethnicity – and yet at the same time keep the perspective of childhood. If your basic concern is opportunity structures and inequality, then life course analysis is the most fruitful perspective. You have to talk to kids, however, and not only use the longitudinal studies. We also have to remember that we have so many childhoods, we cannot assemble a bunch of middle-class kids and term it, 'the voice of children'. We have to be aware of this kind of 'othering', where some categories of children are understood to represent childhood. Acting as though groups or categories have common voices is a way to camouflage the diversity of interests and perspectives. This does not imply that groups do not have things in common.

When you combine perspectives and methods you also have to combine theories. A challenge, especially for sociology, is that we have 'theories' not always rooted in extensive empirical analysis. I remember sharing an office with a guy working with statistics in UNICEF, he said that he had had a very strange experience when he had spoken to a sociologist about some empirical analysis. The sociologist had said: 'I don't work with empirical analysis, I am involved with theory.' From the perspective of natural science this is silly because you have to test the theory. In sociology, however, it can be like this, 'No, I work with theory, I compare Habermas with Giddens and Bauman.' Theories are not neutral, they are loaded with meaning. If you use Foucault you will think that people are exposed to discipline, if you use Bourdieu you will find that social class is inherited. If you use a different perspective you may find something else. So we have to start with the empirical work and gradually construct theories; this is what is called grounded theory. Of course, we bring perspectives with us; but if you start your analysis with empirical patterns and reflections on empirical findings, then bring in different theories and perspectives, re-read the data and so on, you do your best not to just answer questions embedded in a specific theory. Grounded theory doesn't mean that you merely listen to people and try to keep it close to the ground – the point is to elaborate theories. Of course you can use a feminist perspective, you can use a class perspective and so on, but then you have to be very explicit and state that, because another perspective may bring other results. Then we are back to reflexivity. We do need theoretical elaboration, and the fact that we cannot find 'The Truth', does not imply relativity; we identify something as more correct than something else by processes of verification; even if such processes of verification/falsification are self-corrective.

CS That makes sense. Ivar, how do we include the global community of people working in Childhood Studies? Is that another challenge? I am thinking about places like India, Brazil, China? Childhood Studies up until now has been very much about the affluent world (we are very conscious of that with this book). How do we bridge that gap?

IF Well, I have some experience because I was one of the founders of Childwatch International and also the journal *Childhood*. If you look at the studies that are coming from different countries, for me this illustrates that we have to build theories from empirical groundings. Often we take our surroundings for granted. I remember one of the first years of *Childhood* when the school age in Norway was lowered from seven to six and a lot of people in Norway were against that. We had some articles coming into *Childhood* saying that this will hurt children because the period of play will be shorter and so on; but referees who were used to school starting at the age of five or six, would say, 'You start schooling at seven, isn't that a problem?' [both laugh]. What is natural from one perspective might be a problem from another perspective. For me, the solution to this is reflexivity, recognition of the other and grounded theory. In some countries opportunity structures for different groups of children are extremely different, like when girls are blocked from education or families can't afford to educate their children. In Scandinavia the differences between children is more related to children's capacity to utilise opportunity structures, and the social and cultural resources of families, as illustrated by phrases like 'drop outs'. These are things that you don't fully grasp until you encounter them.

CS That is what has emerged clearly in this interview. Before we finish is there anything else you would like to say, mindful of our aims for the book, before we finish?

IF If I were to sum up, what I think I have tried to say, is that the sociology of childhood, like other things, was rooted in a special period, and the cultural changes of that period. The underlining of the competence and agency of children as well as others is visible in critical responses to the authoritarian family and the 'Schwarze Pädagogik', as well as in neoliberal ideology evolving in the period. For me the focus on children was a political project, a moral project, a normative project and a scientific project. If you want to understand children, not to mention to make policies for kids, you really need to know their situation and development as well their perspectives. This now seems obvious, but in that period it was not always obvious. What is a paradox is that when we were putting emphasis on the competent child and argued that children were often over-protected and not given a voice, a group that really bought this were the guys in marketing. They love to advertise to the 'competent child'. Yet we know that kids under a certain age do not distinguish between television programmes and the commercials. The discussion about protection, rights, voice and competence is quite complex.

The sociology of childhood represented, as I met it, modest knowledge about psychology and other disciplines. During the last 10 or 20 years new understandings of children and children's lives have really been developed through life-course analysis, and studies involving the interaction of genetic and social factors. Look at all the work that has developed, for example, from the Dunedin Multidisciplinary Health and Development Study.[5] A high number of smaller qualitative studies brought to the surface knowledge of different groups, but little on the relationship between the situation when you are one, four, 10 and 20 years old. Life course developments have to be related to context and to societal formation, in Marx's sense. You can find correlations now that most likely were not there 40 years ago because it was a different society. Some studies indicate that boys with behaviour problems when they are small, are more often than others unemployed when they are 25. This is related to the knowledge economy; if they had grown 'into work' with Willis' lads[6] they would have had fewer opportunities, but they would have been integrated into work. Now we have more opportunities and more risk; opportunities requires genetic, economic, social and cultural capital. The correlation between the situation when you're three years old and when you're 25 is also related to societal formation. In the knowledge society parents are working hard to help their kids through. This is not only about social inheritance, as with Bourdieu. Families without social and cultural capital, like Chinese immigrants, weaken the idea that everything is about social and economic inheritance and lack of meritocracy. Their kids do very well not because of their amounts of social and cultural capitals, but because of the parental support and push.

I have to underline that I cannot offer a complete overview in terms of the considerable amount of work that is going on now but there are a series of studies which illustrate how new longitudinal data opens up possibilities for new understanding. Of course, we also need the micro-studies, digging into children's local worlds.

References and note

[1] Mannheim, K, 1952, The problems of generations, in his *Essays on the sociology of knowledge*, London: Routledge and Kegan Paul

[2] Erikson, EH, 1995, *Childhood and society* (first published 1950), London: Vintage Books UK

[3] Berger, PL, Luckmann, T, 1966, *The social construction of reality: A treatise in the sociology of knowledge*, Garden City, NY: Anchor Books

[4] Sen, A, 2001, *Development as freedom*, Oxford paperbacks, new edn, Oxford: Oxford University Press (first published in 1999 by Alfred A Knopf, New York)

[5] The Dunedin Multidisciplinary Health and Development Study includes 1037 babies born in Dunedin, New Zealand between 1 April 1972 and 31 March 1973. Over 1,100 publications have been generated as a result of this study.

[6] Willis, P, 1981, *How working class kids get working class jobs*, New York: Columbia University Press

TEN

Robbie Gilligan

Robbie Gilligan is Professor of Social Work and Social Policy at Trinity College Dublin. He is Associate Director of the Children's Research Centre which he co-founded (with Professor Sheila Greene) in 1995 and is co-director (with Dr Philip Curry) of the Children, Migration and Diversity Research Programme (2006). Professor Gilligan has been the President of Childwatch International Research Network since 2010. He is a member of the International Research Network on Transitions to Adulthood for Young People Leaving Care and is a board member of the European Scientific Association of Residential and Family Care. Since 2009 Professor Gilligan has been a member of the Trinity International Development Initiative steering committee. Professor Gilligan's numerous publications include *Promoting resilience: Supporting children and young people who are in care, adopted or in need (2nd edn)*, published by BAAF in 2009 and 'Promoting a sense of secure base for children in foster care – Exploring the potential contribution of foster fathers', *Journal of Social Work Practice* (2012, 26, 4, 473–86). In February 2013 Professor Gilligan was appointed to the editorial board of the leading journal, *Child Abuse and Neglect*.

Carmel Smith To start, Robbie, will you give me a potted history of your career from where you started to where you are now in your work with children and childhood.

Robbie Gilligan Well, I did a degree in Trinity College Dublin in Social Work – I was motivated to be a social worker and deliberately chose that course. I then worked in the fledgling Community Services in the Irish Health Services that were just beginning and in the early 1970s they started to employ social workers to work with children. In 1975 I got my first job in one of the Health Boards outside Dublin – in fact I was the first social worker employed by the State system in the area where I went to work, West Waterford. Then after two years I came back to Dublin and worked in the inner-city of Dublin which was a very formative experience, working with some very good people and learning a lot about community issues, as well as the very difficult social conditions in which people lived, which made me think a lot about the relevance of social work and how to integrate social work with other perspectives. After two-and-a-half years there I went to work for the St Vincent de Paul Society nationally, a big volunteer charity who at that time had something like 10,000 volunteers working week in and week out, and I was a very young and, in some ways, naive Training and Development Officer. I worked there for about 18 months and then an opportunity came up to apply to University College Dublin [UCD] to teach as a very junior assistant lecturer for one year and to my surprise, got the post. That was extended into a second year and during that second year Trinity College advertised a post and I applied for it and again, to my surprise, got it and here I am [laughs]. That is the very potted version and alongside that I was involved with a range of voluntary committees of various kinds, setting up projects and a lobbying organisation called CARE which tried to make the public case for social reform of children's services long before this became a public issue. Then I gradually became more interested in research. Research was something that I grew into with the realisation that this was actually an important part of the academic role. I think that was partly to do with the time and the Irish experience and the way in which we came late to some of these international expectations which are now, of course, quite intense in our system as much as anywhere else. That has, therefore, been an important influence that I grew up professionally and academically at a very early and formative time in a context that was very different from that to which many other people are exposed in other countries. In some respects it was a much less structured context in which to develop, a much smaller and much less resourced context and I think it has coloured the way I think about a lot of things. I spend a lot of my time resisting assumptions, in some of the bigger countries, that because things are that way in their country that that is the way they are everywhere else. I think I am quite internationally minded; this is a small island and people tend to leave the island and to see the world and so they are exposed to other people's thinking and other people's ideas. That has certainly been the case for me. I have been enriched by international contact but also by being not too narrowly focused on my own discipline. I like to look over the hedge to see what is going on elsewhere and I tend to get a bit frustrated by staying too much inside your own paradigms or your own frameworks.

CS Do you think that is something that social work training and teaching encourages you to do, to include all those different disciplines rather than just stay within one particular discipline?

RG It is difficult to be categorical and say that this is specifically due to social work training, I think there are probably other factors at play as well but yes, I think social workers, or certain kinds of social workers, are very much trained and encouraged to think in an inclusive way about ways of thinking and ways of working. You are trying to bring together a range of experience, a range of expertise, a range of perspectives to discern what might work best or what seems to make most sense. The 'social' in social worker is quite important, meaning that social workers are good at working across boundaries of different kinds, so social workers are probably well placed to integrate, to work across disciplines, to work between professional and lay perspectives and to some extent, to work across cultures. Now, I wouldn't want to overstate that or romanticise it too much, but I think that when I see some of the other disciplines that I encounter they do sometimes seem quite prone to very parochial perspectives where they are only interested in what's happening inside their own discipline, or even within a subset of their discipline, and they spend a fair bit of energy on turf wars with people about what's pure or not pure. Quite honestly, I find that frustrating, tiresome and hard to understand because, at the end of the day, it doesn't seem that important, really. I know it is important in one sense but in the bigger scheme of things I think, for me, a big test always is how does this ultimately affect children's lives? Obviously ideas are important, theories are important but ultimately these are important because they should somehow work their way down to have an impact on the experience of children's lives or the experiences children have in their lives and on the contexts in which children live their lives.[1] While it is very important to foreground children and children's experiences, children belong in social ecologies, they belong in social contexts and they belong in social relationships.[2,3] I think that is increasingly appreciated by many people from different perspectives, but I think there is a danger sometimes of talking in too isolated a way about children and childhood and I think its unhelpful for the field of Childhood Studies and it is unhelpful for individual children to isolate children conceptually in that way.

CS The 'new' paradigm was declared in the 1990s and was very much associated with the sociology of childhood. Will you say something about your awareness of the events leading up to that and how you think that has influenced or changed the way we study and understand children?

RG I am not sure I am well placed to comment on the history of the Childhood Studies movement because I haven't looked at that in depth, but I suppose in a way childhood, historically, was the intellectual territory of psychology. Sociology…, again we have to be careful about this because we can talk in these very universal terms about disciplines such as sociology or psychology, but in many ways these disciplines emerge and develop differently in different national contexts.

CS That is a very important point.

RG American sociology is quite different from British sociology, for example. To take that example, British sociologists might find it difficult in some ways to share a lot of time or space with certain kinds of American sociologists. Sociology probably has struggled to be accepted as a serious intellectual discipline and I think that is unfair. It deserves to be treated seriously, but I think it has been insecure intellectually, because of the reception it has received in the academy – bear in mind this is something over 30 or 40 years and longer ago, so it is probably more secure now than it was then in some respects, but maybe not in other respects like trying to ensure that you get enough students, those are still things that a discipline cannot take for granted. This insecurity thing has meant that sociology has perhaps been excessively precious about boundary maintenance and very threatened or critical in terms of its relationship with psychology which takes a very different perspective. I think some of the sociological critique of psychology is valid because I think a lot of psychology is ridiculously de-contextualised in the way it approaches issues. However, in some respects I think sociology sets up psychology as the 'straw man', they are criticising something that they actually don't know enough about. From my perspective, Childhood Studies has to be multidisciplinary, has to take on board ideas from anywhere that is relevant and it is unthinkable that you couldn't have psychology as an important dimension, not a dominant dimension necessarily, but it has to be a critical component of any serious intellectual endeavour in terms of tackling the issues facing childhood and facing children's lives, because, for me, Childhood Studies isn't just the intellectual pursuit of ideas. It is the pursuit of understanding that will benefit and have an impact on the reality of children's lives and not just children's lives in the west, in minority countries, it has to address the realities of children's lives globally and raise awareness of the realities of children's lives and we need many intellectual approaches to achieve that.[4,5] We need to have people from economics, psychology, law, sociology, geography, theology, even business – any disciplines that can show relevant knowledge about children's lives and children's experiences and that can deepen our understanding, have to have a place at the table. Scholars from many linguistic, cultural and economic backgrounds must be at that table. I think the danger is that the club of scholars is far too exclusive in that it may be comprised of people who subscribe to a certain shared view and that view may be too narrowly conceived and not be sufficiently related to real world issues or sometimes to practitioner perspectives or to the lives of parents, children and teachers who play out the realities of children's lives in so many ways, day in and day out. Aside from excluding other theoretical or practical perspectives in their own context, the danger is in many cases that we don't have enough people at the table from the Spanish speaking world, or the Asian world, or the African world, or the Arab world, or from the non-English speaking white European world, or from the Aboriginal worlds of the countries that have been colonised. There are, I would suggest, a lot of unacknowledged vacant spaces at the table of Childhood Studies.

CS I am going to come back and ask you about looking to the future, but just before we move on to that, will you say something about your own experience of research with children and about the type of training that you received?

RG Well, by today's standards it might seem very surprising or shocking, but I had virtually no training! I think it was a case of learning by doing, learning by listening, learning by observing, learning from the experience of other people and drawing on my experience as a social worker. I think I have learned a lot from supervising postgraduate students at Masters and PhD level and I have been in a management role in a research centre and inevitably you get drawn in to research projects because good research is a lot about managing, not just narrowly in terms of resources, but also managing challenges that arise and how to resolve those. I have learned from other people's work in the Centre [referring to the Children's Research Centre at Trinity College, Dublin], Sheila's [Greene's] work and postgraduate students work, the importance of multiple observations about children and childhood experiences.[6,7] This might seem quite obvious in some senses, but it is remarkable how many social research studies undertaken with children or families are still based on a single interview and I am increasingly sceptical about the value of research which relies on single interviews with informants. The reality is that many researchers meet children and they don't have shared ground and they expect children to reveal all or declare their true inner feelings, or concerns, or anxieties, or doubts, or hopes, or aspirations and frankly, I think that's breathtakingly naive when you think about it. So there are probably two things I bring to the table as a research supervisor: one is to encourage people to think about multiple observations. Getting people's perspectives at different times in response to different events, different moods, different incidents, growing trust, whatever, you may get fresh depth to what is being said. The second thing is that we need to think much more in longitudinal terms or life-course terms, trajectory terms so that we are not just thinking about a point in time.[8] When you think about life-course perspectives, interviewing someone once, when they are 14 or 19 or 21, is a pretty feeble attempt to get a sense of the whole person over time. Now I know that there are resource issues and so on, but I think that thinking like that might help us to be more realistic and more modest in our claims.

CS Tell me about 'reflexivity' in research. What does reflexivity mean to you and how you would recommend that researchers approach reflexive research? I am particularly thinking about postgraduate students or new researchers.

RG Well, I obviously hope that researchers realise that they influence the settings and accounts that they are investigating, that they are not somehow separate from what they are observing and intruding upon. I assume that people are aware of that or I would do my best to make them aware of that. I would hope that they would also be reasonably sophisticated in terms of thinking about the various lenses through which they look at issues and the experiences they are encountering, the influences that have shaped their assumptions, their views and their values and that those assumptions, views and values are not necessarily shared by everyone else and how they can ensure, without discarding them or parking them or rejecting them, that they don't obscure other perspectives. It is quite a challenge especially for newer or younger researchers to get this balance right. However, I don't think it should become a fetish, at the end of the day the important thing is that you gather credible data that rings true for the person about whom you are gathering the data, the people who are in the context and for outside observers. I think the evidence you gather has to somehow resonate and if you spend too much time focusing on your own preoccupations as a researcher you may lose sight of what it is that you are there for. It is rare that you can write field notes right at the point of encounter, which is, usually, say, in a school yard; you step back into an office or classroom or somewhere quiet where you can write notes. They are pretty close to contemporaneous, but they are not fully contemporaneous. The act of writing inevitably involves some element of reflecting on and editing the experience and that gives some distance, but you don't want too much distance. From supervising students, students who 'get it', find it very helpful. Some people find it more challenging than others. It is not that easy to learn to take multiple perspectives, but as you get more experienced and more exposed to life in general you probably begin to see that 'messy is good'!

CS I now want to move on to the current state of the field of Childhood Studies. Is it a multidisciplinary field, an interdisciplinary field, is it a distinct field? Should Childhood Studies have a capital C and S or a small c and s?

RG Personally, I think it should be a small c and s. I am not convinced about having a lot of exclusivity. Now a lot of people may strongly disagree with that, but my instinct is that we shouldn't be too fundamentalist, that what we should be trying to do is to spread ideas. Obviously there will have to be places, centres of excellence where the ideas are really tested and developed and new ideas emerge and so on, but I think that the challenge is to spread interest and spread commitment to some of these ideas way beyond the centres of excellence. In other words, what does the phrase child-centred mean? It trips off the tongue very easily and we could have many debates in the centres of excellence about what we mean, but at the end of the day it is important that a teacher in a village school in Africa, or in an inner-city school in Belgrade, or in an Aboriginal community in northern Australia have somehow absorbed through their training and through their experience some sense of what it means to be child-centred, that actually it is reasonably true to what the purists meant or intended in the first place. I think it is very important that we have this idea of reach, that ideas have reach and, okay, some of the people who are at the outer limits of reach may not get the ideas quite right, but their practices may be somewhat better and more child-centred than they might have been if they hadn't been exposed to these ideas however weak the transmission might be by the time the ideas reach them. I think the challenge is not just to distil ideas but to transmit them. For me the issue then is how do we transmit effectively? That requires us to widen the community of people who are concerned, not narrow it. I think that we have to have a community of Childhood Studies adherents or activists who include the people who operate at the centre of the centres of excellence, but there are wider circles stretching out and spreading ideas into different communities of practice and communities of enquiry, which, ultimately, I hope, would influence the thinking and practices of ordinary parents and ordinary teachers and ordinary social workers, ordinary care workers, foster carers, students and children themselves. That seems to me to be the ultimate test. If you think about engineers, of course you need top schools of engineering, but the ultimate test of engineering ideas, in broad terms, is whether bridges around the world are safer as a result of the transmission of the ideas about how to build bridges that have come from the centres of excellence. That is a simplistic analogy but similarly in medicine, there is still a lot of work to be done on what forms of hygiene are most effective or under what conditions do you achieve best hygiene, what practices and so on, but ideas about hygiene have been transmitted over generations and across many cultures and languages and have had an impact on public health. So I think we have to think in those terms, how we make sure that those ideas are transmitted in ways that ultimately resonate in the lives of children.

CS So: feedback loops from those on the ground that would inform the thinking in the centres of excellence?

RG Yes, I think that is absolutely right. I think part of the challenge for all academics is to stay in touch with reality. Of course many people will jump on me and say that there are many realities. Okay, but whatever reality you wish to relate to that day, are you in touch with it? [Laughs]

CS That reminds me of C Wright-Mills and the sociological imagination and seems relevant whatever discipline or whatever professional practice you are involved with as a researcher?

RG I have a favourite question I sometimes put to students when they come in with ideas about research studies. There is always the issue of them wanting to change the world and I say maybe just change one practice in one place or one classroom or whatever. I often say to them, if you were standing at a bus stop and you were to turn round to the little old lady beside you and say, 'I am thinking of doing a study on x' would she say, 'That sounds a brilliant idea and I can really see why you are doing that' or would she look blankly at you? Obviously there are limits to this, but at the same time does this idea pass the test as an issue or as a question to explore? At some level we have to be answerable to the little old lady at the bus stop, this is not just our private, privileged, exclusive business.

CS That's interesting. So children should also be feeding back to us that what we are doing is important?

RG Yes.

CS Before we finish, Robbie, is there anything that I have missed or is there anything else you would like to say?

RG I know that you are convinced about the importance of the practitioner perspective in a lot of this work and I very much share that. I see myself as someone who is both a social work academic but also as a person who is interested in children's issues and childhood so maybe in some ways I could be called a childhood studies person (with a small c and a small s). The interface between social work and Childhood Studies is a reasonable way to describe my position at the moment, but I have been struck over the years in supervising people and talking to people about research, how often the people who have got professional experience working with children seem to make very good researchers. It almost raises the issue of whether you really have to have been a something in the lives of children and families whether as a teacher, or as a care worker, or as a psychologist, or as a social worker, or whatever, but that you have actually spent time working in systems and that that is almost an essential prerequisite for researching. I know that people put an emphasis on formal research training and the conventional route now of a Masters and PhD, but we also need to remember that you do need some real world experience. There is a danger that if since the age of four you have been in educational institutions and, at the age of 30 you have your PhD, but you have never set foot outside the classroom in a sense, does that make you a good researcher?

CS Should the start of research training then be to just go out and work with children in whatever setting or just be with children?

RG I think so and also to somehow be exposed to different social contexts than the ones in which you have grown up. So if you have been reared in a middle-class family, gone to a middle-class school, lived in a middle-class community, gone to a middle-class university then maybe you do need to work or operate in a few other social worlds in order to really have a sense of what is out there. I suppose the other thing that I would want to mention again is, that I have been influenced in this by my exposure to the work of Childwatch International,[9] but I was drawn to Childwatch by the same ideas. We really don't sufficiently acknowledge how tiny a proportion of the world population lives in the wealthy minority countries. The great majority of children live in majority world countries and the realities, experiences and the positive and negative aspects of those lives are not being reflected adequately in the debates in Childhood Studies, capital c, capital s or small c, small s. There are honourable exceptions to that in terms of people who make a serious effort to bring those perspectives to bear,[10] but, broadly, we are much too preoccupied with the realities of children in the minority world. That raises lots of issues and reflects the fact that many of the researchers are operating in the minority world and it is difficult to cultivate research expertise in the majority world, that's local to the majority world. I think if Childhood Studies as a broad church, a broad field, is to thrive we have to find ways of broadening the base of the community of scholars so that they are not just people who are white scholars from privileged backgrounds in the minority world.

References and notes

[1] Gilligan, R, 2009, *Promoting resilience: Supporting children and young people who are in care, adopted or in need* (2nd edn), London: BAAF

[2] Gilligan, R. 2012, Promoting a sense of secure base for children in foster care – Exploring the potential contribution of foster fathers, *Journal of Social Work Practice* 26, 4, 473-86

[3] Gilligan, R, 2009, 'Promoting positive outcomes for children in need – The importance of Protective capacity in the child and their social network' in (ed) J. Horwath, *The Child's World – The Comprehensive Guide to Assessing Children in Need*, (2nd edn), pp 174-184, London: Jessica Kingsley

[4] See Childwatch International Research Network, and publications at www.childwatch.uio.no.

[5] See Young lives: An international study of childhood poverty, and publications at www.younglives.org.uk

[6] Greene, S. and Hogan, D. (eds) (2005) *Researching Children's Experiences: Approaches and Methods*, London: SAGE

[7] See 'Growing up in Ireland' – a national longitudinal study of children growing up in Ireland, at www.growingup.ie.

[8] Gilligan, R, 2009, 'Positive turning points in the dynamics of change over the life course', in (eds) JA Mancini and KA Roberto, *Pathways of Human Development: Explorations of Change*, pp 15-34, Lanham, Maryland: Lexington Books

[9] See note 4.

[10] See note 5.

ELEVEN

Roger Hart

Roger Hart is a Professor in the Environmental Psychology and Geography PhD Programmes at the City University of New York (CUNY) and director of the Center for Human Environments and the Children's Environments Research Group. Much of his research focuses on understanding the everyday lives of children in relation to the physical environment, particularly for those living in difficult circumstances. He has also been concerned with supporting international development agencies to find new ways of enabling disadvantaged children to express their concerns as a way of better fulfilling their rights. This has lead to current research on the kinds of children's organisations in many countries that demonstrate high levels of self-governance by children (http://crc15. org). His many publications include the influential *Children's participation from tokenism to citizenship* (UNICEF, 1992) and *Children's participation: The theory and practice of involving young citizens in community development and environmental care* (UNICEF, 1997). He is currently writing about his return to work with the children of his PhD ethnographic study of a New England town, *Children's experience of place*. A book and film is being produced about this research with the parents whom he knew as children, and with their children, on how childhood has changed over one generation and how parents think about and handle these changes.

Carmel Smith To start, Roger, will you say something about yourself and your background – a potted history of where you started, to where you are now in your work with children and childhood?

Roger Hart My work with children doesn't/didn't begin until after my undergraduate degree in Hull University in geography. I went to the United States to do a PhD and I chose Clark University because it had a good Geography School for my intended research on squatter settlements in South America. I had been there about a week when one of the professors, James Blaut, who was doing research with children and children's understandings of maps and geographic concepts, approached me. He had a grant with an aeroplane to do aerial photography for the research and I had learned to fly through a Ministry of Aviation 'flying scholarship' in the UK when I was 17. So I had a private pilot's licence but I never dreamt that I would be able to use it. It was amazing...talk about the USA as the land of opportunity! So my research assistantship job was flying the plane, doing aerial photography and working with children. I greatly enlarged some aerial photographs of the city to work with a group of second and third grade children in a school. I put the giant aerial photographs on the floor, together with matchbox toys and colour felt pens, to see how far the children could go in talking about geographic concepts when using these materials. I had never worked with children before and it was exciting for me to discover how much I loved working with them. I recall that after that single session I realised that I would be somehow working with children for the rest of my life. I was interested in questions of how children came to understand the geographic world and how they understood space, but it was really the joy of being with the children that I think was dominant. So that was my beginning and I learned a lot because Clark University was the founding home of not only geography in the United States, but also of developmental psychology and these were the two big departments (by the way, Clark was where 'Child Study' began in the 1880s). This was the late 1960s, early 1970s, and interdisciplinary experimentation was part of the zeitgeist of that time and so I worked with three or four other wonderful students and faculty to experiment with putting these two fields together.

I was inspired by one other event at that same time. A professor came to visit Clark from Detroit named Bill Bunge. He was conducting a radical form of geography in which he worked with communities to collect their own data as a basis for change. It was an early form of participatory community research which was very effective and he was working with the African American community of Detroit. Some of his work was on structural racism and how the children of this community were being treated compared to the children of the suburbs. Although this was not participatory with children, it was participatory with their parents and what was profound for me was the idea of engaging with people in research on issues of social justice that were of concern to them. So that was an equally important early formative influence.

Overlapping with my thesis research I was reading heavily about spatial cognition in children and along with my friend, Gary Moore, I conducted a comprehensive review of theories of the development of how children mentally represented the world beyond their horizon.[1] In the course of reading for this review I realised that if I really wanted to understand children's geographic worlds I needed to go well beyond the spatial cognition work of psychologists. So I started to read everything I could find that might be relevant to an understanding of the geography of children. One day I was in the university library, doing my normal exploring of the stacks, when I serendipitously came across a monograph by Jeanne and Stuart Altmann, called 'Baboon ecology'.[2] It was a wonderful naturalistic account of baboons and I sat in the stacks and read it closely. It amazed me that they had even got to the point of theorising the cognitive mapping of baboons in relationship to their spatial behaviour. I thought, 'My goodness, these people know more about baboons than we do about children, certainly in terms of spatial behaviour but also about what are the meaningful places to them in their environment and how they navigate between them.' The next morning I woke up and said, to myself, 'I'm going to find my baboon troop [laughs] and do a naturalistic study with children.' While it was now very clear what I wanted to study, I now had the difficult task of how to do the research! It was 1972 and I could find almost no guidance from anthropology or sociology or any field about how to study children in the wild. I had to invent it.[3] So, some of my reactions when in the 1990s, I heard of the new 'Childhood Studies in the UK and the paradigmatic shift' was, 'Well, where have you been?' I think that for anthropology, and for sociology, we should speak of the bigger change being about the 'discovery of childhood'.

CS That is actually a helpful link, Roger. Will you now say something about the evolution of ideas in the preceding decades leading up to the, so-called, 'new paradigm'? Why did things come together when they did that made the time right for these ideas about children and childhood to suddenly be on the map in a way they never were before?

RH I don't know, I wasn't in the UK at that time but I've generally thought of it as being related to two major forces. One of them was the political climate in the UK where there was a national concern over what was happening with children and childhood – I don't know what the timing is exactly, but if it hadn't become the Prime Minister's concern by then it was certainly the nation's concern. What was the date of the James Bulger incident?

CS I think that was the early 1990s.

RH And when is the time that Childhood Studies is considered to have been born?

CS That's interesting.

RH So, there was a growing fear of and fear for children, the two went together, that was being expressed in the media. One classic marker of the changing nature of childhood in the UK was the loss of children's independent mobility. I remember that I came to London to give a talk about this in 1979 based on my observations that the restricted independent mobility that we had then in urban America had come to the United Kingdom.[4] It wasn't, however, until 1990 and the publication by Hillman on the loss of children's mobility that this became one of those classic markers of how children's lives have changed. Then, on the other side, there was this sense of danger from children, because of what happened to James Bolger. So these currents were taking place and perhaps led to the funding of research on children by the government of Tony Blair in the 1990s – that must have been important to the rise of Childhood Studies in UK universities. And that's not small; money being available for grants through the ESRC, and so on, is ideal if you are trying to establish a new field. Alongside all of this was the paradigm shift in how children should be viewed, called for by the global movement for children's rights.

CS What about in the States? Were there links in the States at that time between those of you who were working with children?

RH No. There was definitely a delay. We took notice when we started to see the books coming out by Allison James, Alan Prout, Chris Jenks and so on. There wasn't an immediate uptake. I don't think we had any sudden awareness of changing childhood at that time like Britain had, and the Convention on the Rights of the Child wasn't being debated at all – but that's another story!

CS I now want to ask you about your own approach to research in the area of children and childhood?

RH My own approach to research is constantly evolving. When I began my PhD study I realised that I needed to learn what children did, where they went and so on, but I also needed to know about their experiences – how they valued the landscape and places and how they put it all together into a meaningful personal geography. I didn't quite realise how radical it was then to just work with children and not with their parents; I felt I was just doing what I needed to do. Although I was reflexive on these issues in my book, I think that if I were writing the book for a Childhood Studies audience today I would have written more. Now that I have returned to do research with these children and their children, more than three decades later, my whole strategy has had to be different.

CS Which theorists have been influential in your work over the years?

RH Initially Piaget was an important influence because I was focused on how children mentally mapped the world. But after that I read widely in child psychology. Sadly, until recently, sociology and anthropology were deserts for insights into children and so I read about childhood anywhere that I could find reference to children's lives, including autobiographies and novels. My greatest mentor died recently, his name is Colin Ward, I am just in the middle of writing an essay about him on how brilliant much of his thinking was about children and how far ahead of his time he was.[5] Colin Ward was Britain's most well known anarchist but he was also a planner and an environmental educator. For those who work with children, his best known book is *The child in the city*, but he also wrote *Streetworks* and *The child in the country*. *The child in the city* was an evocative account of how much children themselves have the desire and competency to self-manage their lives when given the conditions to do so. Colin was the first to say that he was not an academic theorist of childhood, but his insights about children's strengths and capacities and his ideology on how we should build on them in how we work with children were more inspiring to me than any academic texts.

CS You went to CUNY [City University of New York] in 1975 and that has been your academic home since?

RH Yes. I've thought of moving back to the UK many times but the CUNY Graduate Center has been a wonderful work environment that would be hard to find elsewhere. I've only ever had PhD students and so I've been able to work with them and learn from them as fellow researchers.

After arriving in New York I thought, that I would now be able to do research to influence urban planning for children, but it didn't take me many months to realise that I wasn't going to be able to transform residential planning in America by conducting ecological studies about where children played and expecting planners to read them! I did gradually discover, however, that by working through community organisations and schoolteachers I could engage children and their caregivers in research to help them achieve modest changes at the local level. So I became enamored of the potentials of being a researcher who could do research with residents of communities (both children and caregivers) so that they had an improved basis for political advocacy or direct actions to improve their environments. After the UN Convention on the Rights of the Child was adopted by the UN in 1990 UNICEF asked me to write an essay on children's participation because the participation articles were difficult for many to interpret. Later they asked me to write a book on children's participation in sustainable development and that was even more directly connected to all of this local practical community work that I had been doing for years in New York, together with my close colleague, Selim Iltus. Most of my research had been so much based in the process of real practical change in the form of planning and design of the environment and there had been little time to pull back and communicate it to fellow academics. I do enjoy theory-building, though, and am happy to see from the extent of referencing of my writings that some academics see it as relevant to them, but that has usually not been my main goal. I think, because of my father's influence, that I am deeply driven to be practical and when I have had time to write I have typically done so in a way that I thought was useful in guiding change for children in some way.

CS And that's what makes it…because good practitioners literally offer the best of both?

RH Those professionals who work closely with children on a daily basis are my stars; those are the ones I work with and learn from the most.

CS I now just want to move on to the current state of the field, Roger. What are the tensions and dilemmas for Childhood Studies now? Is it a distinct field, is it multidisciplinary, is it interdisciplinary?

RH The idea of integrating the social sciences and humanities to better understand children and childhood has been excellent. I see Childhood Studies as a field that has done a good job of changing the way research on children and childhood is conducted, but I don't really think it matters too much now whether it survives as a distinct department or as a cross disciplinary programme within a university. My identity isn't associated with any particular field, but if I were to start again today I would probably choose to work in a Childhood Studies department. I chose to study geography in university in England because it offered training across disciplines, but I now work in an environmental psychology department and, in spite of the way psychology is attacked by the field of Childhood Studies, my particular programme has been an excellent interdisciplinary home. The reason I have a sanguine view of Childhood Studies is my reflection on what has happened to my little field of environmental psychology. After being established at the end of the 1960s, the expansive growth of environmental psychology in the 1970s was not sustained because it was largely based in interdisciplinary institutes. When money dried up these interdisciplinary institutes were cut out and I suppose that would be the fear if Childhood Studies was based in institutes rather than departments. We survived as a named programme in New York because although we were interdisciplinary we were housed within a department of psychology. Although environmental psychology barely survives as a named field today, many people continue to work across disciplines on the psychological dimensions of environmental issues. I am confident that whatever structure is adopted for Childhood Studies in universities it will survive as a significant interdisciplinary field of study because it has shown its worth.

By the way, while we are on the subject of the identity of Childhood Studies, I hope it will include psychology! Your book will, I suspect, be very important in showing that while a greater interest in studying children in a cross disciplinary way has been fostered by this movement it wasn't exactly a new paradigm. It was more, I would say, an explosion of interest in children and childhood by sociologists and anthropologists which picked up on existing ways, that some people already had, of working with children and gave them a collective form and name. By the 1990s many developmental psychologists had already changed their orientation away from studying the universalism of individual children's development and were investigating children in ways that were contextual and which recognised children's agency. As I said before, I think that in trying to establish an identity for a new field, it was unfair for the pioneer Childhood Studies writers to so aggressively declare that Childhood Studies was entirely contrary to what all of psychology was about, especially when sociology and anthropology had been doing so little for so long to even address children.[6]

Related to this issue of the relevance of psychology, many researchers in Childhood Studies like to say that the idea that children develop is one of the dreadful errors that psychology has thrust on the world, but this, however, is a gross overstatement. It has led to the strange idea that you really shouldn't think about the different capacities of children of different ages when you are designing methods to work with them – and that is of course ridiculous. I have had to develop all kinds of new ways of working with young children and they have been closely related to the developmental capacities of children to take the perspectives of one another and to communicate their thinking effectively. It is true that psychology has consistently tended to underestimate the competence of children but I know from direct experience that one has to find ways to listen to three-, four- and five-year-olds differently to how one listens to twelve- and thirteen-year-olds. Is this perhaps why these age groups have not been studied much in the field of Childhood Studies?

CS That's interesting. The last thing I want to ask you about is the majority world; majority world children and majority world scholars. You have always had an international flavour to your work, what do we do to make sure that those children and those childhoods are more included in the field of Childhood Studies and are more visible?

RH Well, that's a great question and I am glad that there are efforts to correct the way we worked with children in the past in the majority world countries. I am really critical of the way the discipline of psychology works in the Third World. By far the majority of journals on child psychology in the world are produced in the English language in minority countries, most notably in the USA. As a result scholars in majority world countries are steeped in western theory when they examine childhood in their own countries. This is entirely unacceptable. I can give you a very strong anecdote about that if we have time.

CS I think it would be very helpful.

RH When I was doing research on children's clubs in Nepal for Save the Children Norway, two different graduate students, doctoral students, came to see me in Kathmandu: one from a Scandinavian country and the other from New England, USA. They were doing PhDs on mother–toddler interaction in play, they came at different times, and they both had the same kind of complaint: they couldn't find enough examples of it and it didn't seem to be happening and how could they get it [laughs]. I said, 'You have probably got the wrong question because from what I have seen of Nepali children (not middle-class kids in Katmandu but in the rest of the country) they are being raised by older children.' They said, 'Yes, we saw a lot of children with children.' I said, 'Well, that might be a really interesting question. There are thousands of studies of parenting with children but how many studies have you ever seen on how children care for other children?' They explained of course, that their professors were studying mother–toddler interaction in play and wanted some comparative studies from another culture! I strongly encouraged them to conduct research on an issue that arises from within the culture they are studying and suggested to them that in the process they might be able to help Nepal with an issues of importance to their country – like the issue of children as caregivers of their younger siblings. Sadly, it is very rare for students in majority world countries to be trained to do work which tries to build indigenous theory on childhood. So even Nepali students if they study at PhD level will commonly go to a British or an American university and use our theory and methods to go back to apply them in their own country. This is a dangerous intellectual hegemony in the study of childhood that needs to be corrected. Fortunately, there are some signs that Childhood Studies has really tried to do better with that by working within universities of majority world countries to build capacity such as the 'Young Lives' team from Oxford University working in a number of majority world countries and the Trondheim, Norway and Trinity College Dublin teams doing capacity building in Ethiopia. I have had to face this issue of the hegemony of western theories of childhood and children's development in my own work. It has been frustrating for me that when I am invited to a majority world country to talk about children's rights and participation they always want me to give a lecture. I offer to have a dialogue but they insist that they must have a lecture. So I have had to learn how to set up dialogue-style lectures with very large audiences!

I have to admit that I remain very uncomfortable that my writing on children's participation in society has been translated and broadcast so much when I really do not understand the issue in cultures very different to my own. For example, I know that children's participation in Asian countries is very different to that of the west and I believe it has a lot to do with the more collectivist nature of these societies but, for reasons that I mentioned above about western dominance of academic publications on childhood, I have not been able to understand the phenomenon well. Please allow me to offer a little personal history on this issue. I first wrote about children's participation with my colleague, Robin Moore, in three volumes of a newsletter on the theme of children's participation for the International Year of the Child. I drew the ladder of participation in that newsletter and Selim Iltus, who was a new graduate student at the time, redrew it in the attractive form that is now so well known. After we printed the newsletter I got an order for 500 copies from UNICEF and was very disturbed that it was to be distributed to all of their field offices. I called them to explain that the writing was all drawn from minority world countries and it wouldn't be good to distribute it in the majority world. The woman who was coordinating community participation for UNICEF explained, however, that she had never thought of children's participation and that she now realised that UNICEF offices needed to think critically about this notion. After insisting that it was not respectful to send it out when there must be so many good examples of children's participation, in different ways in majority word countries too, and I gave the examples of the Sarvodaya movement in Sri Lanka and Nyere's project on youth self-reliance in Tanzania. 'Okay then, we'll send you there' she said! So off I went to Sri Lanka and met the head of the Buddhist-inspired Sarvodaya movement. It was a community self-help movement that began by first training teachers to get children involved in their communities and then expanded this kind of work to all other members of the community. In hundreds of villages all over Sri Lanka children were involved in managing water wells, helping to build them and then decorating them, cleaning them and monitoring them. When I talked to the children I learned that they were all in this Sarvodaya organisation and there was really no choice about what they did. They were all managing water wells so it looked to me like regime-organised participation rather than the truly voluntary activity that we called participation in the west. Nevertheless, the children seemed to be making valuable contributions to their community and feeling good about it, and themselves, in the process.

Since that time I have seen many similar amazing examples of children managing projects with one another to a degree that it is difficult to imagine in Europe or North America, where the children don't have the opportunity to initiate such projects themselves or to make decisions to change them. So, for example, when I go to Japan and see how very young children set up and manage their classrooms to have lunch when there's no teacher present – its phenomenal. It is most effective, but it is not participatory in the sense we would call it – there is no ownership of the decisions. To say that they don't 'do participation' in Japan because it doesn't look like our form of participation is wrong; but I am not much more informed now about what children's participation means in Asian countries than I was 30 years ago. This is just one example of the kind of fascinating, and important questions that I would like to see networks of Childhood Studies scholars address in their international work. The thing I think I like the most about the organisation *Childwatch International* is that it is trying to build the capacity of majority world nations to conduct child research. As part of this effort it has involved institutions like our Children's Environment Research Group in New York and your Trinity College Dublin Children's Research Centre in a supportive role to help build indigenous research capacities in those countries. We should also recognise that those of us who do research on childhood in minority world countries also have a lot to learn about childhood from understanding differences in childhood in majority world countries. I have tried to illustrate this in my two books for UNICEF on children's participation.[7,8]

CS Roger, is there anything else you would like to say before we finish, particularly in relation to graduate students or new researchers coming into the field?

RH I always like to encourage graduate students to own their own research questions and not let them come from the literature or from a professor. Let them be questions that they profoundly believe are important ones to ask, including things that they may have uniquely observed themselves and they shouldn't let methodological determinism control where they go. We haven't talked epistemology today but I am really a kind of epistemological pluralist. I have undertaken many different kinds of research but that's not because I am agnostic about theory it's just that I really do believe that I have to bring a different approach to different problems. As for methodology – be comfortable inventing it.

References and note
[1] Hart, RA, Moore, GT, 1973, The development of spatial cognition: A review, in R Downs, D Stea (eds) *Image and environment*, Chicago, IL: Aldine–Atherton
[2] Altmann, SA, Altmann, J, 1970, Baboon ecology, *Bibliotheca Primatologica* 12, 1–220

[3] Hart, R, 1978, *Children's experience of place: A developmental study*, New York: Irvington Publishers (distributed by Halstead/Wiley Press)

[4] Hart, R, 1987, *The changing city of childhood*, Publication of the Annual Catherine Maloney Memorial Lecture, City College of New York, http://cergnyc.org/publications

[5] Hart, R, forthcoming, Children's right to the city, in C Burke, K Jones (eds) *Education, childhood and anarchism: Talking Colin Ward*, Abingdon: Routledge

[6] For a good example of writing on how some of the core principles of the 'new paradigm' of Childhood Studies existed in psychology, see the 1979 essay by William Kessen: The American child and other cultural inventions, *American Psychologist* 34, 10, 815–20.

[7] Hart, R, 1992, Children's participation: From tokenism to citizenship, *UNICEF Innocenti Essays* 4, Florence: UNICEF/International Child Development Centre

[8] Hart, R, 1997, *Children's participation: The theory and practice of involving young citizens in community development and environmental care*, New York: UNICEF and London: Earthscan

TWELVE

Harry Hendrick

Dr Harry Hendrick is an Associate Fellow at the Centre for the History of Medicine at the University of Warwick. He recently retired from the Department of English at the University of Southern Denmark. During the course of his career Dr Hendrick lectured in social and economic history in the UK, USA and Sweden. His main research interests are in the history and sociology of childhood and youth and his numerous publications include *Images of youth: Age, class and the male youth problem, 1880–1920* (Clarendon Press, 1990); *Child welfare: England 1872–1989* (Routledge, 1994); *Children and childhood in English society, 1880–1990* (Cambridge University Press, 1997); *Child welfare: Historical dimensions, contemporary debate* (Policy Press, 2003); *Child welfare and social policy: Essential readings* (Policy Press, 2005). Dr Hendrick also wrote chapters in key Childhood Studies texts including, 'Constructions and reconstructions of British childhood: An interpretative survey, 1800 to the present' in *Constructing and reconstructing childhood* (James and Prout (eds), RoutledgeFalmer, 1990; 1997); 'The child as a social actor in historical sources: Problems of identification and interpretation' in *Research with children: Perspectives and practices* (Christensen and James, Routledge, 2000; 2008); 'The evolution of childhood in western Europe c1400–c1750' in *The Palgrave handbook of Childhood Studies* (Qvortrup et al, Palgrave, 2009).

Sheila Greene Maybe we should start with a very general question, Harry, about the origins of your interest in research to do with children and childhood. Perhaps you could tell me a bit about your early career?

Harry Hendrick I'd always had a sense of injustice regarding my schooling and I wanted to be a 'progressive' teacher after having read AS Neill, the radical educationalist. I'd left school at 15, but after a few years clerking and labouring, I decided to attend evening classes in order to get into teachers' training college. During this time I was very active on the left of the Labour party, CND[1] and the Committee of 100. Once at college in 1963 I found it so awful, however, that I left after a term. No doubt my political opinions and my critique of traditional teaching methods made me very dissatisfied. Along with a few others I was regarded as a trouble maker and 'above myself'. My final encounter came when one of the staff said: 'There are people like you, Mr Hendrick, in every college' – she wasn't paying me a compliment! So, after studying at night school and technical college I ended up at Warwick University, where I was well-taught, and I remained to do an MA under EP Thompson from whom I learned that good polemics required scholarship. I then started teaching at Oxford Poly, and began a part-time PhD on late nineteenth-century unskilled workers at Sheffield, which I finally completed in 1986. I developed the thesis into *Images of youth*, a study of working-class male adolescents, which was published in 1990.

In the late 1980s I went to a conference in Cambridge where I met several of the pioneers of child study: Alan Prout, Allison James, Judith Ennew and the pipe-smoking Jens Qvortrup. Alan and Allison said that they were putting together a volume on the sociology of childhood and could I do an introductory historical chapter? I didn't really know much about childhood at the time, having focused on adolescence, but I got to work on it and became deeply involved because I could see how issues pertaining to the child's world connected with my political outlook. Soon after *Images of youth* came out, I was asked to do a couple of other essays and subsequently found myself writing a general history of child welfare.[2] After the Cambridge conference, I attended other gatherings, including a couple in Denmark. I then received an invitation from Bengt Sandin at Linkoping in Sweden to give a couple of lectures, which was the start of a long relationship with his child study department, where for several years I taught a history module on their MA. So I could say that I came to Child Study via a forked road: the Scandinavian and what I think of as the 'Cambridge' route.

SG Did you see them as on two different pathways?

HH No, no. I didn't really have much of a sense of where I was! I felt very ignorant about the sociology of childhood and equally uncertain about the history of childhood since my research had been on adolescents. I think I was the sole English historian in the group and felt rather isolated. Although I was delighted to be included, I didn't feel that History was taken seriously – and I still don't.

SG Although Aries and others had happened

HH I think in some respects Aries has made more impression on people outside History than within the profession. He was, I suppose, influential in the 1970s, but he never made much of an impression on me. Of course, he's a fixed reference point, but there had been so much criticism of both his methodology and interpretation that I didn't and don't now feel obliged to incorporate him in my thinking. Having said that, the matters he raised certainly stimulated further research.

SG So he wouldn't be much debated among historians?

HH. Well, not among historians of the modern period. The medievalists, however, have always been very agitated by his claims about the concept of childhood and queued up to dismiss his propositions. Similarly, with DeMause, he was ridiculed as a rather primitive psycho-historian; often unfairly, I think.

SG For your introductory chapter did you have to create it all yourself or were there sources you could immediately use?

HH Back in 1989–90 there wasn't that much to work with. The 'history' of children and childhood tended to be found in histories of the family by people like Stone, Pollock and Houlebrooke, and in work on education, the industrial revolution and the welfare system. I had met Hugh Cunningham and I knew he was working on his excellent *Children of the poor*, which came out in 1991. There were also very helpful studies by Pamela Horn, Steve Humphries and James Walvin, as well as equally useful accounts of juvenile delinquency and 'child rescue' by Pearson, Manton, May and Behlmer. That may sound a fair number, but set against the scale of 'historical writing', it wasn't much.

SG Is that because history of childhood would be seen as part of social history, which wouldn't have a huge profile in History?

HH In part, yes. The big issues in social history were gender, class, sexualities, industrial relations, oral history, topics like that. However, since History was still rather a conservative subject at the time, the feeling remained that social history was a 'soft' option and as it struggled to establish its academic status, children barely figured at all. Even now, it's not very different. I'd be hard put to name many current historians of childhood writing in the UK (it's a different scene in the USA). I think of Colin Heywood, who writes about France, and Hugh Cunningham and me as the 'old guard' Among younger scholars, I can think of only three in the early modern/modern periods: Hannah Newton, Joanne Bailey and Alysa Levene. Palgrave has, however, recently launched a History of Childhood series, which suggests that they see the subject as having a future. A number of interesting studies on children and childhood have been published by literary and art historians, many of whom are in the Ashgate series. A few feminists also have an interest in the history of childhood, often focusing on girls, people like Carolyn Steedman and Anna Davin, but I think it's relatively sparse when one considers other subject areas and the place of child study in other disciplines. And where university teaching is concerned, there are relatively few fully-fledged history of childhood courses.

SG What does this tell you about the discipline?

HH Since it has neither political punch nor a student base, historical child study doesn't get much notice and perhaps because of this it doesn't attract many of the best PhD students. One of the problems is that as children don't constitute a market for either courses or books, they're not in a position to make their presence felt, certainly not as a force within universities. This is the crucial obstacle politically, one which in some respects is insurmountable. Fundamentally, it's about the absence of children as an organised political constituency.

SG What about the rights of children?

HH That's never become part of serious political discussion; it's been sidelined into social policy areas of family, schooling, child protection and so on. In these areas there is an enormous left-wing feminist influence that privileges women's standpoints and often crude class analyses. The Left in general has little interest in children's rights, leaving it open to undue influence from feminist 'knowledge', which is often critical of the concept of rights. Consequently, there is a tendency for feminism to skew the 'research' in a certain direction, so that some questions are asked and not others – for example, those involving the difficult areas where women's and children's interests conflict. It's a case of adultism in feminist clothing!

I mention this because in the book I am writing currently I quote Ann Oakley, who says that at the end of the day it will be men rather than women who will 'defend' children's interests.[3] Childhood Studies should pay attention to this insight. The connection between women and children is so ambivalent and their interests are so often intertwined that it's difficult for feminists to see any other perspective than their own. The failure of Childhood Studies to address this clash of interests suggests either a surprising ignorance or, dare I say it, a kind of moral cowardice.

Children's rights have never had a political base to ensure that the concept was included in the political conversations that have been conducted during, say, the last 30 years. From Thatcher's Britain onward these debates have been about class, race, gender and feminism, culture, social policy, and the role of the State which, though they had an impact on children, were rarely focused on them, except perhaps in two areas: juvenile delinquency and child protection, and even here, it's usually been in terms of their alleged threat to society's wellbeing. Thus we've had debates about the criminal child, the evil child, the 'feral' child, and so on – much of the discussion being under the influence of the New Right in the 1980s, followed by the hysteria around the Bulger case in 1993, and then, from 1997, children were absorbed into New Labour's 'renewal' of civil society, involving the remoralising of families and the redefining of 'childhood', together with its social investment policies. Children were treated as little more than social capital available for neoliberal schemes. Of course, in certain respects children accrued some benefits from these policies, but it was in the context of all the contradictions inherent in 'welfare paternalism' rather than from the standpoint of justice that treats children as persons with dignity.

SG That seems like a political issue to me.

HH It is political in the sense that children are being talked about and legislated for, but it's usually as part of a broader programme; not for their own being. They usually figure in relation to some 'other'. For example, my feeling is that social policy writing on social investment in children is focused on either women's or family welfare, gender equality, the so-called work–life balance, institutionalised childcare, or neoliberal concepts of personal responsibility. Even Jane Lewis, probably the most influential feminist social policy analyst, and hardly a champion of children's rights, has conceded that children *per se* are not always given the consideration due to them.[4]

SG But it is telling us something, that absence?

HH Oh yes and that's why I'm rather pessimistic about the future. Childhood Studies has been around since the late 1980s and, as I suggest, it's hardly made a significant impact on the political culture, on social theory, or as a university subject. As I see it, perhaps the majority of student courses dealing with children are vocational: 'early childhood studies', many serving to propagandise non-maternal childcare to a student group that is largely girls and mature women. It's hardly revelatory to say that 'children's work is women's work'. No surprise, then, that the subject, I mean Childhood Studies as a discipline, has little academic status. In part because it's seen as a female subject, but also I think because it's been associated with Education, a subject that has also struggled historically for academic status. Of course, there is the wider issue affecting these matters, namely the adult-centric cultural perception of children both inside and outside the academy.

SG But, for you, there must have been intellectual excitement in this area at some point?

HH Oh yes, in terms of my personality, I think, I quite like being the odd man out. I like the idea of struggling on, spreading the word, as it were; trying to raise the political and academic profile of the subject (and, of course, I'm by no means alone in doing this). For a time in the early 1990s, I thought the word would be easily spread; now I don't think so.

SH But you thought there was potential then. Did it not fulfil its potential?

HH I don't think it fulfilled its potential – either academically or politically. Childhood Studies, unlike other areas of recognition politics, has never become an intrinsic part of the Liberal or Left political scenario. In a word, Childhood Studies has been swamped by the crises of late modernity, particularly as represented in universities and publishing, and it doesn't have the political, academic or cultural clout to keep from drowning – except, as I've mentioned, as a vocational enterprise.

SG Do you think that was inevitable or was it just the way academic politics works?

HH. Well, I don't believe in inevitability! Unfortunately, Childhood Studies came in the 1980s at the tail-end of post-1960s 'permissiveness', by which time identity politics or 'the politics of recognition' had already been colonised by feminists, gays and lesbians and multiculturalists and others, each of which, in developing as 'new social movements' enthralled the Liberal/Left. Moreover, where critical social policy is concerned, as I've said, the left perspective was long ago taken over by 'recognition politics'. A small group of second wave feminists, certainly in GB and Scandinavia, however, did adopt Child Studies and brought with them much of the humanistic universalism that characterises the best of feminism. Nonetheless, one of the principal theoretical influences, it seems to me, remains adult-centric 'life politics' of the Giddens variety. Child theory was not developed because there was no political mass movement pushing for a means of analysing relevant matters to do with the personal and the political. Of course, I recognise the preliminary work of people like James, Jenks, Prout, Lee, Qvortrup and Alanen in trying to theorise childhood, but I think it was too little to make a significant impact, and too divorced from organised politics. Nor do I have much hope for the so-called 'new wave of Childhood Studies' with its fondness for 'hybridity' and 'multiplicity'. Moreover, for all the supposed interest in History as claimed by the Childhood Studies pioneers, there has never been a concerted effort to integrate historical understanding or to write a historical sociology, with perhaps one or two exceptions. Nor have historians of childhood been much better at integrating sociology knowledge into their work. Matters may improve now that Lawrence Brockliss and George Rousseau, the editors of the new Palgrave History of Childhood series, run a multi-disciplinary child study seminar series at Oxford. But I doubt it.

SG Do you think historians missed out because they did not reference Childhood Studies? And what has Childhood Studies done for the history of childhood?

HH I don't know how they regard it. For my part, although I'm suspicious of much of so-called interdisciplinary study, I have to say I find it quite useful [both laugh]. Obviously, I like the way I'm trying to do it in the book I'm currently writing.[5] Generally speaking, it has been very important for me reading those I regard as pioneers: Alanen, James, Jenks, Mayall, Prout, Qvortrup, Woodhead and the legal theorist Michael Freeman, who's done so much to advance children's rights. I'm certainly making a conscious effort to incorporate their ideas and findings, as well as those of other social scientists. These perspectives are critical to my undertaking; they help me to produce what I'm calling 'contextual frames' through which to analyse the historical development of parent–child relations.

SG Are there still debates in the history of childhood such as the clash between the dark legend and the white legend that you mention in your chapter in the Palgrave Handbook?

HH Well, I think they're more or less in the past now. It was, however, always more to do with family history than that of childhood, particularly what I think of as the book-length rant from Linda Pollock , *Forgotten children*. She was bent on rescuing parents from the criticism found in De Mause[6] and Stone.[7] What's revealing, however, is the favourable reviews it received: it sounded like a collective sigh from reviewers who now felt that they'd been vindicated as parents! Pollock bolstered what I call the 'parents always do their best' school of thought, much of the evidence for which came from parental testimonies as to how they felt about their children's sickness, death, education and so on. It was a classic example of taking the documents at face value. I hope that my use of twentieth-century sociological and psychological insights into parenthood will help me to produce a more nuanced historical account of parenting. The majority of histories of the family, however, are not histories of either children or childhood, and we should be careful to note the difference between family history and that of children, and not allow the former to write the latter.

SG Are there historians of childhood going back further in history, say to the classical era, or looking at non-European countries?

HH. Well, I've been speaking about British histories. Of course, there are several important European histories of childhood in English and there is a useful bibliographical guide in Cunningham's 2005 text.[8] There's a much broader range of non-European study in the USA, as there is of the medieval period. There are also several accounts of childhood in the classical world. However, my knowledge of US publications is very limited.[9]

SG Maybe it is a matter of academic fashion and it will come back again?

HH No, I don't think it will. These academic fashions are often determined by the general political–social context and there are other questions around now which are considered more pressing, there's certainly a much greater emphasis on globalisation and the globalised child in sociological, anthropological and developmental studies. But I'm quite parochial. I think we still need to work on the history and sociology of British childhood and children and how these categories have been affected by our contemporary anxieties. What we do know is that our world has undergone several fundamental shifts concerning every conceivable aspect of our lives – and, we have to remember, of children's.

It seems to me that the reference points for political discussion in the 1960s are now largely irrelevant, at least as they were posed then. When I was a student at Warwick in the late 1960s, along with many others, I wanted to change the world. I don't mean to be the jaundiced voice of woe, but students no longer frame the 'issues' as we did; in fact, to a large extent they no longer think of issues as amenable to political change. True, some of them are concerned with single issues, such as the environment, 'sexuality', or famine relief, but I doubt that these are seen as 'political'. I taught in Denmark for several years and found the students there, as here, rather indifferent to the world around them. As one bright spark said to me, with a benevolent smile, 'It's not the '60s any more, Harry. It's all changed. We've moved on.' And my temptation was to say 'And a bad thing too!' [laughs]. Of course, the comparison of earlier historical periods with our contemporary world is part of a larger debate about what many years ago Christopher Lasch called 'the culture of narcissism'; a debate that continues to resonate in the work of, for example, Richard Sennett and other critics of 'the therapeutic society', and the so-called 'politics of recognition' as debated between Nancy Fraser and Axel Honneth who, while by no means denying the importance of 'recognition' for human dignity, are equally concerned, as I am, with matters of justice.

This is on my mind because of what I'm working on at the moment, which deals with late-modernity and the therapeutic state. In the last 40 years we've experienced such profound changes – all the familiar areas examined by Beck, Giddens, Bauman and others – that to talk about Childhood Studies or the development of children and childhood outside the framework of these social and political changes doesn't make any sense to me. In many respects I'm very critical of feminism, but I'm also impressed by the way it advanced its ideological position politically, intellectually and culturally. Feminists recognised from the earliest days that they were involved in politics, although I think the slogan 'The personal is political' has back-fired in many ways, reducing feminism and its favourite ally, psychology, to an off-shore of neoliberalism, especially for working-class women. At the time, however, the slogan was useful in helping to constitute and privilege feminist 'knowledge' within a grass roots political environment. Childhood Studies has never understood 'politics', however, and here I risk offending people. In my view the majority of the participants were either naive or politically uninterested – unlike in other recognition studies, where there was an immediate connecting and finely tuned thread between the defining features of these sub-disciplines and politics inside the academy and throughout the broader societies in which they found themselves. Childhood Studies has never grasped the brutal cut and thrust of the political–cultural dialectic; it's too polite.

SG But isn't there direct connection to social policy, which is next door to politics.

HH Absolutely, but the connection has to be made by Childhood Studies practitioners. In my view, that's not been done. For example, the feminist debate on the 'ethic of care' as it relates to children has never been properly examined by Childhood Studies. I see the care ethic as being what George Lakoff, the social linguist, has called a 'frame', which is deployed by feminists to determine the terms under which the ethic is perceived and discussed and to advance their agenda. Childhood Studies should produce its own 'frame', thereby setting an alternative agenda. Unfortunately, the truth is that many in Childhood Studies have no interest in debating the issue since they adopt the feminist perspective.

SG Does that present a challenge to someone like yourself?

HH It certainly does. In a way I'll be disappointed if I don't ruffle many feathers with this book [both laugh]. Aside from organised conservative forums, I see myself as confronting two sets of opposition, the first of which saddens me: the liberal/

left consensus, sections of which display an intolerance of children, if not a kind of child-hatred – what I term 'adultism'; and second, the sectarian left, notably the likes of Frank Furedi[10] and his associates from the defunct *Living Marxism*, who would leave children to the whims of their parents as they continually complain about the decline of parental authority in the face of state intervention in the home, and lament the social work focus on child abuse and protection.[11] Similarly, Aric Sigman, the pro-smacking 'authoritative parenting' psychologist, when quizzed about his views, replied: 'My friends in the Socialist Worker's Party don't find the idea of more control and hierarchy a problem'.[12] Furedi occasionally hits the mark, but he's fundamentally an irresponsible libertarian. He and his colleagues have been compared to a stopped clock – it's broken, but it's always right twice a day! Again, I wish that Childhood Studies would engage with the Left's (including feminism's) ambivalent attitude to children, if only in terms of the problematic influence of our therapeutic culture and its somewhat contradictory dialectic with neoliberal ethics.

I think we should consider the views of Nancy Fraser in her debate with Axel Honneth over recognition politics, when she argues not against this form of politics as such, but that it should not be allowed to obscure the technologies of 'redistribution' – what she calls the 'postsocialist' condition. Similarly, we in Childhood Studies should not allow it to obscure what I claim are often its malevolent effects on children; we should ask how legitimate can such a self-interested politics be when so often it suppresses the interests of children who are particularly vulnerable to various forms of exploitation. I fear that the Left, in its obsession with 'identity' and 'the self', coupled with its largely uncritical relationship to the 'psy complex', has left children unprotected or at best confined them to the sympathetic but politically innocent arms of child protection and rights advocates. In truth, the Left, lacking as it does a coherent and morally bounded set of moral principles, has too often been opportunistic: it neither *thinks* about children, nor campaigns for *their* dignity – because there's no apparent political reward in doing so.

SG So what about the future? Do you think Childhood Studies is going to fragment into separate but quite sturdy elements or is it about to disappear?

HH I think it's a little of both scenarios; but more likely the latter. It seems to me that the bulk of the sociological work in Childhood Studies is empirical. We've had a surfeit of micro studies from sociologists, anthropologists and geographers, but we lack the multidisciplinary or interdisciplinary macro approach needed to deal with the larger theoretical and political practice questions. There are important exceptions, as I've indicated, and good work has been done on agency, participation, recreation, time and space, familial relationships and so on. Agency and participation, however, are fundamentally about power and justice – barely investigated by Childhood Studies; whereas participants in recognition politics grasped the issues and understood the necessity for organised struggle. Childhood

Studies risks becoming merely another sub-discipline lacking influential public and academic status, not least because, as I've said, it has failed to address the pressing issues of our time.

Again, I don't mean to ignore those scholars who have made preliminary efforts in this direction. I return to Oakley's essay: women's studies came out of 'a point of rupture' between experiences and consciousness, which turned women into a political force *and* provoked academic enterprise. This has not happened to children; and given the age range of childhood, it is unlikely to be replicated. What, then, in relation to Childhood Studies is our ultimate goal? The question Oakley asked has not, I think, been answered: is it to provide knowledge to be used by children in their struggles, or is it to advance the careers of practitioners?

SG Do you think that it is because you are slightly on the outside that you have this perspective on Childhood Studies?

HH Yes. But I also think this way because I begin with political questions through which to frame adult–child relations, and while these are lodged in the messy arena of emotional subjectivities, they're also always connected to power, authority and justice. I take my cue from Tolstoy who, when considering the social condition of Russia in the 1880s, asked: 'What shall we do now and how shall we live?'

References and notes
[1] Campaign for Nuclear Disarmament

[2] Hendrick, H, 1994, *Child welfare: England, 1872–1989*, London: Routledge

[3] Oakley, A, 1994, Women and children first and last: Parallels and differences between children's and women's studies, in B Mayall (ed) *Children's childhoods observed and experienced*, London: The Falmer Press

[4] Lewis, J (ed), 2006, Introduction, *Children, changing families and welfare states*, Cheltenham: Edward Elgar

[5] *Parental narcissism in an insecure world: Neoliberal ethics, social change and the rise of the 'parent education' business, c. 1940s–present*

[6] De Mause, L, 1976, *The history of childhood*, London: Souvenir Press

[7] Stone, L, 1977, *The family, sex and marriage in England, 1500–1800*, London: Weidenfeld and Nicolson

[8] Cunningham, H, 2005, *Children and childhood in Western society since 1500*, Harlow: Pearson Education

[9] A useful guide to new publications can be found in the reviews section of the US *Journal for the History of Childhood and Youth*.

[10] Furedi, F, Bristow, J, 2008, *Licensed to hug: How child protection policies are poisoning the relations between the generations and damaging the voluntary sector*, London: Civitas

[11] See also his and similarly inclined publications from the Centre for Parenting Culture, University of Kent, and numerous pieces in SPIKED online.

[12] *The Guardian*, 19 September 2009

THIRTEEN

Allison James

Allison James is Professor of Sociology, and Director of the Centre for the Study of Childhood and Youth at the University of Sheffield. She is also a Professor II appointment at the Norwegian Centre for Child Research, Trondheim; member of the advisory council for the Centre for Childhood and Adolescence, Cyprus College; and Vice-president of the International Child and Youth Research Network. Professor James is internationally recognised as one of the pioneers of the 'new paradigm' for the study of children and childhood that emerged in the 1990s. Her numerous publications include the seminal work *Constructing and reconstructing childhood* (co-edited with Prout, Routledge, 1990; 1997); *Theorizing childhood* (co-authored with Jenks and Prout, Polity Press, 1998); *Research with children: Perspectives and practices* (co-edited with Christensen, Routledge, 2000; 2000), *Key concepts in childhood studies* (co-authored with James, SAGE, 2008). These texts have been foundational in the evolution of ideas in the field of Childhood Studies.

Carmel Smith To start, Allison, will you tell me about your background and training and how you came to work in this field?

Allison James Well, I did a joint degree in sociology and anthropology at Durham and all the way through my undergraduate years I was very interested in sociology. Then, in my last year, I had a very inspiring teacher who made me really get to grips with anthropology so I was teetering very much between the two. For my undergraduate dissertation I did a sociology dissertation comparing Victorian children's literature with twentieth-century children's literature and looking at the images of childhood between those. I was interested in literature and I was heavily into semiotics and the sociology lecturer said: 'I think you need to rein this in a bit' and pointed me in the direction of children's literature. So it started there and then I was going to do an MA in Media something-or-other and instead I was persuaded to do a PhD. I think it was a continuation, really, of that interest and because there had been quite a movement that was just beginning to do anthropology in Britain and I felt...'Fly the flag'. That is where I started and I did my PhD in a mining community in the North-East of England and one thing led to another after that.

CS And what about your research background? Did you receive specific research training in terms of methods and fieldwork?

AJ We are talking 1977 and at that time if you did anthropology it was a kind of ritual – baptism by fire! You were sent off to the field and you learned on the job and that was it. I was doing an anthropology PhD so it was through reading other people and seeing what other people had done and, obviously, through having good supervision. My supervisor was a marvellous and inspirational man. He was a Middle East specialist, actually, so nothing to do with children, nothing to do with the north-east of England but a very fine brain – I still have his picture up on the wall.

CS Who influenced you theoretically?

AJ I have always been into interpretive sociology and interpretive anthropology. In terms of mentors I would say Clifford Geertz is the person who inspired me the most in terms of a theoretical perspective through anthropology. I used to read his article 'Thick description' again and again to remind myself of the importance of sticking to my guns in terms of an interpretive paradigm.[1]

CS Tell me about your research with children and how you work with children?

AJ My research just developed out of my undergraduate and postgraduate work. I did straight participant observation and ethnography for my PhD so my next project was where I really began to think about more formal research methods with children. I was researching in schools using interviews, not something I had done before, so I had to find ways of working with children that would work in those settings. It was then that I began to think more about how you actually can go about doing research with children. The one decision I made very early on was that I would take at face value everything that the children told me in the same way as you would take it at face value with adults. Once you go down the line of saying: 'Well, they are only five therefore, is it true?' in my view you are lost because that is then pre-judging what children say. Whether it is right or wrong is not really relevant. I am not after some kind of objective truth; I am after what this particular five-year-old is saying and how we can make sense of it. One of the main difficulties in this area of research is that everyone has their opinions about children because they have all been one!

In terms of communicating with children I think the notion of waiting to be invited is important. It depends on age but, with little children, it is very much sitting there waiting for them to come to you in the way that Bill Corsaro describes.[2] With older children, depending on the context, you can be a little more directive. I have also learned that if you engage children in an activity they are much more willing and able to talk to you. The other thing about working with children is that they are often just grateful that somebody is interested in them. I think for many children their experiences of adults is of relationships of power and control and to have somebody who is interested in their ideas and their thoughts about the world I think is quite unusual. I think a lot of children are lonely as much as interested actually.

CS Will you now say something about the evolution of ideas leading to the new paradigm, the ideas and events as they developed and came together. Why did the 'new paradigm' emerge when it did?

AJ Well, of course, I can only speak from my own participation in it. I was in a very traditional anthropology department where everybody was going off to foreign lands. I was working in Britain, I was working with children and there was nobody else doing anything like that at all within our department. So I felt that I was ploughing quite a lone furrow, or it felt so to me, at that time. That was 1979, the International Year of the Child, and it was really interesting seeing all that going on and the publications that came out at that time. Between 1977 and 1979 was the period when I was beginning to do my fieldwork. I obviously delved into some of the psychological literature but, bar Charlotte Hardman's article, there seemed to be very little out there, certainly in anthropology, other than rather old texts, stuff written in the 1930s and 1940s. My thesis was a critique of those because it was doing something rather different; they were all the cultural and personality stuff which I think is different from the aims and intentions of what emerged as the new paradigm. As you know, my personal background was anthropology and, beyond anthropology, culture and personality and socialisation theory were the big ideas that were framing, in a sense, where I wasn't going to go. I was going to go somewhere different. Then it was really those meetings in Cambridge in the early 1980s that brought together a large international and cross-disciplinary grouping. They were organised by Judith Ennew and were called 'The Ethnography of Childhood' workshops. Judith Ennew is an anthropologist so there was that kind of anthropological flavour and that was exciting. There were several workshops and all sorts of people came, like Harry Hendrick from history, Jens Qvortrup from sociology, me from anthropology, Alan Prout, Berry Mayall and lots of people from children's rights and so on. We had the most marvellous conversations and it was really exciting. It was actually at that meeting that Alan and I began to talk about what was happening at that event and actually all the contributors to that first volume, *Constructing and reconstructing childhood*, came from those workshops…I think they were all present. That volume was a representation of the discussions that were going on at that time which were international – Benno Glauser was there representing the children's rights perspective. It was just so exciting and you realised that you were part of something that you hadn't thought you were part of until you met the other people who were also wondering what they were doing. Then gradually the whole thing began to swirl together at that point in the 1980s.

CS Did you have any idea at that stage how big the book would be?

AJ No. I remember Judith Ennew saying that Childhood Studies will have come of age when we have a section called 'Childhood Studies' in Dillons Bookshop or Waterstones. Previously if you looked for any books about children they were under 'Psychology', they were under 'Anthropology' or they were somewhere else. Now you go and Childhood Studies is there. I remember thinking, 'That's right, that's what we have got to aim for.' So there was a sense in which we all wanted something to happen and we were all keen to make that happen and I feel we have done it, you can go into bookshops now and see 'Childhood Studies'.

CS Yes, it has come a long way. Tell me about the current field, is it multidisciplinary, is it interdisciplinary, is it a meeting place for disciplines, what do you mean when you talk about Childhood Studies?

AJ I know what *I* mean; I don't think it is necessarily the same as what other people mean. I mean it is a meeting place for different disciplines. So, you are interested in children and childhood, and whether you are a historian, or an anthropologist, or a sociologist, that is actually what you share. I think that is partly because I am an anthropologist and anthropology is a bit of an eclectic discipline and it does borrow and steal [laughs]. In terms of what I do, the book that I am currently working on just draws on what is useful and in a way I don't care where I am drawing it from and I feel very comfortable with that.

I feel more worried about what I think has happened to the field more generally. I don't like the fragmentation and I have written about this in a *Children's Geographies* article.[3] What I feel has happened for certain people and in certain disciplines is that the discipline has reasserted itself. So you are a geographer first, or a sociologist first and you happen to study children, or you are a historian and you happen to do children rather than being interested in children and bringing your discipline to that topic. I am interested in children and childhood and I bring what I can as an anthropologist to that topic, but that doesn't answer the whole question, so I need historians, I need health people, I need other people to help me deal with what I want to talk about in relation to children and childhood. What I feel is that, in some cases, children become a vehicle for disciplinary objectives – so that you are a geographer first and you happen to do children but you could happen to do animals, or happen to do women or whatever. That is my reading of what has happened, on the one hand, and, on the other hand, I feel the applied practice children's rights side has become very powerful and very strong. It is doing fantastic stuff, but I feel that some of that work, not all of it but some of it, is more practitioner based. It is about improving children's lives, it's about helping children get along better and so on, which is a very particular kind of job, but I wouldn't put that into the same bundle of activities as a more academic Childhood Studies. I am not a great practitioner in that sense. What I see is the way in which practitioners, or people interested in helping children become researchers, or helping children do their own projects and so on, they will borrow and make use of the kinds of things that are written in more academic circles. So there is that sort of relationship between theory and practice and I think to bundle all of those into Childhood Studies is slightly problematic because, in my view, they are doing different jobs.

As an academic you have to make your work have impact but it can have impact without having to do the job of people whose job it is…I am not a practitioner, I am not a social worker, I am not a children's rights expert or somebody who could promote…well, maybe I could, but it is not my job to promote children's rights and help children develop their own rights agenda for example. Others might want to draw on something that I might have written and use that, and that's fine, and I might look at what they do and give that as an example to make a more theoretical statement. That is what I mean by interchange, but I do believe the jobs are quite different. Children might do their own research projects, but is that sociology? Not in my view, it is not sociology because sociology is what I do because I have been trained as a sociologist or anthropologist. There is a bit of a muddle I think.

CS One thing I want to ask you about is psychology. Many of the criticisms in your early work in relation to mainstream developmental psychology would be shared by some psychologists working in the field, for example, critical developmental psychologists. Is there a place for those who work in other *psychologies* in the field of Childhood Studies?

AJ Sure. I mean I am currently drawing heavily on Barbara Rogoff[4] and various other people in this new book. What we were getting at in the 1990s was that very traditional framework which is still so dominant in lots of policy and in the way in which people generally think about children. At the moment I am very excited by Jonathan Tudge's book,[5] which I really enjoy, so I think there is a lot of interesting stuff going on in that field. This is in the book and, of course, we had Martin Woodhead there in the original book.[6] It is not that we were against psychology in the way it is crudely put these days; it was against a particular kind of psychology. People like Paul Light way back in the 1970s and 1980s were doing some really interesting work.[7] So it was about the dominant framework.

CS Moving on to the future, tell me how you see Childhood Studies evolving in the future?

AJ I think there is lots of excitement out there, there's lots of interest out there. I feel a little anxious that it might be sidelined, that a lot of the insights that we made and the critiques that we made against a fully developmentalist agenda and so on, are going to be swamped and lost and that we'll, once again, start ignoring what children have to say and ascribing to them age-related behaviours. I think that is worrying if we can't keep on shouting that we have to look at the social context, we have to look at children's experiences. That actually might mean that a five-year-old is much more experienced than a 10-year-old because of their social experiences. I suppose what worries me is that that's very hard, it is easy to say that because they are five they do this, and it gives you a rule of thumb and that's fine, but it doesn't explain the particularities in particular children's lives and, for me, that's always been the interest. All the funding you can get to do research now is for old people, ageing somehow doesn't include children – I don't understand that as it seems to me that ageing begins from year nought and that actually if we are talking about ageing, we need to think of a life-course perspective, we don't simply need to look at dementia. The funding opportunities are fewer and fewer so if you are not doing climate change, if you're not doing dementia, if you're not doing digital worlds, then actually there isn't any money out there anymore really...perhaps crime [both laugh]. So there is also that kind of structural agenda which is very problematic for childhood research, certainly in the UK.

On the other hand, I do find it very interesting that the United States is beginning to wake up to Childhood Studies. Apart from key individuals like Bill Corsaro[2] and Myra Bluebond Langer[8] and so on, it has not been taught in the way that it is taught in Europe and Scandinavia. I find that very exciting that they are kind of picking up the bat and running with it; I see stronger glimpses of that now. I am going to the States next week to Smith College, they have a course on childhood and time, for example, which is really quite interesting and I think Childhood Studies is beginning to pop up in Europe more too. The real problem of Childhood Studies is the lack of translation. There is lots of interesting work going on in Brazil and in Portugal, for example, but we can't access each other's materials and that is problematic. We have tried with publishers to say: 'Well, can't these books be translated so that we can push the agenda forward' but, of course, that's costly. Portugal is a centre and there is some very interesting work going on there, as in Brazil, but it is very difficult to share and, of course, the German tradition is also difficult to share – there is some very good theoretical work going on in Germany. So those are some important structural issues. That sharing that was possible in the 1980s seems to be less possible now.

CS How can we make the field of Childhood Studies more inclusive of majority world children and majority world scholars?

AJ If you go into the development field problems are magnified because children's lives are so pressing in terms of them being hungry and sick and so on, so that, actually, a lot of the debates we might have here seem kind of not relevant because children are dying and that has to be the priority. We are in a much more luxurious position so any tool that you can have that is vaguely helpful maybe is useful in those contexts. I think what is good is that we are getting more researchers from the South being trained and taking that knowledge back which is also important because they have the understanding of their own societies and cultures. So there is that movement which is going on through MA programmes and PhD programmes and so on.

CS So you are hopeful for the field?

AJ Yes and no, I suppose is my answer. I think that it has become less theoretical and I think that's a shame. I am hoping to rectify it with a new book, but we'll see! I don't think we need any more studies of children's playgrounds, we need to see…I'll give you an example, I have a PhD student in dentistry and she is looking at children's experiences of wearing a brace. It is great to have that research because we need more of that kind of stuff in the medical field. We were talking about when children have their braces put on – this was about recruitment I think – and she said, 'Well, of course, I can start recruiting in September/October because they have their braces put on then.' I said: 'Why do they have their braces put on in September/October?' and she said, 'Well, that's because we have always put them on in September/October.' I said, 'Well, if we think of it from a child's perspective, might it not be better to put them on in July so they have got the summer before they go to big school to get used to them?' And that was a really interesting conversation. So there are ways in which one can actually feed in those theoretical perspectives – she immediately got the point so it raises interesting questions for practitioners once you take it from the child's perspective rather than, in this case, simply following a clinical routine. That's what they did and nobody had ever thought to question it before but actually the challenge of bringing children's voices in is that you can begin to question. That for me is so exciting and if we can carry on doing stuff like that then that is really good. So to insert children's perspectives into fields where they have not been before needs doing. We could do it in economics, we could do it about all sorts of big questions, and if we can do that then Childhood Studies won't be sidelined. My fear, however, is that the opportunities might not be there to do that because people still don't tend to think of children as participants in society despite all our efforts. What role might children have say, in relation to the economic crisis? No-one has ever, as far as I know, been really thinking about that and yet they are the ones who are going to have to live with it. If they are eight now they will be 18 in 10 year's time and it is that short period of time…economic crises, sustainability, food insecurity…none of that is going away, it is going to be hitting the children who are eight-year-olds now and we need to know what they understand about it and what they are learning and taking in now. There are some really big and interesting questions, but I don't think the funding is out there to do this research because people can't see it, they can't get that point about children.

CS Tell me about the book project that you are currently working on, *Socialising children.*[9]

AJ The project I am working on now is revisiting socialisation theory; this is my big *bete noir* at the minute. I am trying to see socialisation from children's perspectives.

CS What made you go back to socialisation? You are very brave [both laugh].

AJ I know! I was quite shocked when I opened my PhD and realised that socialisation is in the sub-title. I have been doing the same thing for 30 years basically, I've just taken a long route round!

CS So what has made you revisit socialisation?

AJ I suppose because I wanted to get to grips with some more theory and I didn't want to do yet another project, I wanted to think more theoretically and I realised that actually…of course, we chucked socialisation out, in a way, because we were so keen to get children's perspectives, but of course it is a complete nonsense to throw it out completely because it clearly happens – children grow up and get to know about the world and actually we still haven't got a really good account of how that happens. We know what happens, and perhaps even why it happens sometimes, but we have not really got an account of how that feels from a child's perspective. I went back to look at Denzin's work and, of course, he talks about it in quite interesting ways and I am re-reading that now, the 1970s book,[10] and Corsaro's work, 'interpretive reproductions' and all that.[2] We have got lots of attempts to get back to that all of which are about…they have got children's agency and children as actors in there…but I am having another stab at it in a slightly different way so we will see how that goes!

CS The last thing that I wanted to ask you, Allison, as somebody who has been at the forefront of the field of Childhood Studies with those early books which were so influential, what would you like people, students in particular, to take from your work and how should they take it forward?

AJ This is the big argument I always have with Jens Qvortrup. I think that what is important is the particularity of children's childhoods. Jens and I have always had this ongoing debate and it has been very productive in lots of ways but, for me, that is what I find fascinating. It gives respect to individual children, it allows us to understand them as socially situated people, not psychologically driven individuals but socially situated people who are coping with life in very particular kinds of ways. You can find some patterns, but you also always find the individual child who is doing it differently and making sense of it in a different way and, for me, that feels a very human activity and I suppose that is what I really like. I like that human element that those kinds of perspectives bring, so you get a real insight into how children are experiencing the world. It could be as a group of individuals and as structurally positioned individuals, but not as a great lump called 'children'. For me that has always been the abiding fascination really. You can get two 10-year-old kids and their lives are so different and their views of the world are so different and, for me, that's the great excitement – not the fact that they're 10. So if that could carry on that would be good because I feel that it is only through those accounts that we are going to be able to really…but it is absolutely no good for policy makers, it simply doesn't work but then I think policy is very crude. I don't know what the answer is because you clearly can't have policies for individuals. I think, when you are grouping and categorising children against these very crude measures and then doing interventions into their lives, you actually don't know what the consequences are or how they are being received and I do feel for a lot of children, a lot of the stuff that happens to them is a consequence of the fact that they are just bunged together in a particular category. I am not a practitioner, I am not a policy maker so I can say things like that because I don't have to make it happen, but if I can keep reminding people that children are individuals and that if somehow policy could work better for them as individuals it would be good.

References and note

[1] Geertz, C, 1990, *The interpretation of cultures*, London: Hutchinson

[2] Corsaro, W, 2011, *The sociology of childhood*, 4th edn, Thousand Oaks, CA: Pine Forge Press

[3] James, A, 2010, Interdisciplinarity – for better or worse, *Children's Geographies* 8, 215–16

[4] Rogoff, B, 1990, *Apprenticeship in thinking: Cognitive development in social context*, Oxford: Oxford University Press

[5] Tudge, J, 2008, *The everyday lives of young children: Culture, class and child rearing in diverse societies*, Cambridge: Cambridge University Press

[6] James, A, Prout, A (eds), [1990] 1997, *Constructing and reconstructing childhood*, Abingdon: RoutledgeFalmer

[7] See for example, Richards, ME, Light, PE, 1986, *Children of social worlds: Development in a social context*, Cambridge, MA: Harvard University Press.

[8] Bluebond-Langner, M, 1978, *The private worlds of dying children*, Princeton, NJ: Princeton University Press

[9] James, A, 2013, *Socialising children*, Basingstoke: Palgrave

[10] Denzin, N, [1977] 2010, *Childhood socialization*, 2nd edn, New Brunswick, NJ: Transaction Publishers

FOURTEEN

Mary Kellett

Mary Kellett is Professor of Childhood and Youth and Director of the Childhood, Youth and Education Programme at the Open University, UK. Perhaps best known for her pioneering work to empower children as researchers, she founded the Children's Research Centre to train and support children and young people to undertake their own research. Mary has over 35 years' experience of working with children and young people as a social worker, primary teacher and academic. She holds a number of Adjunct Professorships in Australia and Europe and sits on several national and international advisory panels. Mary has authored widely on a range of childhood and education issues, most notably on children's participation and voice and on child-led research. Mary's numerous publications include *How to develop children as researchers: A step by step guide to the research process* (SAGE, 2005), *Rethinking children and research: Attitudes in contemporary society* (Continuum, 2010); *Children's perspectives on integrated services: Every child matters in policy and practice* (Palgrave Macmillan, 2011).

Carmel Smith Will you first say something about your background and how you have got to where you are now – a potted history of your career to date?

Mary Kellet I have got a practitioner background so I have worked with children for 36 years, but I have only been in academia for the last 15 of those. I started out as a social worker, a children's social worker, I have been a full-time mother for some of that time and I have also been a primary school teacher. It was when I was a primary school teacher that I got completely hooked on research – and when I say hooked, I mean absolutely hooked! I decided that I was going to do a Masters and I just loved doing the research with the children in my class. I then leapt off a cliff, handed my notice in and did a PhD full-time for three years! Fortunately, I got a studentship but I gave up my salary to do it so I was really committed to doing the research. I had an interest in children with special educational needs so my PhD had that focus but I think, even in those early days, that I was already leaning towards empowering children and knew that research was going to get them there. After I did my PhD I worked for a short time at another university and then I came here harbouring, what felt at the time, somewhat of an elicit desire to get children as researchers going, children in their own right! In those days, we are talking 2001, it is quite common now for people to talk about children as researchers but it wasn't then, it was something that made a lot of people throw their hands up in horror. Even in my own department there was a lot of scepticism around competency issues and all the usual barriers, so it has been a gradual journey from that point of knowing what I really wanted to do and just having to climb a mountain really, and it was a mountain, and gradually just eroding away all the barriers; that this was possible and that children could do very valuable research. At the end of 2003 we established the Children's Research Centre here [The Open University, UK] and that was really when things started to take off because we had a home, we had a hub and we have built that now into something that has a good international reputation. The website has around 150 original studies by children so it is really growing.[1] The thing that has probably driven it for me, when I say I got hooked on research, is that it changed me as a person. I found it an empowering process doing research. It made me think in a different way, it opened up parts of my brain that had been dormant for a long time, it changed my attitude to the way I interacted with other people and I think I became a better human being. I thought: 'Well, if research has all these potentially good benefits then why can't we give children the same opportunities, why do they have to wait until they are adults to get the benefits of doing their own research?' That was part of the rationale behind trying to get them off the starting blocks. I was promoted to a Personal Chair in this field in 2008 and that felt like getting towards, or somewhere towards, the top of the mountain. To be able to establish a Research Centre but then to be able to get a Chair that acknowledges that this is a legitimate field of enquiry, felt like finally the sceptics were dissolving away. So that is about where I am on the journey and now it is about consolidation and moving it forward and making many more opportunities for young people.

CS Where did you learn to do research, how did you learn to do research?

MK This is where I fear I am not going to be very good for the data! The modern way, certainly the way we teach research here for any postgraduate student, is quite a formal training in research methods, usually an MSc in research methods and then a PhD. I came the 'learning on the job' route. My Masters was action research, classroom based so it didn't really require a huge amount of reading or learning about other research methods, which I regret as I would have liked to have had that opportunity. My PhD wasn't a good training in research methods at all; it was very much a good training in the research methods that the supervisor said I needed and I didn't really learn anything more and it wasn't qualitative, it was quasi-experimental. So I have come an awfully long way! I have changed directions from…, I had quite a cosy doctoral expertise in a certain area and I kind of jumped off a cliff and decided that *this* is what I really want to do. I needed to get myself up to speed on qualitative research methods because it was what all this was going to be about. I am self-taught in terms of the theoretical and conceptual aspects of qualitative research, but one of the things that I would say is the most important, whether you are an adult or a child learning about research methods, it is actually getting out and experiencing it and I don't think you can learn it from a book.

I also consider the work that I did as a practitioner as being very important in my approach to research. Not just teaching, I don't think I could research with children in the way that I do if I hadn't been a children's social worker because that is a different relationship with children where the relationship is absolutely key to the outcome. So I would say that my approach to research probably started with my first practitioner work so we are going back 36 years really.

CS Tell me about the evolution of ideas and events leading up to the declaration of a 'new paradigm' for the study of children and childhood? Why did it happen when it did?

MK The UNCRC was the watershed that led to a new paradigm for the study of children and childhood.[2] The focus on children as human beings not becomings, on citizens in the here and now with rights that are fundamental to their human status, was a radical shift. Previously children were viewed as part of another: for example, a family or a school, and their wellbeing was negotiated through the proxy of adults.

There was growing discontent with the objective/scientific research design to generate data about childhood suggesting that the premise on which this was based was 'adultist' and wasn't oriented from the child perspective so questions began to be raised about how authentic and accurate such findings were. This coincided with a rise in ethnographic studies which tried to facilitate understanding from immersion in the cultural and social contexts. Key individuals came together during this period, for example, Allison James, Alan Prout and Chris Jenks, theorising what came to be known as the 'new sociology of childhood' by critiquing the adult-centric view of childhood in a similar way to feminism critiquing the male-centric view of society.[3] Key thinkers around generational ordering (for example, Berry Mayall and Leena Alanen) reinforced power issues and absence of participation by keeping children confined to private spaces such as the family rather than public spaces where they might develop a voice.[4] The 'coming together' if you like, of feminist, generationalists, new sociologists and ethnographers created a critical mass that helped solidify the move towards this new paradigm.

This was not happening in isolation, the replication across many countries globally acted as a catalyst. Similar thinking was going on, for example, in Scandinavia, South Africa and New Zealand. In the developing world, NGOs were playing a big part in the spread of a new approach to childhood. Big players such as Save The Children were applying participatory methods in the field at a time when the academics were theorising in their offices.

Approaches to understanding children and childhood had been discipline-specific for over a century, and dominated by developmental psychology and medical research. The growth of a new paradigm was fuelled by the breaking of those chains and the embracing of multiple disciplines to view childhood much more in the round and from numerous perspectives, for example, children's geographies, cultural studies, anthropology, ethnography, sociology, psychology, psycho–social, education.

CS The 'new paradigm' emphasised children as social actors. Given your interest in children as researchers, how do you differentiate between the term 'social actor' and the concept of 'agency'?

MK I think that's a really good question. Agency, for me, is a step further than an acknowledgement of children as social actors. I often talk about participation, voice and agency; participation and voice are different and agency is different again because participation is that act of being involved in something, but that doesn't mean to say you have got voice. Actually, you can participate in participation – voice is about being able to express, to voice it, which is different from participation. Agency is different again, agency is when whatever it is you have either participated in or have a view about, in terms of a voice to express it, that something then can be brought to happen because of that – so it is the agentic part of the process. If something isn't going to happen as a result of expression of voice then there is no agency.

CS So are you saying there has to be an effect?

MK There has to be something that you can trace back to either a result of some participation, if we are talking about children and childhoods anyway, or the way in which they have had a voice about something, because you can participate in just participation and it actually becomes just a meaningless abstract concept, you can have a say and anybody can have a say. I can say what my view is to you and I am having a voice but I'm not being agentic, I am not having any agency unless what I say at some point has an impact or an effect. So adults can choose whether they listen to the voice of the child. The voice of the child can be hollow and meaningless, even though they are getting the chance to say it, if adults then say, 'There, there that's very nice and you were very brave to get up and say that', but then go away and just don't do anything. So it has got to pull through to something that you can look towards and say, 'There was some agency at work there.' It is another way of looking at self-determination, if you like, and I suppose psychologists would talk about self-determination theory but you've got the right to participate is the first thing, going back to fundamental human rights, all of which is actually part of becoming and being agentic in some way. It doesn't have to be in a big way it can be something very small that has happened, or changed, or you have influenced or made people think in a different way but it has had some kind of effect. So I don't think in terms of agency as being just something that children have a right to or that we want to encourage, it has to be something that happens.

I think that is why I stress the importance of practitioner research in the field because the whole meaning of what they're doing, would have an agentic agenda.

If something couldn't happen as a result of their research they would feel that they had failed and yet we wouldn't feel that as academics or theoreticians. We would just pat ourselves on the back just because we had encouraged people to begin to rethink or consider a new policy, whereas in the field they very much need an impact of some sort at the end.

CS Is that why people within the broader Childhood Studies movement, even those who are very much into theory, would say that theory without practice is hollow?

MK I would agree that theory is hollow without practice but where I would be slightly different from some is that I believe the experience of practice has got to inform the theory. It is circular, it is cyclical rather than a straight line that begins at theory and leads to practice. We are too superior, I am trying to think of a nicer word but superior is an accurate word, we are quite superior in the way we think that we dream up all the theory and then we go and put it into practice but, actually, we should be using the impacts and the findings of practice to inform the theory more than we do – I know it does to some extent, it is not as simplistic as I have just said, but we don't do it enough and we don't draw enough on the valuable work that is being done in the field. I think that there has been a very necessary period of time when we've navel-gazed and have done all the theory and got ourselves all these nice paradigms and all the rest of it but actually, without a purpose it is hollow and I think we have to move on from that. We have to really be moving into more applied practice as being a central and a core part of what our understanding should be of Childhood Studies. Again, I appreciate that that's a personal view and it might not be shared.

CS Can I now move on to ask you about the current state of the field? Is it a distinct field, is it multidisciplinary, is it interdisciplinary, how would you characterise the field?

MK Yes, my view is that Childhood Studies is a distinct field, but I prefer to think of Childhood and Youth studies. One of the emerging perspectives is that children themselves see a difference between what they regard as childhood and youth. While there is a unifying legality in that children are legally minors until they are 18, teenagers don't like to be referred to as children, so we should be respecting that there is a continuum between child and adult and youth occupies a large part of this. The reason it is a distinct field is that no other single discipline can authentically convey what it is to be a child because childhood itself is multi-faceted. We wouldn't base all our knowledge about the elderly just on, for example, medical research into the ageing processes of the body – there are so many other social, cultural, psychological aspects of what it is like to be old. It is both multi-disciplinary and inter-disciplinary. It is multi-disciplinary because some discrete disciplines which have their own discrete methods and approaches (for example, ethnography) contribute important perspectives but these are more powerful when they are considered alongside knowledge from other disciplines too, as the complementary bodies of knowledge together create new understandings.

CS Should the field be focusing on children, childhood or both? Some scholars in the field stress the sociological basis of Childhood Studies and argue that the conceptual and theoretical focus should be on childhood as a permanent social and intergenerational category?

MK Rather than children, childhood or both, I think we should be thinking about a continuum where we consider early childhood, childhood and youth and within each of those areas we look at both children and childhood. Both macro and micro are important and I don't think we can separate them because the micro studies that generate knowledge about individual cultural contexts or discrete stages, or ages, or races, and so on, feed into our overall understanding of what it means to be a child.

CS You spoke earlier of 'climbing a mountain' in order to get to where you wanted to be in terms of children as researchers. Will you say a bit more about your personal approach to your work at the moment?

MK Part of the reason that it feels that I am in the right place doing what will hopefully, be useful and valuable to people is a combination, a culmination almost, of all those different personal experiences. Because you are interested in the stories – it is the personal experiences that I have pulled together of being a social worker, a teacher, a mother and with some underpinning in psychology in my academic background – those four things have made an equal contribution, really, to the way I have developed my perspectives and being a mother is just as important to what I contributed to that perspective as being a social worker or a teacher. It is possibly an unusual combination, not many people would do social work and education teaching although they might do social work and academia, and maybe that just gives me a slightly different viewpoint or a slightly more holistic way of looking at the whole jigsaw puzzle. Because of that, the lived experiences of children is what interests me, and anything that will help to get to that more accurately and understand it is useful. Yes, some of that needs to be understanding of childhood and the history of childhood and the way the representations of childhood have contributed to our understandings. I fully accept and appreciate the importance of that, but my ultimate goal is the children part of it, but I wouldn't want to ever separate them and I wouldn't ever want to look at children from only one perspective. I can appreciate when people have done that so that I can go and read medical research about children's diseases and children's illnesses and learn a lot and be thankful that people have gone and done that discrete research, but that was with a specific purpose and with health in mind, so it is only one tiny part that will help me to support the children.

CS What directions do you foresee the field of Childhood Studies pursuing in the future?

MK You have already said that you are aware that the people you have asked to contribute to this book are mainly minority world and that skews the picture somewhat. Childhood Studies is *all* children so we must include majority world children particularly as some of our richest findings come from majority world studies. With modern communications the globe is a much smaller place, so I think the extent of global content in Childhood Studies is set to increase significantly over the next decade.

I wonder, and there is a tension here and I know that you are interested in tensions, how much there will be a contribution to future directions by the less theoretical strands of childhood investigations and enquiries and explorations? That's really from the NGOs and the fieldworkers who we wouldn't normally probably think of in terms of theoreticians or theorisers, but actually they are often doing majority world work. I just wonder whether, as we move forward into the next decade, there will be more of an emphasis on that kind of knowledge that is being generated because of the strong evidence base of it – it's not strong on theory, I appreciate that, but it is very strong on its evidence base and its application in the different contexts which is a strong part of the interdisciplinary nature of Childhood Studies. Looking at the list of the good and the great that you are including in the book, and I would probably include myself as well in this, they are the ones who have contributed to the theoretical constructions. Why do we now need so much emphasis on debating the theoretical nature of childhood and children when, particularly if some of that theory is emanating out of the children's rights perspective, what we should be concentrating on is children's lives and experiences and furthering their well-being and everything else? None of us would be engaged in Childhood Studies, well I hope we wouldn't, if we weren't interested in children and children's well-being. So I do wonder whether Childhood Studies will take a direction that is going to be slightly less theoretical and more applied in terms of the overall balance as we move forward. I, personally, would probably think that that was a good thing because I think we can talk too much, we can argue and debate too much and in the doing of that we miss out on actually supporting some of the children whom we are trying to help.

CS How can we be more inclusive of children and childhoods from the majority world?

MK I think it is going back to one of the points I made earlier about the role that NGOs and applied research in the field has got to play in the longer term and I think at the moment, without being disrespectful to a lot of my academic colleagues, it is not valued in the same way. There is some very good research and fieldwork that comes out of NGO organisations. They are very close to the action in the native language but they are in a position as NGOs to bring that to the rest of the world through English because they are nearly always either English-speaking NGOs or they have got people within those NGOs that are English speaking. If you look at someone like, for instance, Harry Shier who went to work in Nicaragua with the NGO CESESMA, he was an academic from an academic background but he took his academic underpinnings and he was working with NGOs in the Spanish language and then he was able to do a lot of the publications in English.[5] We have got to make sure that we are valuing that and giving it enough of a dissemination platform if we truly want to bring in more majority world findings and studies about children and childhoods.

CS Given the current economic and political climate do you think there is a danger of a shift in thinking about children and childhood, politically and publicly?

MK Absolutely. I think it is a very real threat because you can hit saturation point and there is only so much the general public can take in terms of constantly being bombarded with things about children and young people, children's rights and children's participation and everything else. There is a danger that the general public is going to begin to become fatigued with it all and certainly policy makers. One of the things I have talked or written about, is the fear of the backlash against children's rights. If legislation and policies begin to unpick some of those rights it will affect the fabric of Childhood Studies. There is a danger and a threat there, but even more so if we are not united.

CS Notwithstanding the economic climate, how do you see us moving forward in a positive way?

MK You probably won't be surprised to hear me say that when funding is tight you can cut out the middleman and if you cut out the middleman you are going straight to the children and young people. So we spend funds and money on the middleman activity, but if we go directly to children and young people and involve them more in what we are doing in the actual generation of the knowledge, the collection of the data, then I think we are cutting out some of the funding requirements, some of the resource issues and we are also, but that again is my perspective that may not be shared by everybody, helping ourselves get to a more authentic understanding of what is going on. I really don't think we go to children and young people as a resource enough because, although I wouldn't ever suggest that we should be exploiting children and say that they should all be going out doing research for us, but involving children in research can be done at local and community levels that don't require these very large amounts of funding. We don't always have to be thinking in those terms.

CS Is there anything else you would like to say before we end?

MK When we were discussing some of the current tensions and debates earlier I started to think that we are in danger of coming full circle. Why did we want to create this new paradigm of 'Childhood Studies'? It was because there was so much falling out between psychology and sociology and they couldn't agree on the methods or the approach or the underpinning theory and the absence of an understanding about the cultural context – cultural studies was a big part of the way in which this new paradigm developed. If now that all these different people have got all their different perspectives and they start to disagree too much, the danger is that, if they start to go into silos and camps, we end up where we started and that would be very, very sad to me, because I think it was a big step forward in terms of empowerment. I know that's where I come from really; my ideology is very much based in empowerment of children and young people. Childhood Studies was actually putting the child at the centre, rather than the approach or the theory or the discipline, and we may lose sight of that if we squabble too much. If we are all trying to fight our individual corners about what is most important then we are all contributing to something that could ultimately destroy it all. I think your book is going to be so important because it might actually raise that as an issue.

References

[1] www.open.ac.uk/researchprojects/childrens-research-centre/

[2] United Nations Convention on the Rights of the Child, 1989, Geneva: United Nations

[3] James, A, Jenks, C, Prout, A, 1998, *Theorizing childhood*, Cambridge: Polity Press

[4] Alanen, L, Mayall, B (eds), 2001, *Conceptualising child–adult relations*, London: Routledge-Falmer

[5] www.harryshier.comxa.com/ and www.cesesma.org/

FIFTEEN

Berry Mayall

Berry Mayall is Professor of Childhood Studies at the Social Science Research Unit, Institute of Education, University of London where she teaches on the MA, Sociology of Childhood and Children's Rights. Professor Mayall has over 50 publications including *Conceptualizing child–adult relations* (edited with Alanen, Falmer Press, 2001), the groundbreaking work, *Towards a sociology for childhood: Thinking from children's lives* (Open University Press, 2002) and chapters in key Childhood Studies texts, such as 'Conversations with children: Working with generational issues' in *Research with children: Perspectives and practices* (Christensen and James, Routledge, 2000; 2008); 'Generational relations at family level' in *The Palgrave handbook of Childhood Studies* (Qvortrup, et al, Palgrave, 2009); Professor Mayall has recently written *A history of the sociology of childhood* (2013) and, with Virginia Morrow, has written a book about English children's contributions to the war effort in the Second World War: *You can help your country* (Institute of Education Press, 2011).

Carmel Smith To start, Berry, will you tell me something about your background, a 'potted history' of your career and how you came to where you are now in your research work with children and childhood?

Berry Mayall Well, like very many other people at the Institute and indeed in academia generally, my first main job, apart from some other ones, was as a teacher. I was a Secondary School teacher teaching English to 11–18 year olds all the way up to Oxbridge Entrance and I wasn't trained to do that. I just did it, because in those days, this was way back in the 1960s, you didn't have to have any training, whereas nowadays you do. I then decided to change tack, partly because there were grants available, to do a training course to be a social worker at the LSE. It was an MSc as well as a social work training. It was a lot about the history of the welfare state, we did bits of economics and psychology and sociology and some of it was about research methods. I also worked as a social worker for a few years, but after the MSc I wanted a part-time job because I had a young child and only two jobs that came up that summer, one was to be a social worker and the other was to come and work at a new research unit being set up at the Institute of Education, under the direction of Jack Tizard, an extremely well-known developmental psychologist. My friend said, 'take it' because it was an exciting new venture. So that was the Thomas Coram Research Unit in 1973 and I have been here at the Institute of Education as a researcher since then.

Our work at TCRU in the 1970s was about families with young children and we were interested in how well parents managed with little children in the absence of adequate day-care arrangements and what they would actually like if they had the chance to choose. We did lots of interviews with parents, mainly mothers, and the theoretical perspective that TCRU used was very much that this was empirical fact-finding stuff and we were taught that we must be 'objective'. There was a statistician attached to this outfit, a very well-known statistician, and it was part of his job to make sure that we all did this objective fact-finding method of conducting interviews. During the course of the early years when I was doing this, however, I became interested in the children themselves, because the way mothers talk about children is very much about children as people, not as objects of concern to developmental psychologists, and mothers explain that one of the things that they do is to shift responsibility for daily care, including healthcare, onto the children. I mean, by the age of five children frequently monitor their own health. They look after themselves; if they're tired, they sleep; if they're hungry they eat their food; they go to the fridge to get a drink; they clean their teeth – they are doing quite a lot themselves. So in 1990, with the help of the Institute of Education, which underwrote half of my salary for six years and so enabled me to do this research, I thought I would do some research on what then happens when these five-year-olds go to school. Are they able to look after their health then? How does the school view children's health and healthcare? So I spent a couple of terms in a primary school with the five-year-olds in Reception and also with the Year 5s (aged 9–10). I sat around and discussed topics with them as and when I could and I also went to their homes and talked with their mothers, and fathers if I could get them, with the usual famous problem that you can't actually knobble the fathers! That was where I began on this, what in the end amounted to a programme of research on childhood, because having done that first one I then applied for a relatively big grant, to do a two-pronged study of the status of children's health in primary school. How is it viewed by schools and indeed by the Health Service? So we did a national survey with a short questionnaire and then we did some case studies. We took six schools and spent up to a month talking to everybody concerned including the school nurse, the teachers, the dinner ladies, anyone we could, and the children.

Then I got a grant to do another study which we called 'Children and Risk' which was on the ESRC programme on Risk and Human Behaviour. We were the only people on that programme to be interested in children and again we were talking with children and parents about the home. Is the home regarded by people as a safe place or not and what about the outside world? Then the fourth of these studies was another ESRC one (part of the programme Children 5–16) which I called 'Negotiating Childhood', and that was simply focused on how children themselves understand what it is to be called a child. What does it mean in experience terms? For that one I spent time in primary schools. Those four studies were the empirical basis for the book that I wrote in 2002, *Towards a sociology for childhood*.[1] They are all described at the end of that book and of course those were only some of the (many) studies that I applied for. So that is my history and, as you can tell, it doesn't include research training of the sort that people nowadays more or less have to do if they're going to get a research job. It was more like an apprenticeship, learning on the job. I have also done some teaching at the Institute, on our MA and also with PhD students.

CS Will you say more about your own approach to research with children and perhaps comment on the significant growth in the use of qualitative methods in Childhood Studies?

BM Well in the first place I suppose I have to say that I am not entirely convinced about the distinction between qualitative and quantitative research. As various people have pointed out, when you do what is referred to as qualitative research you generally end up by adding things up and there's nothing to stop people who do large-scale questionnaire-type studies including what some people would call qualitative data in them.

My perspective on doing research with children is that I try to interact with children, taking them seriously as people. There is nothing more to it than that. I think I'm slightly unusual in this field (in the UK) in that as well as thinking of them as people who have valuable experience to tell us about which can make a difference to how we think about policies in place for children, I also think about childhood from a structural point of view, that children's lives are affected, in ways specific to childhood, by large-scale forces; and that children contribute to the division of labour, that they are not in a pre-social stage as presented by some psychologists, they are contributors and it is not only from their school work, it's through the sorts of things they do at home and through what Margaret Stacey calls 'people work'. They are active in relations with other people, other children and with adults. So that's the spirit in which I try to approach conversations with children.

CS What are your views on the concept of reflexivity in research?

BM This comes out of feminism doesn't it? Well I have been accused of not being reflexive. Somebody wrote about a paper about reflexivity and one of the people she took as an example of bad practice was me [laughs].

CS Why?

BM Well I suppose it would be true to say that I am a little bit impatient with all this talk about reflexivity. This comes down, I suppose, to the question of what it is that you are trying to do. I'm not particularly interested in my own feelings about these interviews or my relations with these people actually, or with children. What I am interested in is childhood. I am interested in making political points really, that's what it comes down to in the end. So I think the person was alleging that I should be writing about my experiences of doing these interviews and I think she would probably accuse me, I mean I know her, of being rather crude and simplistic and probably I am. I take the sort of line that a lot of feminists do actually, that there are more important things to do in this world than sit about considering one's navel, essentially.

CS Can we now move on to talk about the evolution of ideas leading to the 'new paradigm'. How did the ideas and events come together from different geographical locations that eventually led to the declaration of a 'new paradigm'?

BM Well, as you know, I have written a paper about the history of the sociology of childhood that has just been published and it can be argued that, in spite of the fact the Americans are not very active at the moment, a lot of the precursor work went on in the United States.[2] For instance, American psychologists went to visit other countries to see what their ideas about childhood were – people like Kessen and Bronfenbrenner and there was a lot of interest in the 1970s about how far psychological paradigms of childhood were adequate. Clearly, and I don't think there is much question about this, a huge boost was given to the sociology of childhood by Jens Qvortrup's five-year project *Childhood as a social phenomenon*. Qvotrup got teams from 16 industrialised countries to consider large-scale factors that affect childhood: the legal position, economic position, how children spend their time and the sorts of statistics that are collected about children. That led on to the first very important book called *Childhood matters* published in 1994.[3] I think what was very important about that study was that the people who worked on it, by and large, were sociologists. Jens Qvortrup had previously worked with Helmut Wintersberger and Giovanni Sigritta in Vienna at the Centre there and had begun to think that adult researchers' work about childhood was seriously deficient because it comprised a very simplistic vision of children as socialisation projects. The sociological movement in the Nordic countries and Austria was paralleled by the work of well trained sociologists such as Helga Zeiher and her many colleagues who wrote a book[4] in which they studied how childhood had changed in Germany over a period of 30-odd years and they looked for understandings of what were the macro-factors that had changed childhood. Jens Qvortrup and his colleagues and the Germany sociologists solidly based their work on understandings derived from sociological study.

Now the development of what you might broadly call childhood studies in the UK came from other traditions. The first people who worked on this and convened some of the very first meetings were anthropologists; they were Judith Ennew at Cambridge and Jean La Fontaine at the LSE. For reasons which, I think, only anthropologists could explain, the tendency was to emphasise the social construction of childhood and children's agency; and that has remained the case in this country today, for example James and Prout 1990. This was an influential book among others that came out in the 1990s, such as Jenks 1996 and James, Jenks and Prout 1998, and they are still regarded as key texts for students. I think there are a couple of things one can say about that popularity: one is that it may be easier for students to understand the social construction of childhood than to do the hard sociological work of thinking about and analysing the relevance of large-scale factors to the character of childhood at different points in time and place. Second, from the point of view of doing research, I think it can be argued that a lot of the research that has been done in the United Kingdom has been poorly funded, carried out by children's charities and certainly driven with the aim of improving children's lives. First, people want to say how terrible the lives of children are: this is one of the things children's charities have to say in order to get money. Second, these people have been activated by the aim of improving the status of childhood and to get more money into childhood. So there has been a tendency in the United Kingdom to focus on small-scale studies: let's listen to children, we want to report what children's experiences of childhood are and we want to improve the character of childhood. I think you could also argue that another important feature of work in this country is to do with children's rights. Now in some countries, notably the Nordic ones, children's rights have, I think, although it is very difficult to say because quite frankly there hasn't been enough work done on it, but I think it is the case that children's rights are better established, more fully accepted, in the Nordic countries than in this country. That means that here in the UK there are a lot of people out there in the NGOs and in the research community, who are dedicated to the aim of promoting children's rights, and the way they do it is again, to listen to children in order to find out how and why children's rights are not respected and to try to pressurise whomever it may be to give better respect to children's rights. So I think, if it is the case that we are going through difficult times in this country as regards the sociology of childhood (though I disagree), I think you can put it down to that sort of history.

On the other hand, of course, it is the case, I believe, that many sociology degrees nowadays do consider childhood and indeed, I have seen A-level papers which include the sociology of childhood and I even went and did a session in a school on that front. The main sociological journals now carry papers about childhood so it may be that this notion that Childhood Studies are in crisis in this country is yet another social construction [laughs] being put about by people, who have been through this development over the last 20 to 30 years and who think social constructionism has reached a dead end, who identify the need for some sort of progress, and who may also want to investigate interesting lines of thought in academic papers. Personally, I think the work done, for instance, for the *Palgrave handbook of Childhood Studies* in 2009, offers a very good account of the state of play in Childhood Studies and it includes many chapters that do address the macro and the micro, not only the opening chapter by Jens himself but there is a whole section on relational sociology, on generational studies which includes important papers by Leena Alanen, Thomas Olk and one by Heinz Hengst on 'Collective identities'. I was asked to contribute a chapter to that section on 'Generational relations at family level' which, as Leena Alanen commented, was a rather narrow remit, but I did what I could with it.

CS From what you have said, there was the more macro approach from Nordic childhood scholars such as Jens Qvortrup, whereas in the UK the focus was on more small-scale research. Looking to the future in Childhood Studies, how can we merge those two strands and do the bit in the middle, as it were, between the structural factors and the micro? What can we do to try and bridge those two approaches or include both in some way?

BM Well, of course, this has been a consideration among sociologists, how do you inter-relate agency and structure. Developing ideas within relational sociology is an important way forward; and one of my students in 2012, for instance, used the work of Anthony Giddens to consider some aspects of this. I think Bourdieu has a certain amount to offer although, of course, he didn't write specifically about childhood, but I think it is possible to go into some depth on what we mean by agency and how far does it include structure and just what are the interrelations between the large-scale and the small-scale, for example, in the work of Bourdieu and Wacquant.[5] This is what C Wright-Mills said in 1959 [both laugh] you have got to relate private troubles to large-scale forces and it is still true – he is the sociologists' sociologist. I think we simply have to go on doing this and it is not easy because, this is perhaps another topic, one of the most important influences on my thinking about childhood is feminism which has, of course, challenged paradigms of research which go on about replicability and validity and reliability. I think one of the things that you can do is to use some of these big sociologists' ideas and use them to try to relate the macro and the micro.

CS Berry, can I ask you why the parallels between Women's Studies and Childhood Studies are not more explicitly examined in the literature? There are exceptions, such as your work and Leena Alanen has written about this. However, more generally, in Childhood Studies why aren't the parallels that we could learn so much from, particularly the debates that went on during the second-wave of feminism, utilised and discussed in the literature?

BM I don't know and I have written about this in several places and Leena Alanen has specifically drawn on lessons from feminism to understand child-adult relations. Of course, it is true that it is still the case, as various feminists have pointed out, that women themselves are a bit wary of taking on children and childhood, so I think the action has to be from the other end, it has to be from the Childhood people who are willing to learn from feminism. I certainly feel that writings by people like Ann Oakley and Dorothy Smith have helped me to understand what we are doing when we are carrying out research with children. You could argue and I myself think, although I am not sure how many people would argue this, that childhood is oppressed by adulthood. I have carried out research where I have not exactly asked children about this, but I have got them to talk about their lives and child-adult relations and they most certainly do see themselves, ordinary British children, as under the control of adults. That, of course, is not a terribly cheerful, optimistic or basically acceptable idea. Clearly, feminism has pointed to the oppression of women by men at every single level of society, and I think you can say the same about childhood. It does represent almost a sort of revolution in how we think about childhood because, though we may have those ideas as highlighted by Chris Jenks in 1996 on 'the demon child' and 'the innocent child', the notion that adults are controlling childhood is not a very comfortable message and yet it can be seen to come, that idea, from harnessing the feminist analysis of women–men relations to questions of child–adult relations.

CS In terms of Childhood Studies now and in the future, are you hopeful that the field will survive? If so, what directions should it follow?

BM I don't know a great deal about university politics, but it seems to me that various versions of what tends to be called Childhood Studies are well established in universities and colleges now. I think it is the case, again I don't know, that people who are training to work in schools, early years and social work and so forth are not nowadays just handed psychological paradigms. To that extent one can say that Childhood Studies which includes an element of sociology is fairly well established. I understand that Martin Woodhead at the Open University and his colleagues are rewriting and updating their course books and that suggests that there is a pretty healthy audience for this sort of thing. On the other hand, I do think that the idea that you can present students with a pick-and-mix, a selection of paradigms to consider childhood, is a step in the wrong direction. This was, in fact, something Priscilla Alderson and I thought about when we were setting up our Masters degree in Childhood, which started in 2003. We thought in the first place that it would be confusing to say, 'Well, this is what the psychologists say, this is what the anthropologists say, the sociologists, the economists, the historians…' and so on, we thought it would be confusing and trivialising. Second, we wanted to advance sociology as a topic and, in particular, to consider the interrelations between sociology and children's rights. I continue to think that we need to press for sociological approaches to childhood. I am not particularly pessimistic about this, I think things are moving along, papers are appearing in mainstream journals and even sociological course books are beginning to appear. In 2001 I went to our local big book shop and looked at introductory sociological course books, when I was writing my 2002 book, and found that none of them, this included Giddens's introductory course, mentioned childhood other than as a socialisation project. More recently there have been some sociological course books which have done so, such as Marsh et al, 2009.[6]

CS Before we finish, Berry, is there anything else you would like to say from your reflections and your experiences particularly for new people coming in to the field?

BM I think it is very important that we try to maintain links with people in other countries. That is getting easier now that English has become…the French and the Germans are all able to communicate in English although we, of course, have not made similar moves in respect of their languages. I think international collaboration and lots of meetings are important, they can be internet meetings, to maintain contact. I went to a meeting recently in Finland, organised by Leena Alanen, and one of the questions that was discussed was what kind of impact could the sociology of childhood make at the level of the ISA (International Sociological Association) and I think it is a problem that there aren't any really high powered people in influential positions in British universities. We haven't got figures like Ivar Frønes, Helga Zeiher and Jens Qvortrup in this country and, as I say, that is a matter, to some extent, of historical traditions, but there is no reason to suppose that we can't have. Actually that is not entirely true, some of those people who have been in this work from the 1980s are now professors of sociology and they include Alan Prout, Allison James and Pia Christensen, but they all trained as anthropologists. One possible line which looks promising at the moment is in considering the interaction, the interrelations between research in the affluent northern countries, the western countries, the minority world and work being done in the majority world. There have been seminars and conferences about this and papers are coming out about it. One of the interesting things about that work is that the majority world is taking very seriously indeed the macro-influences on childhood because of the dire circumstances of many of the world's children. So there was an ESRC-funded set of seminars in Scotland headed by Kay Tisdall and Sam Punch in 2012[7] and one of Allison James's colleagues at Sheffield, Afua Twum-Danso Imoh, has organised some meetings.[8] These papers are reporting on what lessons can be learned both ways, from considering majority world childhoods and minority world childhoods. That is both interesting and important. Of course, as ever, one hugely difficult problem is getting decent amounts of money to do decent quality work in both minority and majority world countries. I think one interesting development, which I am sure will continue in the next few years, is the notion of children themselves as researchers and this is, of course, highly political. A recent report has come out on this (CESESMA, 2012).[9] Harry Shier, who has worked in Nicaragua, and I have argued that, paradoxically, it may be that it is in countries where children are recognised as workers, as productive workers, it may be more possible than in our minority world countries for them to operate as researchers. This is because in spite of the fact that much of the work that children do across the world is menial and even exploitative, they are recognised as contributors to the division of labour in a way in which we *struggle* to get anybody in these affluent minority world countries to recognise. So I think that recognition allows for the construction of research projects by children to be accepted. Harry Shier has acted as a sort of back-up advocate for children helping them to refine their research questions and their methods and then off they go and interview adults – who appear to be willing to talk with them as proper people who have interesting and important questions to ask; they write their report and hold meetings with policy-makers and employers with the aim of improving their working conditions. There has been a bit of that done in minority world countries but not very much. Some of it is, again, to do with funding, it is to do with a lack of adult commitment and it is to do with the power relations between children and adults. Also, of course, children who are actually engaged in productive activity are being forced to think about the conditions in which they work: is it okay for the man who employs them to have a large house up the valley when they themselves are living in shanty towns? Children in these circumstances are faced with political and economic questions.

References and notes

[1] Mayall, B, 2002, *Towards a sociology of childhood*, Maidenhead: Open University Press

[2] For a fuller discussion of this history, see B Mayall, 2013, *A history of the sociology of childhood*, London: Institute of Education Press.

[3] Qvortrup, J, Bardy, M, Sgritta, G, Winterberger, H, 1994, *Childhood matters: Social theory, practice and politics*, Aldershot: Avebury Press

[4] Preuss-Lausitz, U.a.o., 1983, *Kriegskinder, Konsumkinder, Krisenkinder. Zur Sozialisationsgeschichte seit dem Zweiten Weltkrieg*, Beltz: Weinheim

[5] Bourdieu, P, Wacquant, L, 1992, *Invitation to reflexive sociology*, Chicago, IL: University of Chicago Press

[6] See Marsh, I, Keating, M, Punch, S, Harden, J, 2009, *Sociology: Making sense of society*, Harlow: Pearson Education

[7] Tisdall, K, Punch, S, 2012, Not so new? Looking critically at childhood studies, *Children's Geographies* 19, 3, 249–64

[8] Twum Danso Imoh, A, Ame, R (eds), 2012, *Childhood at the intersection of the local and global*, London: Palgrave Macmillan

[9] CESESMA is an independent NGO working with children and young people in northern Nicaragua www.cesesma.org.

SIXTEEN

Peter Moss

Peter Moss is Professor Emeritus at the Thomas Coram Research Unit, Institute of Education, University of London. A historian by background, Professor Moss has a broad range of research interests including services for children, the workforce in children's services, gender issues in work with children and the relationship between employment and care, particularly in relation to leave policy. He also has a particular interest in social pedagogy and radical education. Professor Moss has published widely over a number of decades and his best known works include (with Petrie) *From children's services to children's spaces* (Routledge, 2002); (with Dahlberg and Pence) *Beyond quality in early childhood education and care: Languages of evaluation* (Routledge, 2013, 3rd edn); *There are alternatives! Markets and democratic experimentalism in early childhood education and care* (Bernard Van Leer Foundation, 2009); and (with Fielding) *Radical education and the common school: A democratic alternative* (Routledge, 2011), which won First Prize in the 2012 Book Award of the Society for Educational Studies. He co-edits the book series, *Contesting early childhood*, and is currently editing a book of the selected writings of Loris Malaguzzi.

Carmel Smith Maybe, Peter, before we start talking about the area of childhood, will you say something about yourself and how you came to work in the area of Childhood Studies?

Peter Moss I am not certain that I think of myself as working in the area of Childhood Studies. My work is relevant to childhood and I think that people who are in Childhood Studies are relevant to my work, but I wouldn't identify myself in that way. I came into this field in a way that is both serendipitous and also very difficult to replicate in this day and age; I am a product of my times. I was originally studying history and while I was doing that at university I became involved, through voluntary work, with children who were then called 'mentally handicapped' or, even worse, 'sub-normal'– that was the terminology. I not only did a lot of work with these children, but became very involved in a movement which was concerned to get them out of the really appalling places in which they were lodged when they couldn't live at home, so called 'sub-normality hospitals', which were huge places that could take up to 2,000 children and adults, and were not at all nice. It was a time in the late 1960s and early 1970s when these places and similar places for the psychiatrically ill were coming under question and I became involved in this 'de-institutionalisation movement'.

Through that involvement and campaigning and so forth I met a very remarkable social researcher, Professor Jack Tizard, who was at the Institute of Education and had done some very important work showing that this group of children could, in fact, be cared for applying the same principles and in the same sorts of settings as non-handicapped children and that they were far better off in these more normal environments. So, quite by accident in a way, I met Jack Tizard and when he set up the Thomas Coram Research Unit in 1973 he invited me to join. I had done two years work for him before that on a short-term project, and he now wanted to work on the reform of early childhood education and care. He decided that this was the next field he wanted to reform because he knew, quite rightly, that it was very, very inadequate in Britain in the early 1970s.

What he wanted to do was to show that another way of providing early childhood services was possible and desirable. His first project for his new Research Unit, and onto which I was drafted knowing very little about the subject, was to set up children's centres, which would be a model of how multi-purpose centres could be offered to all local families with pre-school children, free of charge, responsive to the needs of those families and would become important social institutions – like schools. Others at that time were also thinking about this idea and working on it and quite a number of children's centres were set up in England in the 1970s by people who had the same idea.

So there I was, moving down to London and starting my own family, being pitched into this world of early childhood education and care about which I knew very little indeed. Again, this is not something that would happen today as there would be careful selection processes to be followed and you would have to have a very good looking CV. Where I found myself was with somebody who was thinking in a new way about how to provide for young children and their families. Instead of the fragmented, chaotic, inadequate, mishmash of services that then existed, Jack's idea was to develop these core institutions that everybody would feel entitled to use and that would be responsive to their needs. So I never came with the baggage of having worked for many years in the old system, with all its assumptions and ways of doing things – it always seemed obvious to me that children's centres were what we should be doing. Sadly, the governments of the day, both left and right, didn't think it was relevant or pressing, so they never picked up on it though ironically, of course, 30 years later under Gordon Brown, children's centres became *de rigueur* in England and we ended up with 3,500 of them. By that stage, however, the chaotic system had got more chaotic and instead of children's centres being the basis of a universal public system, they were simply on the margins of a predominantly marketised and privatised early childhood system. So I was very fortunate to be introduced to a field, in which I have subsequently worked, without a lot of baggage and with the inspiration and leadership of a most remarkable man and I owe a lot to a way of doing things which wouldn't be possible today.

CS Peter, will you now say something about the evolution of ideas leading up to what is called the 'new paradigm', the sociology of childhood, the social studies of childhood that evolved into Childhood Studies. Your work has always had an international flavour. What happened, what came together that the 'new paradigm' was declared at that particular time?

PM Although I have never seen myself as being in Childhood Studies, I find it to be an important discipline, but only one of many that provide useful perspectives. So as I am no more than a well informed outsider, I am not certain how I can give a very deep or considered view. One can clearly see that it was emerging at the same time as the concept of children's rights and, in some countries, the introduction of Children's Commissioners and so forth but that, of course, leads on to the question of why were these different but connected things happening at the same time. I don't even know when you would begin to put a date on it, but I would have said, although I could be wrong, during the 1980s. It may well have its roots earlier on; there were pioneers, people who were waving the flag well before the 1980s.

I wonder if, to some extent, the emergence of the rights discourse in the 1980s also reflects the resurgence of economic neoliberalism and political advanced liberalism with a very strong emphasis on individualism and rights. I don't know, that could be unfair; but can these developments be entire coincidences? They created an environment in which the idea of the autonomous individual and so forth was perhaps more possible. I also don't know how far it was influenced by the wider 'linguistic turn' to perspectives such as post-modernism and post-structuralism which, of course, brought with them ideas about the social construction of reality and hence the idea of childhood as a socially constructed concept. So those things may all come together and I also don't know enough about what was going on in other countries. I have certainly done a lot of cross national work but much of that was at a policy level, studying early childhood service systems in Europe in particular.

Although I find Childhood Studies, children's rights and so forth important, what has been most important for me has been first of all my understanding of the concept of paradigm. If you had interviewed me in 1995 and mentioned paradigm, it wouldn't have been a familiar concept for me. It was only really in the latter half of that decade through working with someone who has been very important in my work, Gunilla Dahlberg from Sweden, whom I believe to be one of the most important figures in early childhood in the last 30 years, that I came to engage with ideas of paradigm, understood as mind-sets, ways of thinking about, understanding and relating to the world. That introduced me to the idea of the power and influence of the paradigm of modernity in shaping thinking, particularly in early childhood, but also to the potentiality of other paradigms (because there are many others and I am not saying it is either/or), in particular post-foundationalism, which would include perspectives like post-structuralism.

That, for me, has been really important. It helped me in the first place to understand why I found discussions about quality so problematic. In the early 1990s the discussion about quality in early childhood education and care began to spread vigorously and I remember when I first became acquainted with the discussion that I felt very uneasy about it. I wasn't comfortable with the concept of quality but I couldn't put my finger on why. It was through my association with Gunilla Dahlberg and writing a book with her and a colleague Alan Pence, *Beyond quality*, that I came to understand that the concept of quality makes sense from a certain paradigmatic perspective, if you work with the paradigm of modernity, which believes in the ability to come up with objective truths which can be applied universally, and so on.[1] If you locate yourself in the post-foundational paradigm, however, then you have other values and assumptions and beliefs and you accept that there aren't these foundations of certainty, that there are different constructions, different conceptions, different perspectives from which people have to make choices.

That also takes you down the road that questions around childhood, or indeed any other subject, are fundamentally political and ethical because they confront you not with discovering the truth which you then apply, but with deciding between alternative truths, differing perspectives and conflicting alternatives. That way of looking at things, through paradigm, was very important and I would say that the book that I wrote with Gunilla and Alan, *Beyond quality*, which has now been translated into 10 languages, is one of the most important things I have written because it is really seminal in my own development and I think it contributes to what I call a resistance movement in early childhood, resistance to a very dominant modernist discourse.[2] You need only read any policy document in any country or any international organisation to see that discourse, which is about the idea that there are human technologies which can and should be applied prescriptively to achieve certain pre-defined outcomes; if you do that you will get high returns on your investment and then everything will be hunky-dory economically, socially and so on – I slightly parody the discourse, but not too much. Whereas for me now early childhood is about starting with certain political questions, 'What is your image of the child?' 'What is the purpose of education?' 'What is your paradigm, how do we understand knowledge?' and so on. On the basis of answers to such political questions you can then develop your thinking about policy and practice but you don't rely on people like scientists to say: 'This is how it is', 'This is what you must do' and 'If you do that you will get $16 back for every $1 you invest.' So for me, when I think of paradigm and its importance, I am thinking more in philosophical than disciplinary terms. Moreover, I see Childhood Studies as one discipline, and I think interdisciplinarity is extraordinarily important, which is why I find it very difficult to locate which discipline I would say I was in. I would like to think of myself as a border-crosser!

CS Peter, you, and you have also mentioned Gunilla Dahlberg, have been great champions of the importance of early childhood education. There do seem to be issues around the status of early childhood within the broader umbrella field of Childhood Studies. Will you say something more about your more recent work on education and the status of early childhood?

PM I am increasingly interested in education over the life course. My most recent book, which I have written with Michael Fielding, who comes from a secondary education background, looks at how you would envisage an education from birth to 18, or indeed beyond, based on common images, understandings, values, pedagogies and practices.[3] I increasingly get frustrated because I think early childhood is very introverted and inward looking and doesn't engage outside its field. In that way, it is no different to other forms of education – it is just that they are more powerful. I think that if early childhood only spends time talking about itself it will get dominated and colonised, which is what is happening. Early childhood, I would say, is deemed the lowest point in the educational hierarchy and of relatively little interest to other educational sectors. I think people in the compulsory school sector would probably say, 'Yes, of course it is important because it prepares children for school.' I criticise this 'readying for school' discourse in my latest book.[4] Moreover the reality is that people working in the early childhood field are mostly appallingly paid in both of our countries [referring to England and Ireland] and are often very badly educated; their status in the education hierarchy is very low. Last, but not least, early childhood education and care attracts very little real interest from the rest of education, even though I would say that early childhood education, in pockets, probably has some of the most innovative work going on in education.

How that relates to the wider Childhood Studies field I don't know. I wonder, and this is more wondering than knowing, whether there is some suspicion among some Childhood Studies people who, quite understandably, see the danger of institutions that we have designed for children, including the school and the nursery, because of their enormous power and their capacity to govern the child – and, of course, there is a lot of truth in that, schools and nurseries are dangerous. I have a sense that there isn't that much exchange, again I could be wrong, between Childhood Studies people and people working in early childhood because, perhaps, people working in early childhood forget, if they ever knew it, Foucault's comment that everything is dangerous. I think anybody working in nurseries, schools or wherever needs to have that engraved on their hearts because I think institutions are very dangerous. I also think, however, that they have enormous potential and that we need them. I have always tried to walk a tightrope, saying on the one hand that I am aware that they are dangerous places and on the other, that they have great potentiality; therefore we have to pay a lot of attention to how we can minimise the danger and increase their potential. This means challenging what I would call the mainstream discourse, which is highly governing because it is about applying technologies, by technicians, to children to get pre-defined outcomes. That is very, very dangerous and I don't hear nearly enough people, hardly anybody in that discourse, saying, 'but we have to be very wary, indeed we have to think critically on what we are about'. So I understand that concern about the dangers of institutions for children, but I also think that Childhood Studies needs to engage, albeit critically, with what nurseries and schools might be able to do that is emancipatory and creative.

As a post-script, I would add that I think critical thinking is vital and I like to think that that is a faculty which I have become better able to use in recent years. At the same time, I think that hope is also necessary and that critical thinking is not enough.

CS Peter, for new researchers coming into the field, tell me about what training you think they should have? I know that your early research background was closely associated with the policy and practice end of things. It would also be really helpful if you would say more about the importance of critical thinking.

PM I am just going to put that on hold and just clarify something. I would say that the first part of my career was largely taken up with issues of policy and I still have a lot of interest in that field. I am interested in the structuring and organisation of early childhood services and how they relate, for example, to policies on parental leave and so forth. What became important for me in the 1990s was the understanding that you cannot just treat practice as a 'black box' that somebody else knows about, and is of no concern to people doing policy. You have to realise that there are alternatives and that policy in a way has to be at the service of practice. I think one of the problems is that people doing policy tend to have the 'black box' approach to practice: 'There are people who know about that sort of thing...of course, we want quality in early childhood and there is a person up the corridor who knows what that means and how to do it.' While people engaged with practice have, too often, been naive about politics and policy, or not interested, and it only comes up when there is something they don't like very much because it hinders their practice. I think it is really very important, as far as possible, to combine an interest in practice with an interest in policy and systems.

Turning to critical thinking, I think that this is about having a perspective that there are always alternatives and that there are different paradigms and in different paradigms things will seem extremely different; questions that make sense in one, don't make sense in another. I sometimes think that paradigm is so critical that I would almost say, and I don't know how you would do this and not being an experienced teacher this may be of no use, I would almost say that students should be introduced to the idea of paradigm from day one and that, in turn, opens up the issue that the person teaching you is somebody who has a paradigmatic position and therefore you are constantly saying, 'What perspective does this person take?' Then after I understand more about different possibilities, different perspectives, different paradigms I have to make a choice, I cannot just drift through life letting people tell me what I should think and do, I have to make a choice. I then have to realise that I have taken a position, I see the world in a particular way, I can understand that there are other ways and I can respect them, but I have taken a choice.

I suppose my view has always been that I can respect people who choose to situate themselves in other paradigms; but what I can't respect is people pretending that they are just adopting the only way possible to think about a subject – denying paradigm and their own paradigmatic positioning. It is a very difficult issue because I think most students will come to courses very much inscribed with a particular paradigm, because we live at a time when modernity and positivism are still very strong in society and these, unfortunately, contribute to a paradigm – one of whose features is a belief in objective and universal truths and there being one right answer. Actually, the difficult thing about getting paradigm is being able to suddenly realise that it is possible to think and see things in a totally different way, the world turned upside down.

CS And for children's researchers starting off, is their training still grounded in the traditional concepts such as objectivity, reliability and validity which, as you say, come from a particular paradigmatic perspective?

PM Yes, and all the language that people trot out like 'evidence based' and 'programmes' and such like are based on those sorts of paradigmatic assumptions and beliefs. I also think it is then very difficult because it is much safer just to pretend that these things don't exist. I think it is quite difficult for people to suddenly find themselves cut adrift from certainties that they grew up with and I see that as a real issue. In early childhood, for example, I think quite a lot of people, all sorts of people, are not terribly happy with what I would call the mainstream discourse, which I parodied somewhat, and that is why there is a resistance movement that is writing books, writing articles, holding conferences and so on and they attract a lot of people globally. You see that there are quite a large number of people really, not just getting to understand different theoretical ideas within different paradigmatic positions, but doing them in the classroom, which is really important. I think there could be a group of people who might go to a conference and hear somebody like me hint at these things, these alternatives – and then what? There is no system, no back-up to help people and support people to go deeper into these matters, to follow through the realisation that there are alternatives.

I would say that I was enormously helped when I began to grapple with these ideas, lamentably late in my career, by one or two very close working relationships where people would say, 'this is a very interesting book' or I could say to them, 'I don't really understand.' To me that has enormous implications for ideas like professional development, because if you were serious about early childhood workers not being technicians but being critical thinkers and researchers, they need to be supported if they are interested in getting to grips with these fascinating, sometimes slippery concepts and ideas and in seeing how you can put them to work in pedagogical practice. My colleague, Gunilla Dahlberg, has some very interesting examples from Sweden where she has provided something like that to large numbers of preschool teachers. The culture and the climate is such that quite a lot of Swedish preschool teachers are interested in, and able to work with, theories and perspectives which are relatively new to early childhood, for example the theories of French poststructural thinkers such as Foucault and Deleuze, and they find strength from being supported in pursuing that interest. So I think it is a whole sequence of things that need to be considered, which would start from the premise of epistemological and ontological diversity; and how we deal with that is a very big, difficult and unresolved question.

CS During the last part of the interview, Peter, I want to ask you about where we are now, what you see as the current state of the field. I hear you say that you don't necessarily locate yourself within this field, or indeed any particular field, but would you say what you see as the current challenges for the study of children and childhood and what are the possibilities?

PM I think there is a smaller and a bigger answer to that and that is preceded by the fact that because I don't see myself as being in Childhood Studies, I am not very confident in answering this question. I think interdisciplinarity, connectedness, is critical and I suppose this is just raising a fairly obvious problem: that people are increasingly working in smaller and smaller niches. I suppose I would tend to describe myself as a 'Jack of all trades and a master of none' in that I have been able to jump around when I have been interested, read here and read there and follow up; you read in the paper that somebody has done a report on something and think: 'I'll read that' and that necessarily means, of course, that you don't read everything in one particular field.

To me that is really critical because I see two huge problems facing us. One is how we can resist and contest what Roberto Unger calls 'The dictatorship of no alternative', which is all around us today and includes a very rampant and powerful neoliberal political and economic regime into which everything is being sucked.[5] The problem is how can we nurture a resistance movement to that and that would apply to all disciplines in all fields because from my political perspective, this regime is extraordinarily damaging and catastrophic to us and our planet. Within that there is a further problem of how the resistance movement can make its presence felt on the main stage. As I said, read any policy document on early childhood, probably the same on schools, and you won't see so much as a reference to the large body of work by what I would call the resistance movement, the people who are working with different paradigms, different theories, different ways of thinking, talking and practicing. So there are dual challenges: how to sustain that resistance movement and how to move to a much more plural and democratic mainstream politics of education and childhood.

Moving to an even larger scale, I have to say that one of the biggest questions is how we engage with the magnitude of the crises facing us as a species. I read as much as I can around these inter-connected crises: on the environment, global warming and climate change, toxicity, stress on resources, biodiversity being reduced and I think that there is no doubt that we are facing a crisis of absolutely epochal proportions and yet we carry on in every field as if this isn't happening. I have been writing about education and what the purpose of education is, and one of the purposes has to be an education for survival, which is not an original term, several other people have used it.

How do we create such an education? What contribution would Childhood Studies make to this and to our survival as a species? Beyond survival, how can we regain a degree of flourishing which I believe has been undermined by a rapacious and harmful economic regime? Those are my big questions about the future and that is why I think one has to be interdisciplinary, to be nomadic and try to understand what is going on – having, I think it is Mannheim who says this, 'a diagnosis of our time'. This diagnosis is essential even though we may decide to dip into something on a much smaller scale, but we need to have that bigger view. We should not forget that survival and flourishing is the challenge facing children today and children tomorrow.

CS That is a powerful note to end on.

References
[1] Dahlberg, G, Moss, P, Pence, A, 1999, *Beyond quality in early childhood education and care: Post modern perspectives*, London and New York: RoutledgeFalmer.

[2] Dahlberg, G, Moss, P, Pence, A, 2013, *Beyond quality in early childhood education and care: Languages of evaluation*, 3rd edn, Routledge Education Classic Edition, Abingdon and New York: Routledge

[3] Fielding, M, Moss, P, 2010, *Radical education and the common school: A democratic alternative*, Abingdon and New York: Routledge

[4] Moss, P, 2012, *Early childhood and compulsory education: Reconceptualising the relationship*, Abingdon and New York: Routledge

[5] Unger, RM, 2005, The future of the left: James Crabtree interviews Robert Unger, *Renewal* 13, 2/3, 173–84

SEVENTEEN

Alan Prout

Alan Prout is Professor of Sociology and Childhood Studies at the University of Warwick. He has held posts at a number of UK universities, including Cambridge, Keele and Stirling and has been an international Visiting Professor at Roskilde University. He was previously Director of the ESRC Research Programme 'Children 5–16' encompassing 22 different projects. Professor Alan Prout is internationally recognised as one of the pioneers of the 'new paradigm' for the study of children and childhood that emerged in the 1990s. His numerous publications include the seminal work *Constructing and reconstructing childhood* (co-edited with James, Routledge, 1990; 1997); *Theorizing childhood* (co-authored with James and Jenks, Polity Press, 1998); *The body, childhood and society* (edited, Macmillan, 2000) and, as sole author of *The future of childhood* (RoutledgeFalmer, 2005). All four texts have been foundational in the evolution of ideas in the field of Childhood Studies. Professor Prout's recent journal articles include, 'Taking a step away from modernity: Reconsidering the new sociology of childhood', *Childhood: A Global Journal of Child Research* (2011, 1, 1).

Carmel Smith To start, Alan, will you say something about your background – a potted history of your career leading to the publication of *Constructing and reconstructing childhood* in 1990?

Alan Prout Well, there have been several key moments, but I will just focus on two or three. One was at the very beginning of my career when I was working as a researcher in a research project in health education. I was going all around the country interviewing children, parents and teachers about health issues and as I was doing this I was fascinated by the way – they were mums basically, we said parents, but there were very few dads – they would talk about everyday health issues with children, particularly about the problem of how do you make a judgement about whether your child is ill enough to stay off school? This wasn't actually part of our project, but it came up all the time and so I had the idea: 'I can do a PhD in this', because there is a whole issue about how do these negotiations around illness take place in families and what is the children's point of view? In working round this idea I thought that I should read some sociology of childhood books and trotted off to the library to get the books, but there weren't any! Well, there were two actually: one was the *Reader* by Chris Jenks and the other has disappeared without trace, a very slim little volume by a guy in Education who had a shot at it sometime in the 1970s. What I discovered was that there wasn't a sociology of childhood or there was not much of a literature on it. So I thought as part of the PhD project [laughing] why not start writing about childhood from a sociological perspective? Can I make a case for why this is an absence and for why it ought to be there and how useful…? So I started reading around the medical sociology of childhood illness and began to notice that children were invisible and mute, because really it is a kind of sociology of parents in relation to their children, and thought, 'Well, let's try and put children's own points of view.' There is an anthropological teaching on that and there is a range of different things you can go to for some kind of steer on how to go about hearing the voices of those who have been silenced. The particular way I did it was to make the study focus on children's accounts. So that experience was very important to me.

The second moment was when I started to realise that there were other people around the world on to the same idea. My recollection of those times, and really we are talking about the late 1980s and early 1990s, into the mid–1990s really, was that there were scattered individuals all over the world – but particularly in the Nordic countries, in the UK, in America to some extent, in continental Europe, probably other places as well – who thought that they were working pretty much on their own but who gradually began to meet each other. One of the networks that got created were the anthropology of childhood conferences that Judith Ennew organised at that time. They were a way of people getting in touch with each other and discovering that there were people thinking along similar lines. How do networks get going like that? It's capillaries, it's molecular, it's little accidents of people meeting each other and that then coalescing into conferences and so on. A big turning point was the conference that was held in Denmark, organised by Jens Qvortrup and included Wintersberger, Sgritta and a group of other people, at Legoland, which Lego sponsored. That was a big and important event because that really brought, if not everybody, a lot of the people who had begun to learn about each other together (many of the papers were published in Qvortrup, Bardy and Wintersberg, 1994).[1] So the Nordic countries played a very important role in that.

If you are asking about *Constructing and reconstructing childhood*, the reason why I think it took off in an important kind of way was that it was a programmatic statement. It took a lot of the trends and thinking that had already been happening and really that goes back to the 1960s, so the whole interactionist element of that goes back to 1960s sociology. It took these trends, this growing awareness and thinking that many people around the world were beginning to do, and it made a programmatic statement out of it. I think that is why it became an important book – it presented, in a condensed programmatic portable kind of way, a number of key tenets that could be taken up and worked around by anyone wherever they were.

CS That book has been very influential in the field of Childhood Studies and is still the book most commonly cited by people who talk about the sociology of childhood. Do you think that is why the 'new paradigm' is often seen as having been UK led – is that book the connection?

AP Probably. I mean there are other books: Bill Corsaro's textbook[2] which I think was very important, very accessible and brought a lot of that thinking together and was designed for undergraduates, so fulfilled a really good role. Later on Mike Wyness's ([2006] 2011) text is an excellent and very well informed discussion of the field, and recently updated, too.[3] In methodological terms Pia Christensen and Allison James's ([2000] 2008) *Research with children* is playing a leading role, also now in a second edition.[4] Don't forget, however, that another reason that *Constructing and reconstructing childhood* is cited so much is that it is in English and the whole emergence of, let's call it the Social Studies of Childhood, happened against the background where English was becoming the global language and the main language in which academic writing is done and the whole technologies of citation and citation counts and so on, they all work in English. That was nothing to do with that book, that was happening anyway, but it was a kind of wave that was happening.

CS The next thing I want to ask you, Alan, is how your thinking about Childhood Studies has evolved from *Constructing and reconstructing childhood* (1990), *Theorizing childhood* (1998) through *The future of childhood* (2005), to where you are now? So, again, a potted history of where your thinking has taken you?

AP I would say that the main directions are away from sociology and trying to create a sociology of childhood – I still think that's an important task – but I have moved away from that as being a kind of discipline-bound task and towards an openness to multi- and interdisciplinary thinking around childhood. I think that's the future direction, I think it *is* the direction and I think it will be even more so in the future. So I think there are a whole lot of questions about how do we develop Childhood Studies as a multi- and interdisciplinary field? That is where I have moved to and there are many things to say about it that apply to Childhood Studies, which I think also apply to the general intellectual tenor of our times. It is becoming increasingly clear, at least to some people, that the kind of problems that humanity faces simply cannot be addressed except through some kind of multidisciplinary and interdisciplinary effort. I think childhood is a very attractive focus for multidisciplinary and interdisciplinary thinking because it is complex. It is social but it's also psychological, it's cultural but it's also natural, it's about history but it's also about evolution, we are a species with an evolutionary as well as a social and cultural history, so I think we need to bring all of that to bear on our thinking about childhood. That is a very difficult thing to do but we are not alone, it's not the only field where people are beginning to think in these kinds of ways. I think one of the big things is to try and move towards that openness to multi and interdisciplinary thinking about childhood but also to begin to think about what kind of theoretical language do we need to talk about childhood as simultaneously biological and social for example? Because the language that we have inherited from modernist thinking is all about separating those things out and turning them into different, incompatible discourses. We need another language, another vocabulary that encourages us to think about the connections between those things. That is what I tried to do in *The future of childhood*, that is why it is sub-titled, *Towards the interdisciplinary study of children*, it is trying to set out some of the ways and the language in which we could think through multi- and interdisciplinary approaches to childhood.[5] Can I say something about sociology as well?

CS Yes, please do.

AP I am more and more beginning to think that yes, there is a sociological aspect to childhood and yes, it is very important to pursue that, but what kind of sociology? Well, what I would say at this point is, of course, there are many different kinds of sociology and they probably all have a contribution to make but…[pause for thought] how to say this without sounding too apocalyptic? I think there is a problem with the founding tenet of sociology as a discipline that comes from Durkheim's argument that sociology rests upon the idea that social phenomena can only be explained socially – so it is a kind of closed loop that he's talking about. Frankly, I think that is just incorrect and I think by the end of the twentieth century we could begin to see how that is no longer a tenable position in a world dominated by debates like the ecology crisis, the global warming debate on which, by the way, I am not at all convinced of anthropogenic global warming…I think there is global warming, that is just an empirical fact, the question is what explains it? Putting all that aside, there is clearly a kind of crisis at the end of the twentieth century where we are becoming aware of the impact of societies and how they work on things that are supposed to be completely different from them – nature. So we are having to become aware that humans might be a social animal but we are an animal, we have an evolutionary history and evolutionary character, we are filling an ecological niche and that's to do with our social character, our use of language, our use of technology. These are all things that, as a species, we do and make us social. So you can't seal off the social from the natural and this is exactly the kind of thing that writers like Latour are tackling, or one of the things they're tackling. I think we have to take that really seriously so it means that we can't just recycle twentieth-century sociology into childhood, we are not in that place anymore, we are in a different place in terms of understanding, but also in terms of the kinds of problems that human beings face at the moment. If childhood is to become a field of study in its own right it has to place itself inside those developments and be part of that rather than standing a step back from it. That really is the argument in *The future of childhood*, that's what I try and argue. So, yes, sociology, but we have to have an open-minded sociology that is rethinking the basis on which it approaches questions. If we can do that in childhood so much the better, we will be on that wave, not a few waves behind it.

CS The concept of children's 'agency' continues to be used in a number of different ways in the Childhood Studies literature. What do you understand by that concept and what do you mean when you use the term 'agency'?

AP Well, I go with the idea that agency is an attribution that we give to people and things that are seen to have brought about some effect in the social world. Actually it's a question not an answer. I think too much of the literature turns the idea that children might have agency into a statement: 'Children do have agency'. It's probably the fault of Allison and myself in the way we formulated that, but actually I think it is a question, it's an invitation to look, can we see ways in which in given situations, and they are all different, agency can be attributed to the children there? That's how I see it. That's the first thing, let's say it's a way of looking, it is a question not a given answer. Of course, often when we look we find there are ways in which children can be attributed agency and a lot of the work has done that and it's all to the good but it's not enough. The second thing, this is also an argument that's made in *The future of childhood* and also in that book I did on childhood and the body, *Childhood, body and society*, we have to move beyond noticing children's agency to unpacking how that agency comes into existence.

So where noticing children's agency leads us to is another question. Actually this goes back to my earlier point about this much more traditional strand of studying childhood that would put a lot of focus on parents as speaking for children. That is not untrue so the question for the new sociology of childhood might be: 'When parents are representing children how do children enter into that process?' If you like, you can say, 'How do children get their parents to be agents for them?' 'What are the processes through which that happens?' I am not saying that is the only thing we should be asking because I think, many times, children act as agents for themselves, but every time they act they are engaging with other entities whether these are other adults, other children, other machines, other technologies. What are the alliances they are building up in order to create this effect that allows us to attribute agency to them? That is still a very important and not yet properly addressed task although awareness of the need for that has become greater. This is why last time [during previous interview in 2008] I said that I was going to get really fed up if I kept reading more and more papers that say children are agents!

CS I now want to ask you about your assessment of the current state of the field.

AP Well, I think we are in a bit of a lull. The high excitement of the 1990s and even up to, let's say, 2005 seems to have disappeared and after 2008 it kind of got worse because of the squeeze on funding, at least in some countries, which got tighter and tighter – we are in the austerity world. I think those are big problems, I think we are all a bit depressed and, as I was saying to you earlier [prior to the interview starting] we are depressed because we are in a depression and I think this is going to be a period of time that lasts much longer than anyone thinks, it is a 10- or 20-year period. One of the things it raises for me is to think about what were the economic conditions under which this new thinking about childhood arose in the first place? When we look back, actually what we can see is that it came about as we were heading through the boom of the 1980s, 1990s and up to 2008. We were in boom times, the party was on and money was flowing like water, all freshly minted out of nothing, in the form of debt by private banks supported by central banks who allowed that to happen. So what we had was a classic boom, credit boom–debt boom, I should say (when did we start talking about debt and calling it credit?). But it was all part of the creation of this huge debt crisis the consequences of which we are currently living with and you could say, I'll just float this idea, one of the things that happens in this kind of classic debt-driven boom that we have seen, we saw it come to an end in the 1930s, actually we saw it in the 1870s and the 1830s, this thing recurs every so often, always pretty much in the same kind of form. So boom times create expansive thinking, people are open for new ideas, new frontiers and there is a very good side to that, but what happens when you are in a post-bubble contraction? What I fear and what I think is happening, and I think you can see this already, is that new thinking, thinking on the edge, comes at a discount. That's not what people want, what they want is to circle the wagon train and start feeling some security and some certainty – people don't want uncertainty any more, they have had uncertainty and they're ready for some certainty. I think what this could lead to is much more normative thinking in policy and in academic life so I think we should be ready, actually, for a counter-wave of thinking about the rights of children, for example. In the public discourse it is not the sociology of childhood that counts, it is thinking about the rights of children. I think we can see a more conservative public mood around childhood beginning to develop. One of the things we have to do, then, is engage with that mood and that's not to follow it but it's to engage with it. In some ways the biggest danger is that all that new thinking from the 1980s, 1990s and early 2000s gets wiped out and we return to a much more normative set of thinking. I think the task actually might be to treat that as an opportunity. Let's chuck out some of the stuff that when we look back might have been less valuable than we would have hoped, but let's try and consolidate and keep going, maybe by adapting what is really valuable from all that work. Because nothing lasts forever and I think there is much more to come…what's the date today?

CS Tuesday, 23 October?

AP Just for the record: 23 October 2012! I think there is a long way to go and there is probably worse to come in terms of the social and economic climate in the world, but it won't last forever and a more optimistic mood will return. We need to be in a position to recuperate the value and useful things out of that turn in Childhood Studies and consolidate those things and start building them again from a different place. Is that unduly pessimistic?

CS I don't think so. Putting those thoughts on the table is really helpful.

AP I think the social mood is changing in another important way as well, which is more optimistic. I think we are seeing a shift back into a more community and socially minded mood among the population – out of necessity. People are having to relearn what they forgot in the credit boom which is that we actually need each other. We need communal, collective institutions because life is tough and things happen and we need to support each other. Incidentally, I happen to believe that that is also the evolutionary pathway that human beings have taken, our collectivities, part of our evolution. There are historical cycles in this and there are periods when we forget that and we start to believe that it is all about individuals. I think the 1980s and 1990s were such a time, but now the social mood is becoming much more collective. The question is…and I welcome that actually, it is good that we start thinking about what is the social context of children's lives, and ask what the mechanisms are that we need for mutual support and development and all those kinds of things. What tends to come in a period such as we are living through is this more normative view which starts to be developed. Actually I think it is also partly generational. Look back at the 1930s; what did the generation who lived through the 1930s do when they found themselves in positions of influence and also in the politics of the time? What they did was build social institutions, they built the welfare state (there were different versions around the world), but they came through that process convinced that we needed secure social institutions. Maybe that's going to happen again and there are some signs of that. I am very optimistic about the generation of children and young people growing up at the moment, they are much more socially minded and community minded. As someone has pointed out, the baby boomers …invented the personal computer, this current generation invented the social network.

CS That's an interesting observation.

AP It's not my thought, there are some Americans, whose names I forget, who are thinking in this kind of way, but I think their ideas are worth thinking about, how do generations cycle and recycle and relate to each other?

CS It sounds like you are optimistic about new people coming into the field and the way they will take things forward?

AP Yes, I am optimistic about that ultimately. I don't think we are living through a very easy period of history and it could get worse is what I think [gentle laugh], if there is a trade war with China, for example. I do think we will get through it, however, and I think that it is the current generation of scholars who are coming up who will get us through it. What they have to watch for, however, is lapsing into a highly normative mood. Many of the things that developed in the 1980s and 1990s about how we think about children were valuable, they emphasised the agency of children, the particularity of their outlook; all these things need to be studied and I think we need to keep as much of that as we can hang on to in what is going to be a much more conservative time. That's what I think – but I might be wrong!

CS Alan, your work has been hugely influential both to those already working in the field of Childhood Studies and to students. Is there anything else you would like to say before we end, particularly to new people entering the field?

AP Probably millions of things! There is something that I meant to say. The new sociology of childhood was mostly a European phenomenon with some people in the USA joining in, although the ideological climate in the USA is very difficult for people who are trying to approach childhood in this kind of way; nevertheless, some have done it. I also think that there is this question about Asia, China, Australasia, South America – there are childhood scholars in all those areas and I think they've not been included as much as they should have been. Actually, that is one of the reasons why I really wanted to support this journal called *Global Studies in Childhood*, because it seemed to have this global outlook and it was being brought about by scholars in Asia and I think it is very important to link up with them. I have had some contact with them about the forms that childhood take and the context that they are working in – in many different countries, not just China, but China is a big one – I think it raises some really important questions for the western childhood scholars to begin to enter into dialogue about. I think that's really important because although…now I'm beginning to rattle on here…

CS Not at all, please do!

AP The great wave of globalisation that we saw in the last 40 years could recede to some extent. A lot of that economic globalisation was built on a very particular set of circumstances, one of which was the very cheap price of oil. If you are going to do all that global trading things have to be moved around and if you are going to have global supply chains of the length that they got to be, then transport has to be cheap. If you consider that back in the 1990s the price of oil got down, I think, to $15 per barrel and today, I don't know what it is, it's somewhere around $120 per barrel. It is very volatile and could easily dip again, but it may be that the days of that kind of cheap transportation are over. That alone may affect what's happening in economic globalisation. So we may see some kind of shift and reversal of those trends. I understand from what I read that companies are already withdrawing and beginning to build their factories in America again because they see the cost advantages of being back in the metropolis. One thing that won't change, however, is the global communications, so I think that all the technological advances and the processes of cultural and social globalisation are…short of some kind of world war, which is not impossible [gentle laugh] – but short of that, they will continue. So I think globalisation may fade from the intensity that it has got to, but it won't go away and the reordering of the world economy and governance, we have already seen it begin to happen particularly with the rise of China and Brazil and Turkey and India, is going to continue to happen, so we have to engage with that process. I think that means that western scholars have got to start going out and making the contacts. That is not to say that we haven't done it at all, but we have to do it much more intensively. So I would say: be international in your thinking and actually make that mean something by engaging with the perspectives that come from these newly emerging parts of the world. Get in contact with those scholars and take notice, publish in their journals and so on.

References

[1] Qvortrup, J, Bardy, M, Wintersberger, H (eds), 1994, *Childhood matters: Social theory, practice and politics*, Aldershot: Avebury

[2] Corsaro, WA, [1997] 2011, *The sociology of childhood*, Thousand Oaks, CA: Pine Forge Press

[3] Wyness, M, [2006] 2011, *Childhood and society: An introduction to the sociology of childhood*, Basingstoke: Palgrave

[4] Christensen, P, James, A, [2000] 2008, *Research with children: Perspectives and practices*, London: Falmer

[5] Prout, A, 2005, *The future of childhood: Towards the interdisciplinary study of children*, London: Falmer Press

EIGHTEEN

Jens Qvortrup

Jens Qvortrup is Professor Emeritus of Sociology at the Norwegian University of Science and Technology. He was formerly the director of the Norwegian Centre for Child Research and Founding President of the International Sociological Association's Research Committee on the Sociology of Childhood (1988–98). Professor Qvortrup was also co-editor of the journal *Childhood* between 1999 and 2008. Since the mid-1980s, he has been engaged in establishing and developing social studies of childhood, both substantively and organisationally. The work of Professor Qvortrup, particularly his 16-country study *Childhood as social phenomenon* (1987–92), is internationally recognised as being foundational in the body of literature underpinning the emergence of the 'new paradigm' for the study of children and childhood in the 1990s. His numerous publications include the groundbreaking co-authored *Childhood matters: Social theory, practice and politics* (Avebury, 1994); a key chapter in *Constructing and reconstructing childhood* (James and Prout (eds), Falmer Press, 1990; 1997); 'Macroanalysis of childhood' in *Research with children: Perspectives and practices* (Christensen and James (eds), Falmer, 2000; Routledge, 2008). In 2005 Professor Qvortrup edited *Studies in modern childhood* (Palgrave), and in 2009 (with Corsaro and Honig) co-edited *The Palgrave handbook of Childhood Studies* (Palgrave Macmillan).

Carmel Smith To start, Jens, will you tell me about your career, how you came to work in childhood research and your particular areas of interest?

Jens Qvortrup Well, it was not logical that I would end up in childhood research because as a student I based my Masters degree on Marxism and Marxist theory and class theory. It is probably important to mention class theory because that has, in a sense, continued and I have throughout my career, for at least 40 years, worked with social structure. I was working in an Institute with the Soviet Union and Eastern Europe and doing research on income inequality and welfare and so on, in these countries. That was in Denmark, because I am Danish, originally. Then in 1980 I happened to get a job at the so-called 'Vienna Centre' which was the centre that facilitated contacts during the cold war period over the borderline between East and West. That involved working together with people from both East and West Europe. I became the Scientific Secretary of two family projects, one about family patterns in Europe and the other one was about divorce. The people working there were really top researchers in Europe within this field. I stayed there for three years and one observation I made was that these excellent and famous family researchers weren't interested in children, they were preoccupied with parents and talking about how do we make ends meet with these expensive children, children who took our time and blocked our careers and so forth. That is when I got the idea, how come sociologists are apparently not interested in childhood and it should, in my view, be possible to also make sociology about childhood. So the idea came simply from this observation. I didn't know Barrie Thorne or Judith Ennew or anyone else who had been dealing with childhood research. I simply started to think and to read what I could in various areas and to write some papers, I think the first paper was for the Nordic Congress of Sociology in 1983.

CS So, from very early on.

JQ Yes. Then, I had some good friends and allies from these projects to whom I spoke about my ideas and in particular a colleague of mine from Austria, Helmut Wintersberger. He changed from the Vienna Centre to the so-called European Centre in Vienna and he and I put forward a proposal for a project within the European Centre. We were lucky to have it adopted in 1987 as many people on the board were very much against it, but there were some people there who supported us. That was the beginning of the 'Childhood as a Social Phenomenon' project which included 16 countries and aimed to cover the areas we had identified from a sociological and a macro perspective.[1] We didn't really know anybody working in that area, we thought it was new, and we had to stumble in the dark as to who should be the people…I knew Ivar Frønes, I knew a few other people but we simply had to use guesswork. We formed a good group but I would also say there were some who never really came to grasp what it was all about or didn't understand this broader framework and context – they were still thinking in terms of outcomes and how children become good adult people which was considered much more important than how children were living their own lives while they were still children. This idea was very difficult for many, even sociologists, to grasp but I think we were quite successful with this project; we produced a lot of material including 16 national reports, a Statistical Compendium (Jensen and Saporiti, 1992),[2] and the book *Childhood matters*.[3] We ended up in 1992 with a concluding conference in Denmark where we invited everybody we knew who had already done something within this area. It is funny today to know that Chris Jenks had never met Alan Prout and Allison James before they met each other at this meeting [gentle laugh] exactly as many other people met each other for the first time. A lot were German, because it is one of the strongest countries as far as Childhood Studies are concerned and many of them were invited to this meeting. Our proposal in the 'Introduction to a series of national reports' (Qvortrup, 1990) was macro orientated, it was not quantitative in the sense that we didn't carry out surveys or anything like that, it was based on documentary material and very much on statistical material that you could get from statistical offices, from other studies that had been carried out. The statistical part was a special part of it because we wanted to do something with statistics because children were not represented in statistics at that time and we had a programme for how to account for children in statistical terms.

CS So that was, for you, about making children visible?

JQ That was one of the ways to make them visible, to make them be seen in statistical and other social accounting because they were often hidden behind family or fathers and mothers and household and so on.

CS So when did you meet the other names associated with the new paradigm?

JQ The project was adopted and convened in 1987. Judith Ennew was one who had some experience with Childhood Studies before, and Ivar Frønes. Other than this, at an anthropological meeting in 1989 organised by Judith Ennew in Cambridge, I met Alan Prout and Allison James for the first time and they invited me to write a chapter on childhood statistics in the *Constructing and reconstructing childhood* book. The project then started to meet at various conferences and meetings. We then finally had this big meeting in Denmark at the conclusion of the project to try and bring as many scholars together as possible and this was regarded by many as a very important meeting.

CS That was in 1992, it is just helpful to date things?

JQ Yes. One thing also about this history is that coming from class studies, structural research in Eastern Europe and so on, many thought that that was very odd that I switched from these macro studies to childhood but in my view it was also a continuation.

CS Can you say more about that?

JQ I continued with the structural perspectives on childhood and that was very, very important for me because that was a question I wanted to ask, 'What does it mean to think of childhood in structural terms?' Not to put it too crudely, I am not really interested in the child.

CS That makes sense, you are interested in childhood?

JQ I am interested in childhood in its structural form and in structural terms exactly as I was interested in class rather than the individual worker as such. It could be the relations between the two classes, it could be gender between men and women, it could be between ethnic groups. From that also developed the idea of having generational analysis because childhood is not the corresponding structural form to class or to gender, but it must be to adulthood or to old age, it must be in generational terms. My wish was to think in these terms. For instance, we had one section in the project on distributive justice, so that would be distributive justice between the generational groups rather than class and that, of course we can come back to that, leads also to these questions of diversity and plurality versus singularity and so on and what we should favour, because that is one of the things that has been divisive later, much later. So structure is the continuing thread for me.

CS Tell me then in terms of research with children, what do you feel should be the training for researchers coming into Childhood Studies? There has been an emphasis on qualitative research, but as we look to the future what would you say new researchers coming in to the area should be taught?

JQ I think I have written about this a few times in the Introduction to the Series of National Reports but have also repeated in the chapter in the Handbook (*The Palgrave handbook of Childhood Studies,* (2009) that I see childhood as a rather normal thing, it is characterised by normality among humans. There is nothing special about children any more than women or men are special kinds, we all belong to the human kind. I think we can therefore all be studied, in principle, with the same methods but with the necessary differences that there will always be between ethnic groups, or women and men, or small children and big children; there will always be these differences but by and large I think this approach, particularly if you are not going to ask people, makes it possible to think in terms of structure to account for the placement of certain groups in a society.

CS Obviously, Jens, I am not going to ask you in detail about qualitative research because I know that has not been your area of interest.

JQ I am not against qualitative research, I think it is important for Childhood Studies that the field has a wide range of approaches and qualitative agency research, actor research, and structure research all are important and support each other. So it is not about qualitative research or not, structural research or not, it is about whether they are of good quality. One of the problems sometimes with qualitative research is that there is a tiny sample in terms of interviewing very few people. That can be okay, but if one starts to make too wide ranging conclusions from that, rather than simply using that as an inspiration for further research, I think that can be a problem with qualitative research. I have read a lot of this research because I was editor of the journal *Childhood* for 10 years – they were often very boring and repetitive involving small-scale interviewing and so on, but it has its value as long as one knows and is clear that they are not very representative but only, in a sense, have a heuristic value and give some flavour to what sort of structural research can be done.

CS Would you now say some more now about the research that you have focused on in your career, your macro approach, and why you feel it has been useful in advancing Childhood Studies?

JQ Well, I can see that that it has been used and read and so on and I think that is, of course, satisfying [laughter]. I think I never really had a plan as such because I think I have also been very busy organising a lot of things with the project and editorship and being chairperson of the ISA [International Sociological Association] group and so on. It has been my purpose from the very beginning to normalise this research area. You have probably met this idea of human beings and human becomings and so on, and to make children human beings and not to be looking forward all the time and to be able to compare relevant groups with each other. Therefore, if I today were to start over again I think I would probably consider calling it generational research. For me this is the crux of the matter, because if it is not intergenerational then Childhood Studies does not have a future in my view.

CS That is important. So, for you, intergenerational studies have got to be an integral part of the future of Childhood Studies?

JQ That is also why I have had many struggles with people who, when I am writing or talking, ask 'Where is gender, where is ethnicity, where is age?' I have to say that this is not really part…perhaps you can discuss whether you should use age rather than generation, but gender in particular – of course there are differences between girls and boys, but that can also be studied within feminist research and gender research because that is where it really belongs. Because you have to ask, 'Where does childhood belong?' if not in a generational context. It does not really belong in gender research or in class research so childhood is without a home and it has always been without a home and if you want to have a theoretical framework within which childhood is a constituent part then it must, in my view, be compared with adulthood and old age in generational research. You could call it generational research because that is my purpose really. There you will put childhood on a par with adulthood. This is in contrast to the so-called forward looking perspectives, in psychology for instance, where childhood is understood as something which eventually disappears as you grow older. As I have argued on many occasions, childhood does not disappear; a child becomes an adult but childhood remains as a structural form and that's what you have to continue to study. That is why we talk about distributive justice, do children on a broad basis get more or less of the distribution of money, housing, space or other things? This can be compared here and now because childhood is a permanent category. This is also where I have had a fight to say that childhood is not a period, sociologically.

CS So it is a permanent category and then, from your perspective, can be used very helpfully for comparative studies with other groups?

JQ Absolutely, and it can also be compared with itself in the historical context. What is childhood like today compared with childhood 100 years ago, or what is childhood like in Ireland compared with Angola or wherever? You have the same parameters more or less, even if they assume different values – you always have an economic, social, political and technological parameter everywhere, so you can compare on the same scale. Of course, there are different types of values and there you can again compare. So both horizontally and vertically you can make these comparisons; so that has very broadly been a helpful perspective.

CS As I listen to that it sounds very sociological, yet can Childhood Studies then claim to be multi-disciplinary or interdisciplinary? It seems, as it has evolved, that Childhood Studies has become a home that many disciplines would like to be part of, but the project you have just spoken about and your interests sound to me very sociological. Can those who do not have a sociological background fit into Childhood Studies?

JQ I am a sociologist and when I started out my programme it was to see whether there could be a sociology of childhood. The crucial point is whether you accept what, in my view, is new about…let's call it the 'social studies of childhood'. Of course, it would be arrogant to say that we were the first ones to deal with children because psychology has been there and psychiatry, paediatrics and so on. However, I think there is a crucial difference between developmental psychology and us and that is why I think we have the right to say that something new has happened. Psychology is preoccupied with the development of the individual child from birth to adulthood and there are huge libraries containing such studies. That is not only a fact but it is also legitimate – it is simply a different approach and there is nothing wrong with that. However, interdisciplinarity cannot simply mean a melting pot for anything; it must have an agreement of approach.

CS What about childhoods? [Both laugh] This is something about which a lot has been written. How do we incorporate this notion of childhoods into how we research and analyse data on children?

JQ One shouldn't be too rigid. In many respects you can accept that there are many childhoods if you think in terms of history, the Third World and even here in our own country you can talk about childhoods. The point is, as far as I am concerned, that you should be looking for what is common to children and childhood rather than what is divisive, because there is something that is common to their lives: they are all under the majority age, they are all institutionalised during this period, they are all schooled, they are all incarcerated in buildings, domesticated, and so on. So you can mention a lot of things that are common to children that make them different to adults so this is, again, a generational matter. In that sense I would prefer the singular term simply to find out what is the commonality. Then the next step, if you have accounted for the generational perspective, you can start to split up childhood, but then you will immediately see that it becomes difficult to compare with adulthood because the first claim is to split up girls and boys and different age groups and ethnicities and classes and so on. Everything, of course, is relevant; but these divisions you can do already within class research, within gender research, within ethnic research and so forth. In that sense there are, of course, childhoods, but I am only worried about the future of childhood research if you are not really taking care of what is unique to Childhood Studies, namely, that it is generational and therefore its singularity vis-à-vis adulthood. That is why I am insisting on the singular, it is clear that there are as many childhoods as there are individuals, as there are children – this is an obvious point but it is also a trivial point.

CS Jens, would you now say, when you reflect on all the changes that have emerged during the course of the last 15 years, what you see as the current challenges facing the field? What are the key themes and strands that you would pull out and say: 'These are the things we are really going to have to look at'?

JQ In terms of particular issues or in trends, the direction it should take and so on?

CS I suppose first of all, if the field is to stay together under some umbrella and avoid fragmentation, what are the issues that those currently working in the field need to grasp, need to really look at in order to move forward? What are the bones of contention between people?

JQ I think I have partly answered that…I could put it in a negative way and say what one should not do to begin with [laughs] and that is the fragmentation. That is exactly what we are talking about if you are continuing to think in these plural terms and always say that you cannot generalise. So often you hear: 'You cannot generalise, you cannot talk about children in general terms, there are so many childhoods' and so on. My understanding of social science and science in general, is that its purpose is to generalise. If you cannot generalise why are you studying? It is exactly so as to make commonness out of the most diverse material; that is what research is about. Therefore, I would say fragmentation is the really big danger. Diversity claims go right down to the single person sometimes – that will destroy…but that would be the same with all other branches of sociology. I think, therefore, that following this characteristic is the question: 'How do we make sure that we do not end up in fragmentation, what do we do?' That is of course, to find something that is common exactly as was the case in gender research as was the case with class studies, you have to find…I wouldn't say an 'opposite group'…I have quoted sometimes, I don't know if it is in the material that you have, an article about minority research by Louis Wirth from 1945 which gives a wonderful definition of a minority. It includes, for instance, that you can recognise the differences between groups in that you have a group that is suppressed and a corresponding powerful group that is not necessarily the enemy, such as white people versus black people, and it can be various powerful ethnic groups versus others without power, and so on. Accordingly, childhood's corresponding dominant category is adulthood, which is not to say that all children have different interests to adults.

It is very important to make a distinction also between a micro level and a macro level, if you like, although some people don't like the use of 'micro' and 'macro', but I think they are useful to think in terms of, for example, the family level on the one hand and the structural level on the other hand. I am coming to this idea right now because to talk about childhood and adulthood in terms of hostile groups is not always true and particularly not at the family level where, of course, there is great solidarity between parents and children. Most of the time, hopefully [laughing], that is the case so that is a different perspective than if you think in terms of the structural level where you have adulthood versus childhood. You could say on the one hand, the personal level, the family level and other… you can think in terms of emotionality, sentimentality and so on because that has been growing, some people would say, yet on the other hand, you can think in terms of, to quote the German sociologist Kaufmann, who talks about the structural indifference and structural recklessness towards childhood in modern society, which in a sense does not really care for children.[4] Corporate society does not have the obligation to care for children but nevertheless childhood is critically important for corporate society. It is important therefore to move forward and to make sure, if it is possible, to get economics and political science involved in childhood studies because they are very strong, particularly economics. I have sometimes written about reproduction and production and said that while they have historically been separated from each other, we should rethink and say that even if society has modernised, there is still such a thing as reproduction, there is still such a thing as production and they remain dependent on each other. How do we make it clear that even corporate society is dependent on somebody reproducing the population and social life of the population, and what about those who are now, more and more often, without children and who still believe that they have the same right to get a pension paid by other people's children and so on? So there is this inter-connection which I think is very important. That is the big macro terms that you never find in small-scale anthropological studies and we should try to move forward in that direction in my view. There I am not very optimistic; I don't really see how that will come about.

CS That's interesting. So, for you, an important part of moving forwards involves understanding the underlying political economy of childhood in that context because, as you said earlier, economics underpins everything? Have you any thoughts about how Childhood Studies might continue? What do you think is the most probable direction?

JQ That is very difficult to say. I think the trend has been more in the direction of small-scale I am afraid. I think what we started out with as childhood projects 25 years ago you would not really find very often now, these macro approaches. That is underlined also by this discussion of singularity and plurality because those that underline the plurality thesis are in the vast majority micro oriented and they are not really interested in these macro things because they keep saying that we cannot generalise and so forth. I am not too optimistic, but can I mention a few younger people who are really…

CS Please do.

JQ Belonging to a structural orientation there is Johanna Mierendorff from Halle in Germany. There is also Daniel Cook, in the United States, he is in the diversity camp, but doing wonderful studies and research. Of course there are many young people around and it would be odd if some of them did not also think in these plural terms. I hope that young scholars in future will do more than just focus on the child and children; I hope they will also read broad sociology, political economy and other things. I think what inspires me often is when I read sociologists who have nothing to do with childhood. Recently I have quoted Stinchcombe who is a sociologist of organisations and oil and things like that, but he is a wonderful theoretical person and we can learn a lot by reading these other people.[5] If you end up just having a narrow interest in your little, unique child or children you will never be able to broaden out the scale and the scope of this area, and then I think it will wither away.

References
[1] Qvortrup, J, 1990, Childhood as a social phenomenon: Introduction to a series of national reports, *Eurosocial Report 36*, Vienna: European Centre
[2] Jensen, A, Saporiti, A, 1992, Do children count? A statistical compendium, *Eurosocial Report* 36, 17, Vienna: European Centre
[3] Qvortrup, J, Bardy, M, Sgritta, G, Wintersberger, H (eds), 1994, *Childhood matters: Social theory, practice and politics*, Avebury: Aldershot
[4] Kaufmann, F, 2005, *Schrumpfende Gesellschaft: Vom Bevölkerungsrückgang und seinen Folgen*, Frankfurt: Suhrkamp
[5] Stinchcombe, AL, 1986, The deep structure of moral categories, eighteenth-century French stratification, and the revolution, in AL Stinchcombe (ed) *Stratification and organization: Selected papers*, pp 145–73, Cambridge: Cambridge University Press

NINETEEN

Irene Rizzini

Professor Irene Rizzini is based in the Department of Social Work at the Pontifical Catholic University of Rio de Janeiro (PUC-Rio), Brazil. She has worked for many years with organisations responsible for social policies and programmes for children in Brazil and abroad. In 1984 Professor Rizzini founded the Center for Research on Children (CESPI) which has since become the International Center for Research and Policy on Childhood (CIESPI/PUC-Rio) of which she is Director. Professor Rizzini's publications include 'A new paradigm for social change: Social movements and the transformation of policy for street and working children in Brazil' (with Klees and Dewees) in *Children on the streets of the Americas* (R. Mickelson (ed), Routledge, 2000) and *Globalization and children*, 2004 (co-edited with Kaufman, Kluwer, NY, 2004) She has a chapter (with Kaufman) 'Closing the gap between rights and the realities of children's lives' in *The Palgrave handbook of Childhood Studies* (Qvortrup et al, 2009). Professor Rizzini has served as President of Childhood International and as a member of the editorial board of several journals including *Childhood: A Global Journal of Child Research* and the *International Journal of Social Welfare*.

Sheila Greene Perhaps you could tell me about the start of your career, Irene?

Irene Rizzini Well, it's a long story. I was the daughter of a doctor, who later became a botanist. Botany was my father's passion. I learned to be a researcher through botany, observing how botanists did their research with plants. I thought I would be a botanist since there are several botanists in my family. When I was about to go to college at 17, however, I decided to work with people.

When I was a child my father dedicated some of his time to a closed institution for children. There were about a hundred children, including babies, in this place. I used to play with them and that had a major impact on my life. I could see that they were different from me, they were poorer, they were darker and they were called orphans. I quickly learned that they were not orphans, they had parents, sometimes they had both parents. That was a huge shock: 'How can you live in this place if you have parents?' Another issue that hurt me was that I could see how the adults in the institution treated the children like they were nothing, as if they were retarded, as though they were not good kids. They had to always be on their knees thanking the adults for taking care of them. And those people were religious, so I listened to them pray and talk about God, and then attack the children, literally. They did horrible things, humiliating them. So I said I want to do something about this in the future, so I cannot be a botanist.

At that time, the 1970s, in Brazil, like all over Latin America, we had a very violent, military dictatorship that lasted from 1964 to 1984. So basically we could not study areas that were connected to politics or social understanding. So psychology was the option I chose because I wanted to be able to do something and I needed to use words that were not only emotional words about what I felt and thought. I remember as I started working as a young psychologist, informing journalists, putting my life at risk, about the maltreatment of children in institutions.

When I was studying I was always struck by the fact that there was very little written by Brazilians about our children, so our literature was based on research done in the US and a lot in the UK. While I was a student I was working with children who died because of deprivation, who died because they were missing their mothers. The doctors would say 'Diarrhoea' and I would say, 'There is no way this child died of diarrhoea.' The child had not been eating for a week because the child was mourning the loss of her mother. So you can imagine, I was about 17 years old and I was talking to doctors, talking to judges and they said, 'Quiet, you are just a kid, you don't know anything', and I said, 'Well I know something. I know you are writing something wrong on this piece of paper and it's not fair'. So I disturbed a lot of adults at that time and I thought I am not going to win this war by just crying about the injustice done to people. I needed to get out of psychology – though I always valued very much my training, especially in psychoanalysis. That is why I decided to study abroad. I had the opportunity to go to Chicago. So I went to the School of Social Service Administration at the University of Chicago, and at first it was horribly disappointing. I had the feeling that I was talking about something that nobody understood. People had no idea about the reality of the lives of children in my country.

I wanted to give up, but two things happened. One was that the university's Department of Media and Communication was offering to work with people to produce videos. I knew that there was a large institution with 800 children that was closing down and I wanted to interview people who were working there. So I proposed to the university that I would make a video about alternatives to residential care. I produced the video and I met wonderful people and learned so much. The second important thing was that I took classes on public policy and a couple of the professors got very interested in Brazil. I wrote about Brazil and they would read my papers and question me about everything. They were fantastic. In Chicago I had my first more serious training in research, which also really helped me.

In 1983 I got back to Brazil, back to my university. I convinced the Rector to give me a space where we could think about Brazilian children. I told them we had to produce a body of knowledge about Brazilian children. Originally, as I said, the research centre started with me and students. I have always worked with students. When I moved to the Catholic University of Brazil in 2002 I brought my team and the centre became the International Center for Research and Policy on Childhood (CIESPI).

The ideas that I had when I created CIESPI were completely connected to my own trajectory, as well as to the country's historical moment. Since 1984 the Center has always been a non-profit organisation, linked to a university but completely independent financially. That gives me and my team the freedom to publish and to get the resources we need to do the work that we think is important. At the same time it is has been linked with universities that I trust and that trust and value my work. There are two new dimensions to CIESPI that I wanted to make very visible. One is that it is an international centre. In the early 1990s I was very involved with Childwatch International and, through them, linking our work to research centres in over 50 countries. I soon became a leader, a leader is what I am. I enjoy starting things, but I want to work together with other people, other networks. In my work I have always had an interdisciplinary approach, I work with architects, I work with engineers, I work with chemists [laughs] – whoever is interested in young people.

The second focus for the Center is on producing knowledge aiming at policy. That second dimension gives us the identity we want: an international centre which informs public policy. We want to use empirical data to inform public policy.[1] This is not an idea that comes easily to any country where politics depends on the power of a small group of people. A very unequal country will always concentrate the money, power and property. They do not want to change because they have all the privileges and are used to having them. To break that is very hard. We want to do that through children, in part because they represent the present, but they also represent political change for the future. A lot of them still suffer simply because they were born poor and that is unfair.

The focus on disadvantaged children is a priority for us. Today we also have students in CIESPI from the favelas in Rio who managed to get into the university and we want to prepare them to be able stay in their communities and work there. I think we are now the seventh strongest economy in the world but still 42 per cent of the children are born under the poverty line. Brazil is one of the five most unequal countries in the world. It wants to be modern, it wants to be rich, but we have to be able to redistribute wealth. It is awful.

SG Are you optimistic that things are changing or will change?

IR I am very optimistic, that's why I am here after 30 years. I studied the history of children in Brazil and that gave me a political dimension and a context. I have that understanding of how things change slowly and also I am totally aware of how much it has changed. I am optimistic and realistic, too, changes don't happen overnight. You need persistence, and continuity. We are very much aware of how much we helped effect certain major changes in our country through our work with children and youth. Since we started we have become a reference point. It is really fantastic. What is produced is used, in all parts of the country. We say that very humbly because that represents a lot of work and persistence in a country where discontinuity is so present. If you have a fantastic social programme or policy that is disturbing to central power, in the next election, when there is a new party or a new governor in power, the first thing they do is to destroy everything that the others put in place.

SG So have you seen an influence of your way of working on other South American countries or on other centres in Brazil?

IR Oh yes, very much so. In Brazil people come to work with us, and we work within different coalitions. One of the main ways people come together is through the Latin American branch of Childwatch International.[2] Childwatch has lost its main funds but the Latin American Childwatch group continues to meet every year. It is our ninth year working together and there are nine countries which are regularly involved. There is a real dialogue there, there is mutual impact.

SG It seems to me that you have been used to working with a whole range of research methods including policy analysis and secondary data analysis.

IR That is correct and sometimes we have to be really creative about new methods. For example, we did the first study with street children in 1980, interviewing them on the streets, several years before the notion of action research and the idea of listening to children's voices became so important.[3] I would also say that we are working with a lot of limitations as well. We often face the challenge of working with people who are poorly trained in research, particularly when it comes to quantitative approaches. That is why we have developed three areas on our web site with data resources.[4] Most of it is in Portuguese and we can't afford to get it translated into English. We developed a data resource on indicators, developed specifically for policy makers and journalists, people who have little time and find it hard to read complicated tables and graphs. We have another kind of data resource that is on the history of legislation on children in Brazil from 1822 to today. Finally we have an online site that we call 'The context of early childhood' where there are several tools for key actors to think about the first years of life – a variety of information to get people to think about what should be the priorities for young children.[5]

I did the first study on street children as soon as I got back from Chicago. During the military dictatorship children would not be on the streets. There were 'orphanages' packed with children, they were just thrown there. Two years later when we said we would have to close these institutions, since these children were not abandoned or orphaned, the children started to become visible on the streets. I kept reading in the newspapers that the children on the streets were very dangerous. The media referred to them as delinquent, abandoned, dangerous children – they were not called children, by the way, they were called 'menores' – minors. This term had and still has a negative connotation. It was all so absurd that one of the main newspapers in Rio once reported that 'minors' had attacked 'children' at a school. They were all children of the same age, but those who 'attacked' were seen as 'minors'. The minors were poor and black and they lived in the periphery of the city, they were seen as the 'delinquent' ones. So we started to discuss this terminology with whomever we could, including the media. We spent a good deal of time looking at the national statistics and I came to this idea that the children we call minors in Brazil were in fact the majority since a large percentage of them was born in poverty. So that was a huge shock when I started publicising it. I was asked 'What do you mean?' 'I mean that those we name as minors and whom we see as not human, in numbers they are the larger percentage of children'. 'We are talking about this great nation that we want to be, so what does that mean?' That idea created a big impact.

The second major idea that caused impact as a result of our research had to do with children who lived and/or worked in the streets. This was around the early 1980s. The children were being arrested because they were seen as delinquent and abandoned. So I said 'OK we will talk to the children'. So I recruited my undergraduate students and we interviewed 300 children on the curbs, on the streets. Nobody told me how to do that kind of research. There was no rhetoric about 'Giving children a voice'. In fact I don't think you give a voice to anyone. I don't think you give children a voice; you might be able to give them the opportunity to speak and help disseminate that voice in spheres where people do not want to hear. And that's what we did. We started explaining that the children, instead of being delinquent criminals, were the ones doing the job that the State was not doing. So we were able to prove that around 90 per cent of the children gave all their money to their families. These children were very young and the vast majority were black or brown and lived in horrible circumstances, basically trying to survive and help their families. They spoke and we made the country listen to what they had to say.

So from that study on we had several other studies and produced materials and a few videos, the last one being the one that we are announcing on our web site currently, 'When home is the street' [Quando a casa é a rua].

SG When Childhood Studies developed in Europe, did it bring a new influx of ideas or support for you in any way?

IR That's a very interesting question. It took me quite some time and many invitations to understand that I was part of this group, which became what was known as Childhood Studies. It took me several meetings with various international groups to understand how important it all was and how lucky I was to be part of all that. I had several chances to meet and work with scholars who were well known, such as Allison James and Barrie Thorne, colleagues from European and Scandanavian universities. At first I thought I was invited to join the group on Childhood Studies because there were few Brazilians who could speak English, who had been abroad and who had published so much about children in this part of the world. But you get into a circle and then you get known. And then I realised that it was wonderful, I just grabbed all the opportunities. Brazil is our centre but I care about children throughout the world.[6] Everything I experience I bring back. Always, since childhood, when I learn something new I put it to use immediately. Sometimes I think I need a bit more structure, a bit more of a base, a bit more support, but I am already putting new knowledge into action, talking, spreading the word. Then I realised, it is not totally what I am bringing back to Brazil, it is what I am taking to people as well, a constant flux of exchange.

SG Are there bits of Childhood Studies, depending on how one defines the paradigm, which you find helpful and others that you don't?

IR This is a bit harder, because there are ideas that I still struggle with, and that still bother me, like giving children a voice and child participation.

SG Why?

IR I find it disturbing. I mean the way the discourse on child participation spread to so many parts of the world as if it were a new discovery – that children did think and have something to say – a 'voice'. You can see from what I told you that I learned from my own childhood. Having heard those children who told me about what adults did to them, I was totally convinced from the beginning that they have very meaningful ways to say things and that these things can be so disturbing that they have to be shut down. So it is not about giving someone a voice. It is about why people do not listen and do not want to be disturbed by the way children question things; for example, the way children say things straightforwardly that are totally inappropriate from the perspective of an adult, like saying 'Mummy, why are you lying?' in the middle of a party. So in Childhood Studies I got attracted to the group, but I did not feel I had to fit in any category.

SG You did spend time as an editor of *Childhood*.

IR I was invited to be one of the editors because they needed a voice from the South. I was interested in doing that as a way to help other scholars from countries like mine to have access to a good international journal. I kept questioning what I heard in conferences from writers and researchers who had spent a week in a country doing interviews, but not even mastering the language and then publishing their articles in those journals, while the professionals from those same countries often had their papers turned down. I had many fights because I kept saying 'This is not serious international work, it should not be like this'. In CIESPI, if people from other countries want to do research on Brazilian children they have to spend at least six months with us, a year is better or even more. Without speaking Portuguese we do not take them, for they are not going to be able to write about my country, I'm sorry. Through *Childhood,* during almost 10 years, I worked with other colleagues from Latin America and Asia and Africa helping them to improve their papers. I finally could not do it any more, it took too many hours of my week, but I wanted the idea to thrive and it did and that meant almost mentoring people in other countries so that their work would be accepted and that was a very beautiful part of my work. Two dear friends were responsible for my international career: Francisco Pilotti from Uruguay and Sharon Stevens, whom I met at the Trondheim centre in Norway. Sharon was a wonderful soul. Unfortunately we lost her a few years after we met.

SG Could I just ask you about the South in relation to Childhood Studies and what it means? Many people see it as still a problem, this huge imbalance between the Global South and the Global North in terms of the strength of research.

IR Yes there is an imbalance and with Childwatch I did my best to help a bit. I found a lot of resistance, although we did have a large group from the South in the network. We from the South, so to speak – for there is a lot of diversity among us – in general are behind, especially when you are talking about public education. That is true. I know good education is a problem in many countries, but in some of our countries it is indecent. Some of it, however, is also more subjective, it has to do with ways of understanding apparently the same phenomenon. Different interpretation of the same phenomenon is related to cultural differences, but it was often labelled simply as poor research. In the 1980s we still had the emphasis on scientific research as the only model of research. It took us a long time to really question this model and also to question the idea that the research done in the North was the best model for all of us.

Another aspect that is crucial has to do with the monopoly of language. I keep saying this wherever I go. There is some very good research done by people who cannot write in English and who cannot pay for translation. A lot of the papers that came to *Childhood* were papers about Africa, say, but written by a UK citizen. Once we acknowledge the imbalance, things get better. I remember someone describing an analysis of literature on children where they claimed it was a review of everything important that was published over a period of time. I told them that it was a very partial view of what had been produced. You can't say this is how children are portrayed, you can only say this is how children are portrayed according to research in the major journals – in English. That's all you can say.

SG You had other things to say about the Childhood Studies paradigm

IR Let me focus on the child rights framework as an example. There is a very interesting contrast between the North and the South in the use of child rights.

I work with two friends and colleagues carrying out research on young activists in Rio, Chicago and Mexico City, so for four years I have had this incredible dialogue with them. I increasingly realised that when we talk about children's rights here it is very different from what they understand there.[7] There are the complexities of using the same terminology but having very different meanings, different nuances and also different uses. When the dictatorship was over we had the opportunity to start a new process of democratisation of the country. We wanted to kill those roots. It was very interesting, that many of us came to this realisation and to the vision of a new paradigm shift through our work with young people. We had this understanding of the child as a whole being, not an adult to be, but a person who is complete. This was not new to me, it was inside my heart. So the discourse of human rights applied to children – the idea of children as subject of rights – became for us a kind of a strategy to fight for the changes we envisioned to help improve the lives of vulnerable children in my country.[8] So in Brazil we started using the notion of children as young citizens entitled to their full development. That was crucial to call the attention of our country to the fact that part of our population had no access to their rights – not only the children in poverty but also the mothers and fathers and grandparents. This approach helped me to discuss the rhetoric of rights – that everybody should be equal but they are not and they have never been and they probably never will be. The ideas present in the framework of rights and in the Childhood Studies paradigm helped us to change our laws and to change our major policies. Also to change the sad and unfair realities of so many young people in Brazil.

SG Could we talk a bit about how you see the future of Childhood Studies as an academic area? Do you see it as having done its work?

IR I don't know how to answer that question really, in part because I am not so much part of the group at the moment and I have not directed my energy to that for the past few years.

SG I see that, Irene, but you do have a deep familiarity with it. Are you saying it is not that relevant to your work?

IR No, what I am saying is that maybe the momentum was very important some years back because it challenged some very heavy structures and disciplines, but it is not here any more. People in universities are not changing their practices and their structures, and in some ways that is getting worse with all the crazy demands on publishing and fund-raising. I don't know if we still can say that there is a consistent nucleus that could be called Childhood Studies in action. The structures and grants for research continue to be fragmented and absolutely connected to interests that are in opposition to the principles of Childhood Studies. The idea of interdisciplinarity is a good one but the structures in which we operate do not allow it, in the universities, in hospitals, in city hall they continue to function in a totally fragmented way. You cannot do things together in a real way if the budget continues to be separate and fragmented. The idea was very important, however, and maybe in the near future we will have other ways of working in more collective ways. Despite the continuous discourse on rights and equality the structures are not changing to reduce the gap between those who have and those who do not.

I hope that the important paradigms that question structures that benefit only a small group of people will continue, and that other paradigms will emerge that question inequality. My idea for the future is that we continue to be creative in the movement and to be critical and accept that what at one time was very important can be replaced when needed. Nothing is good or bad forever. There will always be a group of people trying to maintain the status quo and a group of people trying to change and question. I hope that from now on we can fully understand, deeply understand, how the new paradigms which became so important around the end of the last century cannot be fixed for ever and that we can allow new waves, new movements, with ideas that are never totally new but fresh, or refreshed. Ideas that will allow us to move in the direction for which we are fighting. It is not about this framework or that framework, it doesn't matter. For me it is the ideas and the practices, including the personal transformation that comes with that. It is the attitude, the personal ethic that matters. I like to think that all those paradigms we created and believed in made a lot of sense and we made a beautiful use of them, but now, if they don't make any sense any more – or some of it doesn't make sense – then it is time to move on. We understand why, and that is our role as academics, to understand why.

References

[1] Klees, SJ, Rizzini, I, Dewees, A, 2000, A new paradigm for social change: Social movements and the transformation of policy for street and working children in Brazil, in RA Mickelson (ed) *Children on the streets of the Americas*, London: Routledge

[2] www.childwatch.org

[3] Rizzini, I, 1994, *Children in Brazil today: A challenge for the Third Millennium*, Rio de Janiero: EDUSU

[4] www.ciespi.org.br/

[5] Ambiente da Primeira Infancia, www.ciespi.org.br/primeira_infancia/

[6] Kaufman, NH, Rizzini, I (eds), 2002, *Globalization and children*, New York: Kluwer Academic/Plenum Publishers

[7] Del Rio, N, Rizzini, I, de los Angeles Torres, M, 2013, *Citizens in the present: Youth civic engagement in the Americas*, Chicago, IL: University of Illinois

[8] Bush, M, Rizzini, I, 2011, *Closing the gap between rights and realities for children and youth in urban Brazil: Reflections on a Brazilian project to improve policies for street children*, Rio de Janiero: CIESPI/Oak Foundation

TWENTY

Annie G. Rogers

Professor Annie Rogers is a clinical psychologist, published poet and painter. She is Professor of Psychoanalysis and Clinical Psychology and Dean of the School of Critical Social Inquiry at Hampshire College, USA. Professor Rogers is a Research Associate in Psychology at Trinity College Dublin, and a member of the Freudian School of Quebec and its Boston Psychoanalytic Circle. She has a private analytic practice in Amherst, Massachusetts, USA. Formerly an Associate Professor at Harvard University, her scholarly work is grounded in an original method of interviewing and analysis. Her research includes studies of girls' psychological development, child sexual abuse and psychoanalytic case studies. Professor Rogers's numerous publications include 'Voice, play and a practice of courage in girls' and women's lives' *Harvard Educational Review* 1993, 63, 3; *A shining affliction: A story of harm and healing in psychotherapy* (New York: Penguin/Viking, 1995); 'Interviewing children using an interpretive poetics' (in Greene and Hogan, *Researching Children's Experience*, London: SAGE, 2005); *The unsayable: The hidden language of trauma* (Random House, 2006), and 'A place for Lacan in critical psychology: Four memos and a gap' (in *Annual Review of Critical Psychology*, 2009).

Carmel Smith To start, Annie, will you say something about your background, training and your experience of qualitative research?

Annie Rogers When I was working on my PhD I worked with Jane Loevinger, the psychologist who founded the theory of ego development. She was strictly a quantitative researcher. During that time I had clinical notes from a psychoanalytic experience of working with children and I kept returning to these notes and looking at them. Finally I signed up for a class on qualitative research that allowed me to make some use of those notes in a thematic kind of way, what was called grounded theory, and then I linked my analysis to literature on working therapeutically with children. It was wonderful to know that such a class could be taught at the time – this was in the mid-1980s – but also it left a lot of questions for me, more than anything else about qualitative work as a mode of research. I had been trained in a quantitative mode that was very specific and very rigorous. Designed into my dissertation, I asked to use some of Carol Gilligan's and Lyn Brown's interview data from the Laurel-Harvard Project, a series of studies undertaken during the 1980s designed to connect a psychology of women with girls' voices, which I used primarily as a way to validate certain scales of my own reading of the justice and care voices in ego development data. This was how I initially made contact with Carol and with Lyn. I didn't use the interviews in any other way other than to make use of some broad categories of analysis in relation to my own data collection and analysis, but I really wanted to go much further. I was very taken with *In a different voice*[1] and I felt as though I could learn something completely different in working with Carol Gilligan. I wrote a grant application to the American Association of University Women for post-doctoral research while I was finishing my PhD. Fortunately, I got the grant and went off to Harvard. I worked with Carol Gilligan and Lyn Brown and others and, in the process, I learned how to do qualitative research. We were *inventing* it, I would say, more than my being trained in it. I also got to know a wonderful researcher, Joe Maxwell, an anthropologist who knew the field of qualitative research with a very different reach, and he directed me to a lot of reading.

In that time and beyond those years, in the late 1980s and early 1990s, what was interesting to me was the clinical world of working with children and, for me, how it began to overlap with the world of doing research with children. That happened especially in the years beyond my post-doc when I was learning to listen for what I came to call 'the unsayable', a kind of tacit knowledge that children were expressing, but not directly. I worked with a group of five doctoral students very closely over a period of years to develop a new method, an interpretive poetics (IP), to try and get at that tacit knowledge. Since then, really, Carmel, my interest has become increasingly psychoanalytic, and Lacanian psychoanalytic at that. This interest in Lacan has led me to make massive changes in the IP method and also to change my way of working with and interviewing children. I am now working on a new book manuscript based on that original method – *Ghost, whisper, trace: A space for the unsayable*. So that is an 'in-a-nutshell' version of the overview of my history as a qualitative researcher.

CS Can I ask you about the evolution of ideas leading to the 'new paradigm'? Although the 'new paradigm' is often associated with British scholars there does also seem to have been a lot of work going on in other geographical locations as well. For example, in the US Bill Corsaro's book had been published and people like you, Barrie Thorne and Roger Hart had been doing work in this area for some time. When were you first aware of the sociological material that was being written in say, Norway or Britain? Was that at a later stage from when you had been doing your work with children?

AR Yes, I would say in the late 1980s. If I were to say what feels the most accurate to me is that there were different pieces that were developing in parallel, not necessarily in close communication with one another, that eventually converged on this new interdisciplinary field of Childhood Studies. It doesn't surprise me that people would have different accounts, different timelines and different experiences [gentle laugh]. When I think back to that time I certainly knew the work of Barrie Thorne because I was interested in her studies of gender in the playground.[2] I'm not necessarily the best historian, I have to say that up front, in the sense that I was moving from having worked within a very traditional paradigm with Jane Loevinger within an ego development framework and quantitative studies and adolescents. When I moved to work with Carol Gilligan that group was really in the midst of inventing, or rather reinventing, the method that had been called a 'Reader's Guide', to try and understand how to listen to adolescent girls in particular, and the invention of a 'Listening Guide'- a way of reading language by highlighting particular meanings in a single reading and letting others fall to the background, and trying to discern in that way different voices, or a kind of polyphonic chorus of voices, within an interview.[3] Its influences were in part Mikhail Bakhtin and the idea of a dialogic self,[4] it certainly came from within feminism and the idea of listening to women's and girls' voices initially. Then, for me, as I continued with that work, it was very strongly influenced by psychoanalysis because that had been my training as a child clinician. I became increasingly interested in what was not being said and the things that were impossible for children to say and therefore, the invention of the IP method and the concept of 'the unsayable'. So that's a trajectory that, because it has a trajectory into psychoanalysis and 'the unsayable', starts to spin off in a direction that Childhood Studies has not yet moved.

CS You have referred to your interest in psychoanalytic ideas and position yourself within the Lacanian School. Where would you stand on the traditional concepts of objectivity, reliability, validity?

AR Well, in Lacanian psychoanalysis it goes back to Freud's idea that we are each a split subject, split in our knowledge of ourselves, that each of us construct a consciousness and an ego narrative, a way of navigating the world on the one hand and on the other hand, there are pieces of our experience that are constructed through the unconscious. The unconscious is in our speech, as opposed to hidden away somewhere else, and also in our fumbled acts, in our acts of forgetting. The way that the unconscious is arranged, what is driving us is also hidden to us, so in that sense our memories, what we remember as having happened in reality, having happened objectively in some sense, is in fact, an illusion. It is all subjective. It is all nuanced by this experience of the unconscious. I truly don't believe in objectivity. At the same time I am not a naive realist or a naive relativist – neither one. I think that there is such a thing as getting multiple takes, multiple perspectives on any experience and that an accounting of experience itself, let alone a layered reading of it, gives you a much richer and less narrow picture than is possible if you just say: 'Well, here is my take on it' as if to say simply that version stands. I don't consider subjectivity simply as an idiosyncratic account or story. In terms of reliability, in qualitative research one interviewer, one researcher is simply not replaceable with another. There is no real reliability in qualitative research, but again that isn't to say that you can't build an interpretation drawn from evidence and ask someone else to look at your interpretation and to pose questions or challenges to it, as a way of enriching that perspective. For me, that is really the only kind of validity that is open to qualitative researchers, this kind of transparent accounting, or transparent enough accounting, that it can be read critically by someone else. Beyond that, reliability, validity, objectivity? I think that they are huge illusions that have been brought over from the world of quantitative research, where they were already illusions [joint laughter], into a world that doesn't suit them.

CS Can I now ask you specifically about your experience of research with children. How many years and what types of research with children have you undertaken?

AR Well, this is the point where it is actually a little scary to think about the number of years [soft laughter]. My first research with children was actually with infants, I did studies of mother–infant interaction in the early 1980s, straight out of my undergraduate degree, completely in a quantitative mode, looking at behaviours. This experience also allowed me to look at what was happening between babies and their mothers in the first year of life, which seemed enormously interesting to me, and the chance to hang out with babies! Then my work took a turn, in terms of working with children. Since the early 1980s I have done clinical work with children which would seem to be separate from research, except I was being trained in a psychoanalytic way of working with children. The result was that I was bringing transcripts and notes to a supervisor three times a week, which made it feel very much like an intensive research project in itself. That psychoanlytic supervision experience definitely spilled over into my thinking about how to do research, because part of my task was to interpret, while staying very, very close to the children's words and actions.

Then my next experience was working with Carol Gilligan and Lyn Brown and the Harvard Project on Women's Psychology and Girls' Development, doing some interviews with the Laurel-Harvard Project with adolescents and children. I then directed a project called: 'Strengthening healthy resistance and courage in girls'. Carol Gilligan, Normi Noel (a gifted teacher from Shakespeare and Company) and I were meeting the small groups of girls and doing things in the arts and theatre. Carol was the Principal Investigator of that grant and we worked on the research together for four years all together. It was quite a shift to me initially when I went to Harvard and began to do this research. The shift was away from a form of clinical listening that I had become pretty comfortable with to a much more active kind of questioning and also, at least initially, following a protocol of questions, as opposed to following the child's lead. Even in the years of the Harvard Project we began to modify this method by making the interviews fairly flexible. Then I did a longitudinal study with children called: 'Telling all one's heart' in which we greatly modified interview protocol methods. During this time, around the mid-1990s, it is interesting how my interviewing began to once again converge with my clinical way of listening, which was always in the background as a tug.

CS Say some more about how your theoretical framework informs the way you work with children.

AR When I meet with a child, whether it is clinically or whether it is in a research relationship, there are some things that I pay attention to because of my immersion in psychoanalysis. For example, I ask what is his or her reading of me? 'Who am I to this little person?' It has nothing to do with them finding out who I am actually, and much more to do with how I can discern how they are reading me through their responses to me. I also assume that, like all of us, children sense that there are some things they can say, and some things they can't say. So I read them for reading me for what is receivable. What can I receive from them? If I can, I find the limits of what I am hearing, and try to jiggle it up in some way as if to say: 'Ah, but you did realise this here's another opportunity?' in a sense to the child – not saying it directly but…For instance, there was an experience I actually had while I was still with the Harvard Project that illustrates this idea of making an opening or opportunity for a child. There was a point where I was sitting with a little girl and going through the interview protocol and I thought: 'This is not what she is actually thinking, this is not getting me anything that really sings to me.' So I put the protocol aside and I just played with her a little bit…I can't remember exactly what it was but I put my questions aside and I just played with a set of ideas with her, away from the protocol, and it just…it made something happen between the two of us, because I think she read me for the first time as: 'Oh, this is someone who will be playful and who will let me go where I want to go with this.' There was a time when I was interviewing sexually abused girls both here in Ireland and in the US and some of them really couldn't speak about some experiences. Rather than pushing them to be able to do that, I would ask questions around that curious territory of the unsayable. I literally asked them, 'What happens to the things that you can't say, do they just disappear for you or are they with you in some other way?' I was reading the child or the adolescent, through their reading of me, and also thinking of that young person as someone who necessarily has to censor to live in society, and because of that, who has an unconscious, who has access to all kinds of tacit knowledge that can be invited into a social space, at least in a limited kind of way, and I think especially so with the promise of confidentiality.[5] These ideas are very much on my mind when I am with children as a researcher or as a clinician – I don't make that distinction very strongly any more.

CS When you go into a research context how aware are you of topics that might have an impact on you? Is that something you think about and prepare for before going into a research environment?

AR Yes, very much although you sometimes can't predict how an interview will affect you. When I was interviewing sexually abused girls, in Ireland and in the US, I did not at first calculate how crucial it was going to be that after any interview was over I had to build in at least two hours in which I was not responsible to be somewhere or do something, simply because the interviews had a very powerful effect on me. There was a period in my life when I was really interested in doing research on physical and sexual abuse, but I knew both for myself and for children, that I couldn't. I could do it clinically but I could not do it as an interviewer and then leave that child. So I think it matters that when you are going to open something up, especially with a child, that you know you can, in some way, navigate that territory. A lot of people want to speak with children about experiences that have deeply affected their own childhoods – an experience of grief or chronic illness or all kinds of things that children experience as children. As adults we want to understand children's experiences. We all know the research that has that kind of quality [gentle laughter] and I do think it is important that researchers have come to a place in themselves where it is possible to receive another person's story as very distinct, a very different one, as well as one which may call up all kinds of things emotionally.

CS Can we now move on to the current state of the field. Is Childhood Studies multidisciplinary, is it interdisciplinary, is it a distinct field?

AR I think at the moment it is more multidisciplinary rather than truly interdisciplinary, in large part because fields have not learned terribly well yet to speak to one another. We are still mostly educating graduate students in single fields rather than multiple fields at once. So I think that is a piece of it. When I think about the field of Childhood Studies, some of the most exciting work is by people who are pushing the field outside of sociology and into very new directions. So I think of the work of my colleague at CUNY [City University of New York], Wendy Luttrell, who has been interested for a very long time in the way children portray their experiences through visual means, through photography, through art – mostly through photography but also through art; or I think of my colleague at Hampshire College, Rachel Conrad, who is exploring children's subjectivities through poetry. My own work is very much at the edge of Childhood Studies and psychoanalysis so it pushes the field into new directions. I don't think that it's a settled field, I think it's a field of the future and hopefully, a field of the future that will begin to really allow different disciplines to take up a common enquiry about children's experiences, or children's subjectivity, or children's experiences in cultural contexts in ways that we don't even imagine right now because most of us have been trained within a single field.

CS You have touched on this already, Annie, when you said that the field of Childhood Studies of the future is probably hard for us to conceptualise. Will you say something about the tensions, dilemmas, challenges that we will have to navigate in order for the field to move forward?

AR I think one of the huge tensions, from my point of view, is that the field wants to understand children's experiences from the child's point of view, but each of us has a version of our own childhood, from a different time and space, that we bring to our studies, as well as the overlay of ideas about what childhood has been and is now. The result is that we can't really accurately get at the child's own experience of childhood other than simply repeating what children tell us [laughs] and in repeating what children tell us, we necessarily select some things and leave out others. Of course, what children tell us is completely shaped by the relationship and what questions get posed and what works and what doesn't work in terms of creating an atmosphere where a child can speak. It's doubled and redoubled, especially when you get into the younger ages, by children's lack of language and facility to speak to the fullness of their experiences. For me that is an overwhelming truth of childhood itself. Which is why I am actually so interested in psychoanalysis, in the unconscious, in the idea that children will speak and portray and play things out very indirectly. I admire my colleagues who are interested in children's art and in the world of poetry in relation to childhood because it opens up a different register for trying to meet children in their experience and it's a meeting rather than a notion that somehow you can gain access to childhood as it's lived. I think another place that is very exciting is the possibility of new ethnographic methods that really will allow us to know something of the experience of childhood in new terms. What that would look like in the future I really don't know because we are entering a world in which the way things are recorded and shared in the world is changing. I can't even imagine it to be honest [laughs], but that central tension of the child's experience, trying to approach and to give voice to the child's experience, that impulse that that's possible still exists, on the one hand in the field, and on the other hand, in the sense that it is all filtered and that we are missing big pieces of children's experiences. That is much more the side that I see myself on.

CS What about psychology, Annie? Where do you see psychology fitting in to the field of the future? I think there is some recognition now that it can't just be left out of the picture, that would be throwing the baby out with the bathwater, but for psychology in the future do you think there is a role and what useful role could psychology play?

AR That's such a difficult question because, at least here in the US, the psychologists of the future are saturated in neuro-psychology, cognitive psychology, laboratory psychology, as if everything about human experience can be measured, observed, known. Even in clinical programmes, psychology students are not trained carefully in interviewing methods or in methods of interpretation. I think psychology as a field needs to be part of Childhood Studies, but it's not part of the current paradigm within psychology. As for myself, I am teaching courses to undergraduates in psychoanalysis rather than psychology because I am so deeply disaffected from my own field. I don't know…it seems to me that, if anything, Childhood Studies will have to bring something back to the psychological study of childhood itself and shake up that field in some new way for those two fields to have anything to say to one another.

CS There are some people within the field of Childhood Studies who believe that we should be studying childhood rather than children. Micro/macro is perhaps a bit too crude as a way to portray it, but there does seem to be this division. Is there room for both?

AR Yes, I think there's room for both. Studying childhood as historical and cultural conceptions of childhood is important and compelling, and studying children is equally compelling, trying in some sense to understand something of the experience of childhood itself. In fact I think if you throw out one or the other you have a very odd picture of children as [laughter] dismembered from childhood.

CS At present the field of Childhood Studies is predominantly white, western, American and European and yet, of course, most of the world's children live in the majority world countries. What we can do to make our work more relevant to the lives of children living in those contexts and also in terms of greater inclusion of majority world scholars? It does seem to be a huge gap in Childhood Studies at the moment.

AR It's another way in which I think the field of the future is something that is very difficult for us and even our generation to imagine. I hope that the digital age will open up education to people around the world in a way that we have never seen before and in doing so, I hope that adults in countries around the world will begin to be intrigued with their own culture, their own version of childhood and their own children. Rather than the field, as it now exists, trying to incorporate or bring into itself variants of what childhood can be and what it means around the world, I hope that there will be a proliferation of new scholarship and new studies in a way the field can't imagine right now. In fact, I do think the primarily white, western American/European world view will come to be seen as one of many views. Will it be done by our generation in the field as it now exists? I really don't think so and I hope not, I hope it will be taken up by others.

CS The last thing I wanted to ask you, Annie, is, do you have any advice for new researchers coming into the field or anything else you would like to say?

AR I think this is very important, how to speak to the next generation of students and this is how I try to teach. I would say don't begin with loyalty to a field or a set of ideas, but with pressing questions that lead to a path of enquiry and let the path of enquiry guide you, the sources you draw on, the fields you pay attention to and what references you use to get started. Let your work have some trajectory that leaves a trace in the world, that it is not just for the production of knowledge itself but work that leaves some trace in the world. I think young people themselves, the next generation of people who will take up this work, that's their own impetus anyway [laughing] – to have an impact. The thing that really dismays me is all the effort to try to get this next generation to follow in a path we have already made, rather than to clear a path for them to make their own way in a way that is truly original and will meet the sense and the needs of the future. One of the things most striking to me, in terms of the generational exchange, is that we know from psychoanalysis that children from any generation have to take up and work with most centrally whatever has been repressed or censored in the previous generation. In that sense I think the field of the future will have to pick up the pieces of what we, the people who created this field, have left in the dust, have really not understood, have distorted or just left behind. Again, that's the spirit of my teaching. I am delighted you are doing this book in the sense that it is both historic and it has that reach into the next generation of people doing work on childhood.

References
[1] Gilligan, C, 1982, *In a different voice: Psychological theory and women's development*, Cambridge, MA: Harvard University Press
[2] Thorne, B, 1993, *Gender play: Girls and boys in school*, New Brunswick, NJ: Rutgers University Press
[3] Brown, LM, Gilligan, C, 1992, *Meeting at the crossroads: Women's psychology and girls' development*, New York: Ballatine Books
[4] Bakhtin, M, 1986, *Speech genres and other late essays*, Austin, TX: University of Texas Press
[5] Rogers, A, 2006, *The unsayable: The hidden language of trauma*, New York, NY: Ballantine Books

TWENTY-ONE

Nigel Thomas

Nigel Thomas is Professor of Childhood and Youth Research at the University of Central Lancashire, UK, where he is also Director of The Centre for Children and Young People's Participation in Research. Professor Thomas practised as a social worker for 20 years, and has since taught and researched extensively in the field of children's welfare, rights and participation. He has worked with children in care, young carers, school pupils and members of youth councils, using a range of innovative methods. His publications include *Children, family and the state* (Macmillan, 2000; Policy Press, 2002), *Social work with young people in care* (Palgrave, 2004), *Children, politics and communication* (Policy Press, 2009) and *A handbook of children and young people's participation* (with Barry Percy-Smith, Routledge, 2010). He chairs the Editorial Board of the journal *Children and Society*, of which he was formerly a co-editor. He is a Visiting Professor at Southern Cross University, New South Wales.

Carmel Smith Nigel, will you start by saying something about your background, how you came into children's research and about your research training?

Niogl Thomas I am always a little conscious of not having had very much by way of formal research training. My first degree was in Politics and Philosophy and I think what that gave me was a logical approach and also an understanding of, at some level, some of the issues around the relationship between data and theory and the kind of slipperiness of concepts like objectivity. I was taught by a very good sociological theorist and epistemologist and that left me, I think, with quite a good understanding of those kinds of fundamental issues and that really helped years later when I started doing research. When I did my Social Work Masters there was a research methods module as part of that which, like a lot of social work students, we, in a way, tried to avoid engaging with [laughter], but I suppose it left a bit of a residue. I then spent 20 years in social work practice – generically most of that time, but latterly with children and families. In the late 1980s, when I started to get itchy feet, one of the things I did was sign up for a course in research methods. I went along to this course and it was really the first serious formal training in research methods I was conscious of having. It was a five-day course over five weeks, but a lot of it seemed very familiar, as I had picked up a lot of these concepts along the way. I came out of that feeling that I didn't necessarily know how to do research, but that I had a reasonable understanding of what different methodological approaches were about, what quantitative research was *about* and what qualitative research was *about* – and I could relate that to my undergraduate understanding of how you ask questions, how you answer questions, what constitutes knowledge and all those aspects that are sometimes quite difficult to grasp. So I guess that my understanding came from those experiences of formal training, some reading and thinking, really, and reading lots of stuff within my discipline and outside my discipline. Then I managed to make the shift from social work into academic work. I initially signed up part-time to do an MPhil, and then it turned out that the place where I was going to do the part-time MPhil had a part-time lectureship going where they wanted someone who knew about the Children Act. I applied for that and got it so I then had a base partly in the academic world and partly still in the field. I stayed with the local authority I was working with as an adviser for a couple of years part-time and started to get into this MPhil research, which was around decision making processes when children are in care, and from there started learning on the job. I am a great one for making it up as you go along and seeing whether it works or not, really!

CS You have mentioned objectivity, where do you stand now on those traditional research concepts of objectivity, reliability and validity?

NT I suppose I am a kind of critical realist really. I haven't read huge volumes by Roy Bhaskar, but from what I understand that critical realism is saying, that is pretty much where I would stand. So, reality is socially constructed, but it is socially constructed in interaction – by people engaging with each other. This applies not just in discourse, but in practice, although it is socially constructed within limits and there is a kind of reality with which we work.

CS Can I now move on to research with children? I know that you have done a lot of research with children. Did you have any training on researching with children specifically or is that something that again has evolved in your work?

NT It has evolved. Some of it has come out of practice because a lot of my practice is with children. It is interesting because when I first started talking to children as part of my MPhil research which turned into a PhD, it turned into quite a big project, but it was initially fairly small scale, I found myself kind of adopting my idea of a researcher role which was very much about having a questionnaire, having a tape recorder and being fairly formal, really. I did a few interviews with young people in the care system and was disappointed at how little I got from them. I guess it was when I was sitting listening to the tapes and transcribing those interviews – doing your own transcribing is a fantastic way of understanding what has gone on in an interview because you pick up all sorts of things that you weren't aware of at the time – I started to notice what was going on in the interaction and realised that there must be other approaches I could take to engaging with these children that would make it easier for them to engage with the process and talk to me. The key moment was when I kind of gave myself permission to be a social worker rather than a researcher and started using some of the skills and techniques and tricks that I had used as a social worker in engaging with children. Once I started doing that and stopped being a 'researcher' in a suit then things went a lot better, really!

CS Based on your own research experience and your involvement in training children to be researchers, what training do you think new researchers should receive?

NT I am a bit heretical about research training, really. Because I am not sympathetic to the idea that there is a body of knowledge and skills that you learn and then you go off and start practising, I think that training has to be related to purpose to work. One of the things I have done quite a bit of in the last couple of years is train children and young people in research, and that has always been in the context of specific projects, and what seems to work best for me is to put in the training when it is needed. So when you reach a point in a project where we need to think about ethics, that's when you engage with the young people and think, what's involved in doing research ethically, what kind of rights do research participants have, what would we want if we were on the receiving end of this, so what should we be offering to the people we are working with, what kind of issues are likely to arise? In fact, I am doing that later on today because I am preparing for a session tomorrow with a group of young people with whom we are just about to start on a research project. One of the things…I am trying to put together a basic introduction to methods and ethical issues that is going to have to be relevant to what we are doing on this project, because people don't want to learn something in the abstract usually and, even if they do, they don't necessarily retain it unless there is an opportunity to put it into practice. I think that applies to research students and employed researchers as well. You need the skills when you need them and you need the knowledge when you need it and you can't go away and get it all and then go off and use it. You build up your repertoire over time. Now that maybe a kind of ex post facto justification for my history which has been very much of learning things as I go along!

CS When you work with young people as researchers, do you involve them in the whole process, for example in data analysis?

NT I try…I prefer to involve them in the whole process. I mean, there are different ways of doing it, different things are suitable for different projects and different contexts, but what I am trying to do at the moment is to find opportunities to do work where young people can be involved from beginning to end: from generating the research question to presenting the final report.

CS What theorist or theoretical framework has most influenced the approach that you take in your research work with children?

NT Theoretically I guess the most important for me is Anne Solberg's injunction to ignore age as far as possible.[1] I try not to go in with assumptions about what children will and won't understand, but with an open mind about what they will understand and what they will be interested in, so it is very much a matter of feeling my way in, really.

CS So seeing the person rather than the age?

NT Yes, absolutely.

CS Will you say a bit more about how you conceptualise children and childhood and some of your thinking around that?

NT I conceptualise children as people who are younger than other people who often get called adults – it is not always clear why [laughing] – who may know less than older people, but may also know things that older people don't know, like, what it is like being a child. A child may have less developed abilities in certain areas – but I would come back to the point that that has to be tested in individual cases rather than assumed as a generality – and may have less power and often don't have the practical ability to simply say 'yes' or 'no' to participation in research, for instance, without other people's permission. My approach to that is shamelessly subversive really, I try to get round it because my starting point is that people should be able to decide for themselves about participating in research, provided that research is being done in a way that is ethical and responsible, and while there are lots of situations in which it is clearly appropriate for parents or carers to have some part to play in that decision, I try to avoid situations where parents and carers have an automatic veto. So I guess my conceptualisation is of children as people and people who in principle ought to be given as much opportunity as possible to take responsibility for their own lives.

CS Tell me about how you work with children. The concept of rapport has been in research methods text books for decades whereby researchers are told that it is important to establish rapport. What is rapport and how do you understand it in your work with children?

NT It is not either/or, and it is not a mechanical thing. It is not like when you are interviewing somebody for a job and you ask them if they had a nice journey and that's your way of establishing rapport – it doesn't work like that. You have to engage with the particular person and find the ways in which you can put this particular person at their ease or maybe you can't, in which case you just have to do the best you can with that. So, for example, in an interview or a focus group you have to start with what brings people together, what brings people to this interview or focus group – why are they there? Presumably they have chosen to be there either because they understand and value the purpose of the research and see themselves as being able to make a contribution to that, or because they are simply interested, intrigued by it or because they are attracted by a reward, or because they have been persuaded to come along by a friend or, at worst, because they have been told to come along by a parent or a professional or something. Your engagement needs to connect with the reason why a person is there. If there is a sound reason for them being there, if there is some kind of sound motivation in one of those categories, then if it is not working that is a kind of shared problem isn't it? Why is this not working or how can we make it work? Then it is going to be a matter of the kind of methods of communication that you use.

What we did on the Children and Decision Making project[2] was, we went to both our interviews and our focus groups – we had done quite a lot of work to establish consent beforehand (real consent from the young people rather than proxy consent from other people) and we then went along to those events with a repertoire, a pack of things we could use so that we were able to offer young people lots of choice about how they engaged with us – whether they answered questions, played games, did drawings, told stories   that was for them as much as for us, so we weren't simply presenting something and inviting them to follow along a pathway that we had predetermined. It was much more about working together to establish: 'How can we make this interview work?' We had very few problems with what you might call rapport. I mean we had one or two interviews that didn't work and we had one or two focus groups that got a bit wild, but they were still productive. I suppose the other thing is that if a young person doesn't say anything, that is a huge amount of communication, isn't it? And then you have to start trying to interpret, really.

CS In terms of the researcher–child relationship, is there anything that I have missed [referring to the interview topic guide] from your knowledge and experience?

NT I think you have covered the ground pretty well, actually. I think the question of what we bring from our own experience of childhood into those encounters is an interesting one, and one that people don't really talk about very much.

CS Linked to that, I want to ask you about the concept of reflexivity in research. The professional practice literature is full of references to the 'reflective practitioner', so does that extend to practitioners undertaking research? There seems to be very different approaches across disciplines in terms of how people understand the concept in research, why it is considered important and how reflexivity is practised.

NT I think there is a lot of confusion around, partly because there is semantic confusion between reflexivity and reflectivity. If you talk about reflection, unless it is written down, nobody knows which word you are using and to me there is a distinction between being reflective which means doing some of the things we have been doing in this interview and some of the things we have talked about in this interview, it means thinking about what you are doing as a researcher, how you are handling these situations, reflecting back on that afterwards and thinking about ways in which you could have done it differently. That is really important and overlaps with, but is conceptually distinct from, reflexivity which is about the relationship between me as a person and the research I am doing. I think that is the best way I can put it. It is what I bring into the research by being who I am and having the history I have, the hang-ups I have, the characteristics I have, the preoccupations I have, whatever, and that is all kinds of things. For me, being a researcher with children and young people, I am bringing in my own experience of being a child – when I often found other children quite intimidating or unsettling – and my experiences as a parent. When I first started researching I was a parent of young children or children entering their middle years of childhood and it is interesting that that was roughly the focus of my research at that time, and now, as my sons have grown up, I have found myself doing more and more work with young people – you don't have to be a conspiracy theorist to spot a kind of connection there between biography and research interests! But I think the most important thing about reflexivity is to be aware of those issues, be aware of your own likely impact on the research and people you are doing research with and aware of the agendas you bring to it. It takes me back to that early learning about epistemology when I was an undergraduate, that pure objectivity is an unhelpful fantasy; really, the trick is to be aware of when you are not being objective and to understand that and, as far as you can, to allow for it and use it rather than try and ignore it and pretend it is not there.

CS Can we now move on to talk about the field of Childhood Studies. First of all, tell me about your recollection of the events and ideas which led to the coming together of key individuals to declare a 'new paradigm' including influences from different geographical locations in previous decades. Why did it happen when it did?

NT I think this was something that had been brewing for quite a while. Jens Qvortrup and others tend to imply that the key shift took place in Britain and the Nordic countries in the late 1980s and early 1990s. In fact a lot of important work was done in the USA in the 1970s, by sociologists like Norman Denzin, Gary Fine, Matthew Speier and Arlene Skolnick; a tradition that continued with the work of Frances Chaput Waksler and Bill Corsaro. There is often a bit of 'parallel play' going on either side of the Atlantic in Childhood Studies, although in recent years there has begun to be a bit more cross-fertilisation, especially with the work being done at Camden-Rutgers.

I think Allison James and Alan Prout would rightly remind us that they did not invent but rather 'proclaimed' the new paradigm. The critical ideas they identified, in particular the social construction of childhood and the emphasis on children's agency, were there already; they put them all together in a package, a bit like a literary critic announcing a new 'movement' in poetry. Their collection, *Constructing and reconstructing childhood*,[3] together with Qvortrup et al's *Childhood matters*[4] were probably the most influential books in establishing the new paradigm as a significant part of the academic discourse. Why that happened when it did is an interesting question, but I'm not entirely sure what the answer is. The embryonic 'children's liberation' movements of the 1960s/1970s probably contributed, and the filtering of ideas from the American sociologists mentioned above, together with a general opening up of categories and attitudes around who is a person deserving of consideration, that is in my view a more long-term trend in many societies.

CS In terms of the current state of the field, is it a distinct field? Is it sociology, multidisciplinary, interdisciplinary? Should we be studying children, childhood or both?

NT Oh gosh, those are big questions. For me it's definitely childhood, not children. The category has to be always bracketed and open to question. However, in practice, a lot of the work that goes on, judging by papers presented at conferences, and so on, is less clearly defined than that. I'm concerned in particular that the operating definition of children as people under the age of 18, imposed by the UNCRC, is becoming hegemonic and is obscuring the socially constructed character of childhood even in academic discourse. Sometimes it's helpful to freshen things up a little by referring to 'people currently occupying a space designated as childhood'. I would also say that the field has to be multidisciplinary, and its strength is in being interdisciplinary too, although sociology is almost certainly the dominant discipline.

CS Your work has always had a strong international flavour including in the *Handbook* you edited with Barry Percy-Smith in 2010.[5] How can the field of Childhood Studies do more to include majority world children and majority world scholars?

NT I think there's been a lot of movement in that direction already. We could do more, though, to address the inequalities of access to knowledge, by offering more direct support to majority world scholars, and by persuading our institutions to share their library resources with universities in money-poor countries. We could also try to stop talking and writing as though a minority world childhood is the norm. It's a hard habit to break, with the best will in the world...

CS Looking to the future of the field, what are the tensions, dilemmas and challenges that Childhood Studies is facing? What direction should the field take?

NT There are clearly tensions around agency, that tend to surface around the question how much agency children have in reality, and whether there is a propensity among researchers to exaggerate how much agency children have, or to be excessively triumphant over minor examples of agency. My own feeling is that this debate sometimes cloaks an ambiguity about what we mean by asking whether children have agency or how much they have. There is an ontological/epistemological question about how we understand agency and the relationship with social structure, linked with a conceptual issue around children as social agents rather than the objects of external socialisation. There are also practical/empirical questions about how much freedom of action children have in actuality. As long as these two kinds of questions, which operate on different conceptual levels although they often resemble each other, are not clearly distinguished, that particular debate is in my view unlikely to make much progress.

Other than that, some of the central issues people like Chris Jenks and Jens Qvortrup identified many years ago – being or becoming, one childhood or multiple childhoods, macro or micro as the primary focus of enquiry – are still with us, still being played around with in different ways.

The move to intergenerationality as a focus of study is I think very important, and may even prefigure a fundamental shift in the field. The relationship between Childhood Studies and the disciplines is in my view problematic, illustrated by the continued failure of mainstream social and political theory to regard children as people, a sign of our failure as academics to penetrate our parent disciplines with what we have learned in the past 20 or 30 years. The study of generation is one way in which, for example, sociologists of childhood can re-engage with other sociologists in an area of wider interest; the work of Leena Alanen and Berry Mayall, building in part on Bourdieu, is significant in this regard. It is also an important turn to be taking, however, because it follows from the logic of seeing childhood as a social construction, and offers an escape from being trapped in the still-dominant definition of childhood as a taken-for-granted category defined by chronological age and serving as a natural descriptor of those occupying that space – in other words, an escape from being the study of children, rather than the study of childhood.

Finally, the ethical and political issues generated when we study and research childhood and children in this paradigm demand attention. The relationship between academic study of childhood and engagement in societal structures, processes, relationships and discourse, characterised by James and Prout in terms of the 'double hermeneutic', remains complex and challenging.[6] And the ethical position of children in relation to the doing of research, the tension between protection and empowerment, is, in practice if not in theory, highly problematic.

References

[1] Solberg, A, 1997, Negotiating childhood: Changing constructions of age for Norwegian children, in A James, A Prout (eds) *Constructing and reconstructing childhood: Contemporary issues in the sociological study of childhood* (2nd edn), (pp 126–44), Basingstoke: Falmer Press

[2] Thomas, N, 2002, *Children, family and the state: Decision-making and child participation*, Bristol: Policy Press

[3] James, A, Prout, A (eds), [1990] 1997, *Constructing and reconstructing childhood: Contemporary issues in the sociological study of childhood*, Basingstoke: Falmer Press

[4] Qvortrup, J, Bardy, M, Sgritta, G, Wintersberger, H (eds), 1994, *Childhood matters: Social theory, practice and politics*, Aldershot: Avebury

[5] Thomas, N, Percy-Smith, B (eds), 2010, *A handbook of children and young people's participation: Perspectives from theory and practice*, Abingdon: Routledge

[6] See note 3.

TWENTY-TWO

Barrie Thorne

Barrie Thorne is Emerita Professor and formerly Professor of Sociology and Professor of Gender and Women's Studies at the University of California, Berkeley. Professor Thorne's research and teaching have focused on gender, age relations, childhoods and families, feminist theory and ethnographic methods of research. For ten years she served as US Editor of *Childhood: A Global Journal of Child Research*. Professor Thorne is also a former Vice President of the American Sociological Association and former Chair of the ASA section on the Sociology of Children and Youth and a recipient of the ASA Jessie Bernard Award. In 2010–11 she was a Fellow at the Center for Advanced Study at the Norwegian Academy of Arts and Sciences. Professor Thorne has published seven books and numerous chapters and journal articles in the course of her career including *Rethinking the family: Some feminist questions* (Northeastern University, 1992) and *Gender play: Girls and boys in school* (Rutgers, 1993). The work of Professor Thorne is widely cited in both North American and European literature and she is internationally recognised as one of the pioneering US scholars in the field of Childhood Studies.

Sheila Greene So, if we just start with a very general question, Barrie. Maybe if you would talk about how you got into this area of research in the first place?

Barrie Thorne I told the story a little bit in my book *Gender play*.[1] When I was a graduate student at Brandeis I was involved in the draft resistance and anti-Vietnam War movement, which led me into the early years of women's liberation. I helped create a Women's Studies Programme at my first job at Michigan State University. Then, after I became a mother, I started to pay attention to the worlds of children. I am the oldest daughter of a family of five, with three younger siblings, all of whom were in diapers at the same time. I have always enjoyed being with children, but in the early 1970s I started to notice them with an ethnographic eye. So when we went on sabbatical at a university in California, I had developed the idea of doing fieldwork in a school, so I got access to an elementary school. As I focused on the topic of children and gender, I looked for what was written on the topic and discovered how limited the frameworks were. It was mostly a field dominated by studies of teacher practices, a few ethnographies of school worlds, but not that many, and very little, that I could find, about children's lives outside of school. I later wrote up a kind of manifesto which I called, 'Revisioning women and social change: Where are the children?'[2]

So I came to the subject of children very much though feminism and through the connection of women to children. I was appalled when I realised that the feminist literature mostly focused on children as women's labour, not on children as actors. There was very little about girls, except for critiques of what then was called sex-role socialisation. The Brandeis graduate programme was outside of mainstream sociology; it emphasised critical theory, the Frankfurt School and ethnographic methods. I realised the functionalism embedded in the socialisation literature, referring children to an end point, driven by adult interests and by the question 'How is society possible?' You train children so that they can participate in society, but there is little recognition of children as actors, and experiencers in the present. So I began to think that we needed another way of looking at and studying children. After I had written my manifesto asking. 'Where are the children?', which was published in *Gender and Society* in 1987, Bill Corsaro invited me to a small conference on ethnography with children that he and Sigrid Berentzen had organised in Trondheim, Norway, held just before a global conference on children growing up in the modern world. At that conference I learned for the first time about the UNCRC [UN Convention on the Rights of the Child], if you can believe it! The US has still not signed the UNCRC and you rarely hear about it here, whereas in Norway *everyone* knows about it. I have spent quite a bit of time living and working in Norway and the contrast is just amazing. Later I became an editor of *Childhood* for 10 years. This contact with Europeans who were doing childhood studies gave me many new ideas, and it was very validating. It was heartening and thrilling to be part of this global interdisciplinary network and from then on I spent a lot of time going back and forth to Europe.

Jens Qvortrup, Leena Alanen and others started a research section on the sociology of childhood in the International Sociological Association, which led to a lot of exchange across national borders. Finally some of us in the US, with Gertrude Lenzer at the City University of New York taking the lead, formed an American Sociological Section on the Sociology of Children and Youth, which is still going and thriving.

I have spent a lot of time thinking about a sociology of knowledge question: why did the understanding of children as actors and the affirmation of children's rights more broadly, especially rights of participation as well as protection, take hold so strongly in Europe but not in the US? I thought it was really telling that while some of us advocated for calling the ASA section the Sociology of 'Childhood', the majority wanted 'Children'. Now what's the difference? 'Childhood' calls attention to the social and historical circumstances in which individual children grow up. The word 'children' tends to eclipse social contexts and can evoke a naturalised view of the child. Putting collective practices and the political economy of childhood at the foundation of the field has been harder for Americans to do. I think some of it is because of the deep power of our assumptions about privatised childhood, as well as the lack of a meaningful welfare state. The contrast between a country like Norway and the US is simply phenomenal. Different European countries are positioned variously, the UK being closest to the US in a major symbol of this, which is the rate of child poverty. Our rates are by far the biggest, they are far worse than 25 per cent; meaningfully about a third live in shaky economic circumstances. Unlike the US, most Scandinavian countries have a conception of children as social citizens. When we come to the subject of the future of Childhood Studies, I think ethnography is great but we need more on the political economy of childhood.

SG From what you say, you would like to see more challenging of your own discipline. Do you identify still as a sociologist?

BT I do, I am a sociologist who is critical of positivism. I have engaged with ethnographic, qualitative epistemologies, critical theory, and with critiques of mainstream sociology. I also have had joint appointments, quite deliberately and by choice, in sociology and in gender and women's studies programmes and departments. I didn't go entirely into gender studies because I am a sociologist and I have come to realise it more and more. I love, however, being in interdisciplinary spaces and having legitimacy for singing whatever song feels right. I don't like intellectual policing and disciplinary chauvinism. I am like a time-bomb [laughs] ready to go off if I hear anyone say 'That's not sociology' because that is used to put people down and run them out of the territory; it's ridiculous and authoritarian. The fields of ethnic studies, women's studies, childhood studies focus on devalued groups, so it makes it even harder to launch challenges that go to the heart of other disciplines.

SG You feel that they can readily be brushed off by mainstream sociology or mainstream psychology as peripheral activities.

BT Yes but, guess what? The majority of new PhDs in sociology in the US are women, and we have elected several feminist presidents of the ASA, but Childhood Studies will never be able to build up that kind of power because, although children are a huge percentage of the population, they are not members of the ASA and they never will be.

SG So you are tarred with the same kind of status as they have?

BT Yes you are, yes you are. We have to promote the study of children in sociology with the challenging question: why is the field neglecting such a large segment of the population? In addition, intellectual excitement – having something important to say – helps the field grow, but yes it's certainly marginal.

SG You were saying your own approach has been mostly qualitative?

BT Yes, and theoretical.

SG So would you ally yourself with a particular theoretical framework?

BT Yes, a mix of them. Methodologically my heart and my training are with ethnography and other qualitative approaches. I am strongly influenced by feminist theory, Marxism and political economy. I got a lot of that from being in the political Left. I am also influenced by theories of care

SG So you would have received training in qualitative methods?

BT Yes, we did a year of collaborative fieldwork at Brandeis as our basic methods training.

SG Because it is interesting that quite a few of the people working at an early stage in the field really did not themselves get training.

BT Yes I was lucky to go to Brandeis for graduate school. I had fantastic training, some of it as an apprentice. We also read a lot of epistemology, including phenomenology, Alfred Schütz, for example.

SG A very deep background. So when you look at qualitative research would you be concerned about issues to do with rigour? Would concepts like validity and reliability be relevant to you?

BT Yes, though I would probably use other concepts. It is important to be systematic, to be careful about evidence and inference. I think it is important for qualitative sociologists to understand epistemological variation and ways of knowing and to read about grounded theory approaches, about inductive versus deductive logics, the logic of hypothesis testing and why this discourse is just not appropriate for detailed case studies. Ethnography is not about statistical generalisability or questions about your *n*. In studying a classroom it is important to talk about the size and dynamics of the class. If there is anything about sampling it's about what Glaser and Strauss call theoretical sampling, so you might choose a child to be interviewed because of their position. It is extremely well-informed sampling, not at all random. So I think in order to survive as a qualitative sociologist, it is important to know how to go on the offensive, to not give away the methodological and epistemological turf. All knowledge is situated and we need many research tools. I am grateful for people who can do surveys and find out about the percentage of children in poverty. I can't tell you about that from my methods, but I can tell you about how people cope with poverty, and live it. A lot of energy is wasted in false debates.

SG I know you have had years of experience of working directly with children. Was your approach very much influenced by the kind of training you had or were there certain approaches that you introduced?

BT When I started doing fieldwork in 1976, hanging out with a class of fifth graders in the playground, I began without a lot of reflection about whether it makes a difference that these are children. I had not yet read a really interesting article by Nancy Mandell on trying to be 'least adult' in doing fieldwork with children, but I was doing that, trying to slough off as much of adult status as I could while being responsible and not denying that I was clearly an adult and not a student in their eyes. I sat at the back of the classroom, but I also wandered around and changed my position. I began to be alert to how adults treat children. How we often make little collusive comments. The teacher would try to grab my eye when the children said something that was funny to an adult or which had a double meaning. I would avert my eyes from hers, because I wanted to not be on 'her (adult) side,' which is tricky because you have got to be in the good graces of the adults who own a setting.

It was so different 20 years later, in 1999, when I was doing research in a school in Oakland supported by a grant from the McArthur Foundation. I was older and I also brought with me from one to three other fieldworkers – students at University of California, Berkeley who would tell the children that I was their teacher. So I was a teacher big time, a teacher of older students, who were researchers, and the Principal liked to talk to me in her office, which also put me more on the adult side of things.

The graduate students who worked on this project were primarily not white, they were African American, Latina, and there was a bi-lingual speaker of Cantonese, who herself was from an immigrant family, and a young man who was an immigrant from Vietnam. I wanted to replicate some of the incredible linguistic and ethnic diversity of the students whom we were studying because that was the major focus of the project.[3] The children in the school really liked the younger researchers, and sometimes identified along ethnic lines. Children with Southeast Asian backgrounds sometimes called the Vietnamese American researcher 'cousin,' imputing kinship to him. The African American kids adored the undergraduate student who spent a lot of time with them; she was cool and good-looking and, like the kids, she came from a low-income background. The kids identified with her and saw that they too might be able to make to college. In short, the Oakland project was a very different research experience for me, partly because of my different positioning. I realised I had moved to mother-grandmother-teacher-manager and away from being 'least adult'. Each vantage point yielded distinctive insights – reflexivity in action.

SG So in terms of the communication between the researcher and the child during the research process, is there any particular perspective you take there, in that relationship?

BT I felt somewhat prepared by growing up with lots of children in a Mormon community where there were extensive cross-age relationships (I am an excommunicated Mormon because of my feminism, just to clarify! [Laughs]). I was also prepared by the way I learned how to do fieldwork, no-one said this is only for adults. My dissertation was an ethnography of the draft resistance movement. Some years later when I began doing fieldwork in a school, I assumed that the children were little adults, or something. I didn't say that to myself; I hadn't read Phillipe Aries at the time, who, by the way deserves credit as one of the founders of childhood studies. Mostly, I thought, well, children have their culture too, rather like the tribal approach that Prout and James have written about. They cite my work as belonging to the tribal approach and they are quite right. I just wanted to get in and see how kids constructed worlds. I quickly saw that they had a big hand in constructing gender relations and meanings; they were not just being socialised.

SG It sounds like you are naturally tuned into the idea of reflexivity.

BT Very much so, in the sense of being attuned to the interplay between the fieldworker's beliefs, background, and social position and what she observes and how she interprets that world.

SG So in terms of relating to children as a researcher do you see yourself as being important in the interaction?

BT Absolutely, and in the process of fieldwork I learned a lot about myself. I wrote about this in *Gender play* when I reflected on why my field notes were so obsessively detailed about the most popular girl and the way the rich get richer. She was the one who at recess more often got handed the ball, which is a social resource. And how I kind of got the creeps from the more pariah girls, as I called them, the more marginal girls – and boys – who would cling to an adult. And then I remembered my own middling status in elementary school and how I was aware of it at the time. If you go back to your own experiences in school I think the unconscious is at work. I felt like I was in fourth or fifth grade when I started doing fieldwork. I felt 'childified', as I discovered one day when the school PA system announced, 'Barrie Thorne, the Principal would like to speak with you' [both laugh]. And the kids were all looking at me and I thought 'Oh no, have I done something bad? Am I going to be kicked out?' [both laugh]. He just wanted to ask me how my fieldwork was going. But I thought then, 'Oh my God, I really do feel like I am one of the kids, for good and bad.' That's reflexivity.

SG Have there been some very difficult moments? Topics that were difficult or children that were difficult?

BT Yes absolutely. In Lansing, Michigan, where I did some fieldwork, many of the parents were unemployed automobile workers and I felt guilty as I realised the privileges I had which many of the children lacked – privileges as simple as having a warm coat and gloves when we went onto the playground on cold winter days. I really thought a lot about the shame of poverty. The gap of privilege made me feel that I was exploiting these people; there is no getting round some level of exploitation in research. You try to be ethical and you try to tell yourself 'I want to use this information to make people aware of and ready to take action to challenge poverty', but there is still an element of exploitation and also voyeurism. It was difficult in our interviews. If the shame of social class came out, especially if there was one child from a low income family, I would feel like covering it over and smoothing out the social relations of the interview and certainly not like digging deeper. So that was a problem and also there was a huge element of self-discovery, just realising what a huge bubble of privilege I live in.

SG So is there any other issue you would like to raise?

BT Yes, one other thing about doing research with children bears on the future of child research. In the US, unfortunately the way human subjects (HS) committees operate is often to protect the institution from law suits rather than to meaningfully consider ethical issues. HS committees are badly run, with little attention to precedent and a huge turnover of faculty, who come from all sorts of different backgrounds, on the committees. One committee member told me I couldn't talk to children when I was doing fieldwork because it would violate their right to protection. Couldn't talk to them! That would be far less ethical than explaining yourself to them. I have noticed that in the last five or ten years, if I say to graduate students, 'Why don't you look at the children, why don't you ask the children about this or that?' They will say 'Oh no, I can't do that, I won't be able to get it through the HS committee.' So a lot of work that could be done and should be done is getting side-stepped because of the perceived blockade by HS committees. What is needed is more education of HS committees about how to handle research with children.

SG I agree. Can we talk about the state of the field. Is it a field? What kind of field is it? Where is it going?

BT From what I can see in the UK and Scandanavia, which is where I have the most contact outside the US, compared with the US, Childhood Studies has more of a presence in Europe; there are research institutes, undergraduate majors, and graduate programmes. In the US, as far as I know, there is only one PhD programme in Childhood Studies which is at Rutgers Camden. Some of that is because the UNCRC, which your countries have signed [laughs], has been a wedge to open up and legitimise research with children. In the US children's rights are simply not high on the political or academic agendas. It is infuriating.

OK so what kind of field is it? It has institutional infrastructures, including within disciplinary associations. Much is to be said for having research institutes that really try to promote cross–disciplinary collaboration, although that is hard to do.[4] There are, however, meaningful cross disciplinary collaborations that happen as people find one another and it is all to the good to have spaces, including conferences, where this can happen. In the US there are fewer institutional attempts to be cross-disciplinary.

I think the disciplinary imprint remains very, very strong. I haven't seen the kind of flying-free work one sees in gender studies. There aren't enough jobs to support robust interdisciplinary work on children, nor is Childhood Studies driven by a political movement, in comparison with gender studies, ethnic studies, and LGBT studies. There has always been a political impetus to reach outside departments to support and dialogue in these interdisciplinary areas of study; that's not true of Childhood Studies.

OK, the future of Childhood Studies: I have several observations to make. As I said earlier, I think it is important to keep building infrastructures to support this kind of work, and the more people can do to support one another across institutions and to build up vital centres of knowledge creation and teaching, the better, because it is a marginalised subject and it always will be. We are advocating for a group that we care a lot about but it does not have that extra edge of a political movement, although it does involve politics. I am hoping that in the US there will be more widespread concern about child poverty. Some of the child advocacy groups such as the Children's Defence Fund are working to make this happen and I think that academics should be working on that more.

So that brings me to several substantive concerns. If we take stock of this historical global moment, compared with the 1970s and 1980s, when the so-called new – now it's middle-aged – paradigm emerged, the contours of what is happening to children globally have become significantly worse; the need for rights of provision and protection has never been as strong. Because of global movements of people, there are third world pockets within the US, within London, within Oakland, both in terms of immigrant cultures with very different ideas and practices of childhood but also economically. That stratification really should drive a lot more of our work than it does. As should attention to the power of corporations in shaping children's lives and exploiting them and their families. In addition, cutbacks in social welfare systems and neo-liberalism are widening class divides, with strong implications for children's lives. It is really important that everyone be informed about and be historically reflexive about this historical moment.

So that's one thing. A second is that I think we are ripe for new ways of approaching our subject. That's where a more fully trans-disciplinary, theoretically eclectic mix might be useful. One approach that I think has much promise is to take the example of women's studies, racial ethnic studies, and sexuality studies and the breakthrough when we shifted to deconstruct and theorise gender, race and ethnicity, and sexuality as categories of analysis. There are analogues in these interdisciplinary projects that mine the fields of socially-marked differences and inequalities that cut across each other, as evoked by the concept of intersectionality. The theorising of age belongs right in the middle of that and it is often not even mentioned in litanies like 'gender, race, class, sexuality, religion, nation'. As I wrote in an editorial in *Childhood*, what age brings in from the very beginning, which gender and class do not as quickly, is the theorising of temporality, of time.[5] The word 'childhood' evokes biological time, the time dimensions of developmental change, the biographical time of being in the younger part of the life course, chronological time, movement through life course time and through named age chunks like 'infant', 'toddler', 'teen', which vary historically and culturally. Generational time is also involved, and historical time frames it all. I would like to see more attention to these issues. I also think that we need more reflection on the differentiation of the word 'child', which covers at least 18 years by western uses, and to reflect more on all that that encompasses and glosses over.

SG Those are some challenges. Are you planning to engage actively with any of them?

BT I retired in June 2012 and plan to move on to other things, but I'll continue to take an interest in Childhood Studies.

References
[1] Thorne, B, 1993, *Gender play: Girls and boys in school*, New Brunswick, NJ: Rutgers University Press

[2] Thorne, B, 1987, Revisioning women and social change: Where are the children?, *Gender and Society* 1, 1, 85–109

[3] Thorne, B, 2009, The Chinese girls and the Pokémenon kids: Children constructing difference in urban California, in J Cole, D Durham (eds) *Figuring the future: Children, youth and globalization*, Santa Fe, NM: SARS Press

[4] Thorne, B, 2007, Crafting the interdisciplinary field of childhood studies, *Childhood* 14, 147–52

[5] Thorne, B, 2004, Theorizing age and other difference, *Childhood* 11, 403–8

TWENTY-THREE

Martin Woodhead

Martin Woodhead is Professor of Childhood Studies at the Open University, UK, where he pioneered interdisciplinary teaching in Childhood and Youth Studies. His first degree was in psychology, followed by a master's in sociology and his main research interests are in early childhood development, education and care, as well as child labour and children's rights, poverty and inequality, including theoretical and methodological contributions as well as policy-focused research. He has carried out extensive international research and is a senior member of the University of Oxford 'Young Lives' four country longitudinal study of child poverty. Professor Woodhead has contributed to several of the foundational texts in the field including 'Psychology and the cultural construction of children's needs' in *Constructing and reconstructing childhood* (James and Prout, Routledge, 1990; 1997); 'Subjects, objects or participants? Dilemmas of psychological research with children' (with Faulkner) in *Research with children: Perspectives and practices* (Christensen and James, Routledge, 2000; 2008); 'Child development and the development of childhood' in *The Palgrave handbook of Childhood Studies* (Qvortrup et al, Palgrave, 2009). He was co-editor of the journal *Children and Society* 2003–11, co-edits the *Early childhood in focus series*, and is a member of the editorial board for *Childhood* and advisory board for *Journal of Early Childhood Research*.

Sheila Greene Let me just start by asking you how you got into this area in the first place.

Martin Woodhead I think my journey into child research began even while I was still a child, especially through my attempts to make sense of the culture of a boys' grammar school in Birmingham during the 1960s. Then, while studying psychology at Manchester University I became much more reflective about my own education. That led me towards the radical educationalists of the day – such as John Holt and Ivan Illich. I drifted into research, initially in the field of child development. I started a PhD and was trying to do a very technical thing about mother–child interaction. After one year I was getting nowhere and I dumped the PhD in favour of a job at the National Foundation for Educational Research, which grounded me in doing applied research on education, with a specific focus on pre-school education for disadvantaged children, which is an area I still work on. So, by the mid-1970s I was already doing applied research around children's issues, without being very clear about where my career was heading. Then I joined the Open University in 1977 and slotted straight into the team planning a radical new course *Contemporary Issues in Education*, which was just up my street!

SG Why would you have got involved in, or become aligned with, what has been called the new paradigm of childhood studies, as a psychologist?

MW OK. That was a long journey. Throughout the 1970s and 1980s I remember feeling uncomfortable with my academic identity. It felt fine doing applied research on educational issues because nobody was asking too much about my academic discipline. I was – and still am – a member of the British Psychological Society, attended the conferences, designed and taught Open University developmental psychology courses, and so on, but was always very questioning about that paradigm. I think what was happening was a gradual emergence, through a number of experiences, of a redefining of my identity and then the gradual discovery of kindred spirits. Now what were the elements of that? First, there was my discomfort with positivist developmental psychology. You have to understand that at that time I did not really feel confident to be critical about such a huge body of highly technical scientific research, because I, in a humble sort of way, thought it must be because I am not particularly good at it! A second element was my concern about the narrow cultural paradigm embedded in most research. I have always been involved with international child development issues. Recognising the diversity of ways of being a child goes back to when I spent three months in West Africa living in villages in the early 1970s. So, the first two elements were a critique of positivist methods in developmental psychology plus a critique of the narrow construction of the child within developmental psychology. As you know, I wasn't the only psychologist uncomfortable with many aspects of the discipline. I was hugely influenced by Martin Richard's 1974 book, *The integration of the child into the social world*,[1] and especially David Ingleby's chapter 'The psychology of child psychology'.

A third element in my journey is about becoming more reflective about the way the child is positioned in families, in schools and in social policy, as well as in research. This element crystallised during the mid-1980s in the paper I found myself writing on 'Psychology and the cultural construction of children's needs'. I say 'found myself writing' advisedly, because I didn't at that time have a strong sense that I was contributing to a new paradigm. That chapter was originally published as a journal article in 1987 in the *Oxford Review of Education* before Allison James and Alan Prout picked it up for the famous *Constructing and reconstructing childhood* book. It interests me that I wrote that article completely in a vacuum. I didn't really know what I was doing, I just knew that I was troubled by something to do with the social discourse around children. After all, social policy wasn't my field. I felt I was coming at this as an outsider, but the fact that so much theory, policy and practice at that time was framed in terms of children's needs worried me and puzzled me, and that's how I came to write what at the time I almost thought of as a philosophical piece because it was an analysis of the language being used, long before I had heard of discourse analysis!

SG That was a very significant paper, it still is. You say that you almost wrote it in a vacuum – were there influences, theories, ideas that you can now say influenced you or was it your discomfort with practice and policy, as you saw it, in a very immediate way?

MW OK. My memory of it is as follows. It was a response to the discourses of the day and specifically a very influential popular book published in 1975 by Mia Kellmer-Pringle and called *The needs of children*. It was also serendipitous – I was asked by our next door neighbour at that time – the early 1980s – to do some guest lectures and tutoring in the Department of Social Policy at Cranfield University. So the paper came about through talking to social policy people about the way they thought about children, this construction of children as having 'needs'. As I think back now, it makes me wonder, what on earth was I doing doing part-time teaching in a social policy department when my core discipline was psychology and I was by then a member of the Education Faculty at the Open University? I think this provides the clue to a fourth element of my journey into childhood studies, which is about challenging traditional disciplinary boundaries. Remember I didn't just do a degree in psychology. I went on to do an MA in sociology before I began my aborted PhD research.

SG A lost cause already!

MW Yes, I guess I was a lost cause [both laugh]. I never was a pure psychologist, although I got a first class honours degree in psychology. I now realise the psychology lecturers at Manchester University were wonderfully open-minded and gave me the space to develop my somewhat eclectic and radical interests. The department was run by John Cohen who was rare at that time in taking a stand against the extremes of behaviourist psychology, including refusing to allow his students to do animal learning experiments in his lab. He used to say 'Go to the zoology department if you want to study the behaviour of rats, we are interested in human psychology here!' Those extraordinary three years at Manchester, followed by a year at Leicester doing sociology of education contributed to a certain disciplinary insecurity, but much later I began to feel the benefits and sometimes described myself as a 'boundary worker'. Incidentally, working across disciplines is still really important to me. I love being part of the Young Lives research team at Oxford,[2] it includes economists, anthropologists, sociologists, public health and social policy specialists, as well as me, a sometimes psychologist!

SG OK, so that radical or critical or subversive strand...

MW At root, I have come to recognise the power of my personal and family history, especially Quaker values about human rights and social justice, respect for the individual and for diversity, as well as international development work, and so on. A big concern about children's rights only explicitly came into my work much later, but I would now identify it as an important fifth element of my story. I wasn't self-consciously thinking about rights when I wrote the needs paper. I wrote that paper in 1987 and the UN Convention on the Rights of the Child was 1989. There was of course lots of work around children's rights going on before 1989, but it wasn't strongly on my radar. It wasn't part of my thinking, explicitly.

SG So, at what time did you recognise a coming together of like-minded individuals?

MW It's fair to say that, up until the late 1980s, I felt quite intellectually lonely. For me, a turning point was in 1986 when Judith Ennew organised a small 'Ethnography of Childhood' meeting in Cambridge, and it was the first time that I had been in the same room as a group of kindred spirits, including Allison James, Alan Prout, Jo Boyden and several others. And it was suddenly, 'Oh, we are talking the same language…and we are coming from different disciplines.' For me that was where the idea of a Childhood Studies was born, and at last I felt clear about my academic identity. I felt that I was becoming 'real' in my professional identity for the first time, as in that wonderful story *The velveteen rabbit* by Margery Williams where the Skin Horse says: 'It doesn't happen all at once…You become. It takes a long time. That's why it doesn't often happen to people who break easily, or have sharp edges, or who have to be carefully kept.'

So, I've never had intellectually sharp edges, indeed, I feel myself often a very multi-stranded or chameleon-like scholar. I guess it does all fit together and the Childhood Studies bit has given me a very core sense of what I believe and what I do. It is why I was so proud eventually to be conferred a Personal Chair in *Childhood Studies* at the OU. I have to admit even now I don't see myself as staying within even the broad boundaries of Childhood Studies. For example, several of my recent papers have been about the impact of the growth in private sector schooling on 'education for all' in countries like India.[3] In this work my root concern is about the role schools play in equity and social justice, which I guess ties closest to the child rights strand of my work.

SG So what is Childhood Studies in that case?

MW Well Childhood Studies became identified with a capital C and capital S very, very strongly in the late 1980s, 1990s and 2000s when there was this very, very clear attempt by people to establish a field that embraced study of children and childhood within academic research in a fundamentally different way, and that played out in a burgeoning of books, papers and conferences and eventually degree programmes like the BA in Childhood and Youth Studies I helped get started at the OU. All the elements we have talked about provide the underpinning for this, with at the core a very strong re-framing of the research agenda around children.

SG A lot of people have quoted the James and Prout statement of the key principles.

MW I would go along with those, yes. I have already outlined my own journey. It was that fundamental concern about the narrow frameworks of Developmental Psychology, both scientifically as a positivist regime and also in the way it constructed the child within a very, very narrow conceptualisation. It was about the way, more generally, that discourses of the child frame the child in terms of needs rather than agency or rights and it was more broadly about respecting children as participants in research, in families, in schools, in society. Of course, we inevitably got into big debates about whether we were envisaging a new discipline, or a new sub-discipline, or an interdisciplinary field. I spoke about this in my lecture to launch the OU Childhood and Youth Studies degree, drawing attention to the opportunities and dangers in a 'clearing house model' a 'pick 'n mix' model and a 'rebranding' model.[4] I could see a risk of new turf wars breaking out and I have to admit I was never very comfortable with Allison and Alan framing it as a New Sociology of Childhood, when there were historians, anthropologists, psychologists and others all contributing, including to their seminal book…but I hasten to add this was only an intellectual debate, we continued to be firm friends and allies!

It's probably worth mentioning that there were a couple of experiences around that time that fed into my thinking about children and childhood. First, I was very involved as adviser to the production of a major BBC One documentary series from 1984 to 1990. It was called 'All our children' and billed as 'The world of childhood through children's eyes'. It was incredibly ambitious, with filming from all over the globe, including tracking the early lives of babies born as far apart as Brazil, China, India, Hungary, Kenya and the UK. The series was all about international childhoods and it was about trying to get closer to the experiences of children and get children talking about their lives wherever they were and whatever their circumstances, and included programmes about all the key themes, school, child labour, play and so on. So I was doing all this TV work around the time I was doing more academic papers around children's needs, and around early childhood education as well as designing the OU Masters programme on *Child Development in Social Context*. By 1990 I had already done nearly 20 years as an academic and I have to admit that I was a bit 'burned out' when the opportunity arose to do something completely different! I was living in Sussex at that time with Judith, my wife, and our four children. We had become very involved in Rudolf Steiner, or Waldorf, education during a very fruitful year I spent as a Fulbright Fellow at High/Scope Educational Research Foundation in the USA (that's another story!). Anyway, by 1990, Judith was working as a Special Needs teacher within a specialist residential school for children with 'emotional and behavioural difficulties' and it was run according to the Rudolf Steiner philosophy. They needed house parents to run the big residential unit. So we moved in and had three extraordinary years working with a diverse group of young people from a whole variety of difficult circumstances including some with diagnosed conditions, including on the autistic spectrum. So, actually, just as Childhood Studies was getting going, and during the time that Allison and Alan were getting their book together, I was busy taking time off from being an academic and working with these very disturbed children, who presented us with a huge challenge in terms of understanding the different ways of being a child and trying to be respectful of them, but also in terms of managing their very disturbed emotions and difficult behaviour. I sometimes tend to think of these experiences as a little sideline in my life, but perhaps I ought to bring them more into the story, because this was the one period of my life I worked directly with children.

Shortly after we finished at the school, I received a phone call that took me off into another fascinating episode, a four-country study of quality in early childhood. In 1996 I published the final report of this Bernard van Leer Foundation study as a short book *In search of the rainbow*. It gave me the chance to apply so many of the concepts I'd been working with over the years to the challenge of defining quality in diverse cultures and contexts. There was a small group of scholars doing similar work at that time, notably Peter Moss, Helen Penn and Alan Pence.

As you will realise, my journey in child research feels to be more about serendipity than planning! My next project took me off in yet another direction, but a very relevant one in terms of developing the Childhood Studies paradigm. Jo Boyden asked me to join a small group working on a study of child labour in some of the poorest countries in the world, supported by Swedish Save the Children. It was a very applied piece of work and it had come about from concern about international agenda-setting about working children; the whole ILO movement to abolish child labour; worries about insensitive interventions; not respecting children's contexts, voice and ability to make judgements about their lives. This was a fabulous opportunity for me to try to figure out how to engage with 'Children's perspectives on their working lives' as the final report was called. It connected with a key principle of the Childhood Studies paradigm, namely respecting children as experts in their lives and I felt so comfortable with it, although the issue itself was anything but comfortable. It was highly contentious and at times upsetting to witness children whose work was so clearly hazardous. We were not, however, going to set up a positivist paradigm to look at its effects on their self-esteem and their cognitive outcomes, although I do acknowledge the importance of such work if done sensitively. At one level, the starting point for this research was much simpler. We want to find out from young people what they felt about having to work, the hazards they faced, the feelings of stigma or pride, how far they had choices between working and/or school, as well as their expectations about their future. So that's how we came to do that study, in Ethiopia, Bangladesh, Philippines and countries of Central America. We covered lots of different categories of child labour and piloted a whole lot of different tools for groups in order to engage non-literate young people in a way that was informative but non-threatening.[5]

I struggled for a time to know what methods to use in the child labour research and at that point I was introduced to Robert Chambers' work on participatory rural appraisal, PRA, which was already widely known in developmental studies. PRA had been developed to respect the views of communities of adults, but I thought that it 'applies just as well to children'. A lot of the techniques we used in that study, the activity games we played with the children, were based on PRA.

SG Do you have any comment on your approach to qualitative research? This term, 'participatory research', what does it mean?

MW Mmm…I think I have probably talked too loosely about 'participatory research': I am probably guilty of that. I think probably the features of participatory research, for me, at that time were fairly modest. I was still on a fairly low rung on Roger Hart's ladder of participation! Minimally, I wanted to emphasise treating the child as an informant about the issues being studied at face value rather than for interpretation. In other words, hearing what the child says and not turning it straightforwardly into 'Oh, this is a child with low self-esteem' or 'This child's moral reasoning is only at Kohlberg's Stage 3', but rather, 'This child is telling us important things about their experiences of their life.' That is a more respectful starting point for understanding the way forward in terms of intervention. I now recognise that this is not 'participatory research' in a stronger sense, like in the Children's Research Centre at the OU, where children devise the research, children plan it, children do it, children write it up. In this case we were participatory in the way we positioned children in relation to the research process, and the way we interpreted what they said, but in other respects it was actually a very adult-defined exercise. We knew why we were doing the study, we conceptualised what the issue was, we had devised the research methods, and we wrote up the report. So perhaps this work shouldn't be called 'participatory', but I still think it involved quite a big paradigm shift. I feel very confident about it. Since then I have gone on to do a lots of work in Young Lives and have helped develop the longitudinal qualitative component. For example, Laura Camfield, Gina Crivello and I have worked a lot on understanding children's feelings of well-being and finding tools to get at children's sense of well-being.[6]

SG Do questions of rigour figure largely in your thinking?

MW Yes, I am acutely aware of the weaknesses of the work I've done!

SG Do you take any particular approach to strengthening the research from that perspective?

MW I have not been a very good methodologist. I am far too pragmatic. Small sample sizes, small budgets, research done quickly, with only brief pilot studies – all the sins committed!

SG Yet this research has been productive and useful?

MW Oh yes, I think so. Through doing those studies on child labour, like with the garments workers in Dhaka, one is not trying to say that this is the definitive statement about children in Bangladesh, we are saying, 'These are the voices of a group of children who do the job you are talking about abolishing. Now we may not have a huge sample size, but it is better than anything you've done when you pontificate about their needs within a narrow child protectionist framework.' Of course we could extend it, and lots of other people have, but I think I am just very pragmatic when it comes to that sort of thing, and probably a bit restless, to move on to the next thing.

SG Do you see examples of bad practice?

MW One sees rather weak research endlessly, as well as beacons of excellence. I was *Children and Society* journal editor for nine years with Nigel Parton and then Allison James and Nigel Thomas. We had occasion to publish a few things I wish we hadn't and we rejected a whole lot more, which were very poor. For example, 'We wanted to know about bullying, so we asked a group of children about bullying and here is what they said', without any framing and without any real analysis in any deep sense. I regret that child research has spawned, at worst, some very superficial pieces, without a critical framing or theoretical context; pretty primitive stuff. There are also, however, lots of really strong studies being done, and the extent and range of work is increasing all the time. Let's celebrate the successes!

SG Do you think that developmental psychology, or a form of developmental psychology, has a place in all of this?

MW Oh yes, there is a place, some of the questions developmental psychology is asking are totally legitimate and proper. I made that point in several of my papers.[7] I have tried to put some perspective on participatory research and say 'Let's not throw the baby out with the bathwater.' If you are doing medical research on children's diseases the child is objectified because you are interested in what's going on in their body and brain. That's nothing to do with not being respectful of the child in the surgery as you would be in any human relationship, but don't let's pretend the child is a strong participant in the knowledge-producing process, although hopefully they can be the beneficiary of that knowledge.

SG So where do you think things are now? Do you think there is a coherent field of Childhood Studies?

MW If I were coming to Childhood Studies now I would feel much more confident than 20 years ago. There are handbooks of Childhood Studies, there are textbooks of Childhood Studies, there are courses in Childhood Studies, there are degrees in Childhood Studies, there are research programmes in Childhood Studies, there are people who call themselves Professor of Childhood Studies, so it must be a field! [Both laugh] Whereas, as I said at the beginning, when I embarked on all this I was terribly lacking in confidence about sticking my head above the parapet and I don't think I thought of it as a field. In terms of asking me in a more fundamental sense whether the field is clearly defined, I think that there is a huge momentum of activities around some of the core principles embedded in Childhood Studies. It is expressed, for example, in the submission rates for *Children and Society* which went up and up while I was co-editor.

SG You have written a paper for the UN on early childhood interventions and children's rights.[8] Would you see that strand of your work as part of child research? It seems to me to come from the same mind set.

MW I wouldn't have thought of it that way, but I suppose it comes from the same mind set because of its underpinning in rights and respect for children's voices. As I said, child rights was only really strongly shaping my thinking when I began the study of child labour in the late 1990s, which was all about Article 32.[9] Then being asked to do the General Comment on early childhood, I think at that point I realised that fully respecting the significance of the child rights perspective was to me one of the missing pieces of the jigsaw in our earlier formulations when we were playing with the cultural constructions of the child and the positioning of the child in research. Something was missing. There was a risk of spiralling into cultural relativism. I found embracing a human rights, a child rights perspective, that suddenly made sense, and that linking science to child rights gave a more complete picture because it gave you your grounding in values. It isn't straightforward, because child rights are contested, the UNCRC is contested, but I am a pragmatist in saying, 'This is a crucial landmark towards improving the status and wellbeing of young people, to which virtually all the nations of the world signed up.' And boy, that's a hell of a good starting point, but it's only a starting point, for trying to negotiate around some of the worst violations in a way that is respectful of diversity and so on. That has given me a real feeling of strength to speak about things and be clear about what it means to be trying to work towards better childhoods in a way which is not dogmatic, but is very open-ended but also not naively culturally relative.

SG Just maybe a few thoughts about the future.

MW Leaving aside whether Childhood Studies is getting embedded in the mainstream in Europe and America, that's an issue, but it's not the issue I worry about. What I am still very much concerned about is the imbalances in research and scholarship with the majority world in terms of the development of scholarship in this area. Childhood Studies is still a drop in the ocean in terms of really building global capacity in childhood research, and in terms of expertise around children's rights and development. There are a few exceptions, but far too few. That's a challenge for the next generation.

References and notes

[1] Richards, MPM, 1974, *The integration of a child into a social world*, Cambridge: Cambridge University Press

[2] www.younglives.org.uk

[3] Woodhead, M, Frost, M, James, Z, 2013, Does growth in private schooling contribute to Education for All? Evidence from a longitudinal, two cohort study in Andhra Pradesh, India, *International Journal of Educational Development* 33, 1, 65–73

[4] Woodhead, M, 2008, Childhood Studies: Past, present and future, in MJ Kehily (ed) *An introduction to Childhood Studies*, London: Routledge

[5] Woodhead, M, 1999, Combatting child labour: Listen to what the children say, *Childhood* 6, 1, 27–49

[6] Camfield, L, Streuli, N, Woodhead, M, 2010, Children's well-being in developing countries: A conceptual and methodological review, *European Journal of Development Research* 22, 3, 398–416

[7] Woodhead, M, 1999, Reconstructing developmental psychology, some first steps, *Children and Society* 13, pp 1–17

[8] See United Nations Committee on the Rights of the Child, *A guide to General Comment 7: Implementing child rights in early childhood,* www.ohchr.org.

[9] UNCRC (United Nations Convention on the Rights of the Child), Article 32, see www.ohchr.org/en/professionalinterest/pages/crc.aspx.

TWENTY-FOUR

Conclusions

Introduction

This book presents the ideas and perspectives of 22 high profile pioneers who have contributed to the making of the field of Childhood Studies. These key thinkers provide first-hand accounts of the evolution of ideas leading to the proclamation of a 'new paradigm' for the study of children and childhood in the early 1990s. Reflecting on the current state of the field, they examine the current tensions and dilemmas facing Childhood Studies and also highlight the critical issues with which those working and researching in this area must now engage. This final chapter summarises the experiences and perspectives of these key thinkers and thus contextualises the radical changes in theory and practice that have taken place in the study of children and childhood over the course of the last 30 years. The interviews have captured the diversity of viewpoints that characterise this coming together of scholars from a wide range of backgrounds and standpoints to form a new field. Inevitably there is evidence of difference in orientation and a variation in commitment to the project of Childhood Studies alongside a shared commitment to advancing the understanding of children and childhood.

The 22 interviews in this volume present a mixed picture, both in terms of levels of satisfaction with the current state of the field and on its perceived sustainability in the longer term. Interviewees differ in the source of their dissatisfaction, some being wedded to the value of an ongoing radical critique of all comfortable orthodoxies, including Childhood Studies, and other unhappy because of issues of research quality or lack of acceptance within the academy. In general, there is recognition of the considerable changes that have taken place during the course of the last three decades. Childhood Studies is now established in universities and colleges in many countries and there is a growing body of literature in terms of books, journal material, policy documents and applied practitioner publications. The fact that Childhood Studies now has its own section in many book shops across the world is seen as a testament to the progress and acceptance of the field. Many interviewees, but not all, also highlight the progress made in moving away from the constraints of single disciplinary approaches towards multidisciplinary and interdisciplinary work, this being evidenced by the level of integration between the humanities and social sciences in approaches to understanding and researching children and childhood compared to 30 years ago.

One unifying thread throughout the interviews is recognition of the magnitude of the global challenges facing children and childhood in the coming years. These are particularly acute for children in the majority world but cultural, political and economic conditions in the minority world are also changing childhoods, for good or ill. Notwithstanding the ongoing need for research worldwide, all interviewees acknowledge the partial and restricted views of children and childhood emanating from the current focus on minority world contexts. They are united about the need to find meaningful ways to address the current imbalance between minority world and majority world research if representative accounts of global childhoods are to be presented and understood.

A number of interviewees are more equivocal about what has been achieved and as a result pose a number of fundamental questions about whether there is a future for Childhood Studies as a cogent and distinctive field. These interviewees pose questions such as: 'Have the diversity of interests that are now incorporated under the heading of Childhood Studies become too disparate?', 'Is the field in danger of fragmentation?', 'Is Childhood Studies a product of its time and part of a phase that is coming to an end, perhaps to be replaced with new and different ways of understanding children and childhood?'

Main themes

The main themes to emerge from these interviews are presented in three sections. The first section covers the history of Childhood Studies and the emergence of the 'new paradigm' in the 1990s. The second section examines interviewees' accounts of their research practices and the methodological challenges emanating from the 'new paradigm'. The tensions and challenges facing the current field are reviewed in the third section and possible future directions for Childhood Studies are considered. Each section begins with a brief summary of the key themes and these are then explored in depth using interviewees' own words as far as possible. Where a point has been made by a particular interviewee their surname is noted in brackets.

The history of the field of Childhood Studies

The interviews in this volume show that there is no one shared and undisputed history of Childhood Studies. They also further demonstrate that interviewees' perceptions of the key ideas and events that led to the 'new paradigm' have been strongly influenced by factors such as geographical location and disciplinary perspectives. In particular, the close association often made between the 'new paradigm', 'the new sociology of childhood' and the work of UK based scholars is questioned by several interviewees on the basis that it fails to give recognition to other sociologists, other disciplines and to the range of relevant work that had been undertaken around the world from the 1970s onwards (Alanen; Corsaro; Mayall; Qvortrup; Woodhead). The picture that emerges is of clusters of innovative work being undertaken in many countries and gradual connections and networks being formed. An understanding of this history is essential to understanding the current field of Childhood Studies and why it is characterised by a range of different theoretical and methodological approaches. The question that remains is whether this multiplicity of interests is desirable and sustainable in the longer term?

The 'new paradigm' for the study of children and childhood

In tracing the evolution of ideas leading to the 'new paradigm' in the 1990s it seems that a shift in thinking about children and childhood had been 'in the air' (Frønes) and 'brewing' (Thomas) for some time. The backdrop of the 1960s civil rights movements, increasing demands for the muted voices of marginalised groups to be heard, coupled with changes in political and public discourses around children and childhood, all seem to have played a part in creating the conditions for a new paradigm to be declared and positively received (Cook; Frønes; Hart; Prout). Frønes refers to the 'countercultures' from the 1960s and believes that, 'an essential part of the new paradigm was the understanding of children as subjects and their right to a voice'. He points to the legal developments during that period and the fact that the 'old authoritarian regimes were falling everywhere', including in schools, workplaces and families. All of these created the context for demands for children's voices to be heard both within and outside the academy. In a similar vein, from a US perspective, Cook's sense of the 'new paradigm' was that it arose out of the 'social and civil movements of the 1960s' and from new ways of thinking about 'identity politics' in terms of representation and voice. Cook suggests that the 'new paradigm' emerged as a result of the convergence of generational, political and gender influences. This perspective is shared by Kellett who suggests that the work of 'feminists, generationalists, new sociologists and ethnographers created a critical mass that helped solidify the move towards this new paradigm'.

The interviews in this volume suggest that several important strands of ideas and trends fed into the new paradigm. One major influence was the work of Nordic scholars, such as Qvortrup, Bardy, Wintersberger, Sgritta (1994) and others involved with the 'Childhood as a social phenomenon' project between 1987 and 1992 (Alanen; Mayall; Qvortrup). This grouping took a macro-oriented, theoretical, comparative, intergenerational approach wherein childhood is treated as a permanent structural category on a par with adulthood (Qvortrup). Alanen refers to the work on the project as having, 'opened our eyes' not only to the idea of 'generation', but also to new concepts derived from generation like 'generational order' and 'distributive justice'.

A further strand of influence was the innovative methods of research with children being developed in many countries from the 1970s onwards. Rogers and Thomas both suggest that there were parallel developments on either side of the Atlantic and that these strands, 'eventually converged' into what is now the field of Childhood Studies. The interviews with Corsaro and Hart reveal that they were independently undertaking fieldwork and developing novel approaches in their research with children in the United States in the 1970s (Hart, 1978; Corsaro, 1985). Both were working in relative isolation without a body of literature or like-minded colleagues to consult. Hart suggests that while a 'greater interest in studying children in a cross disciplinary way has been fostered by this movement, it wasn't exactly a new paradigm'. Rather, for Hart, there was an explosion of interest among sociologists and anthropologists into what he refers to as, 'existing ways that some people already had of working with children'. Hart suggests that the pioneers simply 'gave them a collective form and name'. Corsaro had published his book *Friendship and peer culture in the early years*, in 1985, several years prior to the publication of *Constructing and reconstructing childhood* (James and Prout, 1990) in the UK. Corsaro highlights that, at that time in sociology, 'peer culture was for adolescents, nobody ever said even pre-adolescents had peer culture, let alone preschool children'. For Corsaro, the UK pioneers, 'did pretty much overlook my work' and his main influences and connections remained with colleagues in Norway, Italy and the United States.

In terms of the UK pioneers, the early work of Chris Jenks (Jenks, 1982; 1990) was seen as having been an important influence in the development of the 'new' sociology of childhood (Mayall; Prout; Thomas). Prout recalls the period between the late 1980s and mid-1990s as one where there was a gradual realisation that there were 'individuals all over the world' pursuing similar novel approaches and ideas and that these individuals began to learn about each other's work. Prout reflects on how such networks develop: 'It's capillaries, it's molecular, it's little accidents of people meeting each other and then coalescing into conferences and so on.' In a similar vein, James recalls the period prior to the 'new paradigm' as one where she was 'ploughing quite a lone furrow' in terms of her research with children in a 'very traditional anthropology department'. She recalls the excitement in the 1980s of making connections and meeting others who were thinking along similar lines and how 'gradually the whole thing began to swirl together'.

The third important set of influences and ideas which emerged during this period came from the 'embryonic "children's liberation" movements of the 1960s/1970s' (Thomas). Significant numbers of activists and organisations, in many different countries, had been lobbying for children's rights in the years leading up to the 1989 UN Convention on the Rights of the Child (Ennew; Hart; Rizzini). Kellett believes that the 'UNCRC was the watershed that led to a new paradigm'. She highlights that the work of key individuals in the UK, US and Nordic countries did not happen in isolation and that 'the replication across many countries globally acted as a catalyst'. Kellett also points to the role of NGOs in spreading the new approach to children and childhood, in particular some of the bigger organisations who were 'applying participatory methods in the field at a time when the academics were theorising in their offices'.

Reflecting on the crucial events that facilitated the making of connections between these various strands, interviewees consistently highlighted the first Ethnography of Childhood workshop organised by Judith Ennew at Cambridge in 1986 as a turning point (James; Mayall; Prout; Woodhead). That workshop was seen to have provided a forum, for the first time, where people could meet other childhood researchers, learn about each other's work and form national and international communication networks. The follow-up Ethnography of Childhood workshops in subsequent years, together with the meeting organised by Jens Qvortrup and colleagues at Billund in Denmark in 1992, were seen to have consolidated and given momentum to international collaboration (Ennew; Mayall; Prout; Qvortrup; Woodhead). It was at this series of workshops that James and Prout shared their work and forged links with those who contributed chapters to *Constructing and reconstructing childhood* (1990), this being the seminal publication which first proclaimed the emergence of a new paradigm.

As evidenced by the disciplinary backgrounds of interviewees, many disciplines, particularly in the humanities and social sciences, contributed both to the 1990s paradigm and to the continuing evolution of ideas. Consequently, not all interviewees were comfortable with the 'new paradigm' being framed as 'the new sociology of childhood'. This was in view of the fact that several of the contributors to *Constructing and reconstructing childhood* (1990) came from other disciplinary and practitioner backgrounds (Woodhead). Thomas notes that, 'Allison James and Alan Prout would rightly remind us that they did not invent but rather "proclaimed" the new paradigm' in that the 'critical ideas' they highlighted were already in existence. He suggests that the work of James and Prout put these key ideas together in a package, 'a bit like a literary critic announcing a new "movement" in poetry'. This is consistent with Prout's assessment of why the book was so successful. He suggests that it 'took a lot of the trends and thinking that had already been happening' and presented these in an accessible and condensed 'programmatic statement' that could be used in multiple contexts.

Psychology

The portrayal of psychology within the early literature of the 'new paradigm' was questioned by several interviewees. Hart suggests that it was 'unfair' for the sociological pioneers to 'so aggressively declare that Childhood Studies was entirely contrary to what psychology was about' not least when sociology and anthropology, 'had been doing so little for so long to even address children'. Burman sees the 'new paradigm' as 'simply one aspect' of a broader set of epistemological and conceptual and ethical debates that arose in the social and human sciences from the 1970s onwards and which arrived in psychology in the 1980s. She highlights that dominant mainstream psychology is only one of several psychologies and contends that many of the critiques emanating from critical psychology are highly relevant to Childhood Studies. For Burman, it is a mistake to 'privilege or scapegoat psychology as the monster that needs to be ejected or repudiated from the disciplinary debates within Childhood Studies', because she sees psychology as no more problematic than other disciplines.

Gilligan suggests that sociology has 'perhaps been excessively precious about boundary maintenance' in relation to psychology. While accepting some of the sociological critiques, because 'a lot of psychology is ridiculously de-contextualised in the way it approaches issues', Gilligan also rejects the setting up of psychology as the 'straw man'. Instead, he argues that Childhood Studies 'has to take on board ideas from anywhere that is relevant' and sees it as 'unthinkable' that psychology would not be an important dimension in 'any serious intellectual endeavour' to address contemporary issues facing children and childhood. The interviews with Prout and James clarify their thinking in relation to psychology: 'It is not that we were against psychology in the way it is crudely put these days; it was against a particular kind of psychology' (James).

In terms of the continuing evolution of ideas, there was broad agreement among interviewees that what had started as 'the new sociology of childhood' evolved into the 'new social studies of childhood', this being in recognition of the contributions of other academic disciplines and also a range of practitioners to the field. As a result of the input and interest of a growing number of disciplines, including those outside the humanities and social sciences, the field has become known as 'Childhood Studies'.

Researching children and childhood in the field of Childhood Studies

This second section offers insight into the methodological issues and dilemmas encountered by those undertaking research in the field of Childhood Studies. A deeper analysis of the interviews reveals the ways in which the biography of the researcher influences how researchers position themselves in research and in their interactions with children in the research context. What is less clear from the interviews is how researchers take account of these influences in their research work. Concepts associated with the new paradigm are discussed, such as children's 'agency', children's 'voices' and children as 'social actors', as a backdrop to the assertion that a significant change in research focus is required. Interviewees agree about the need for the field to progress into broader, deeper and more rigorous approaches to research. To this end, the parallels between Women's Studies and Childhood Studies are examined and similarities and differences noted.

The biography of the researcher

Given the range of disciplinary and professional backgrounds of those working in Childhood Studies it is not surprising that such a broad and diverse range of career and life experiences emerged in the interviews. The biography of the interviewee emerged as pivotal to understanding the different ways in which interviewees position themselves in relation to their work with children and childhood. The main influences were their personal histories, their disciplinary backgrounds and their professional practice training.

The issue of how researchers' own childhood experiences and personal histories might influence and affect their work has received scant attention in the literature to date. 'I think the question of what we bring from our own experience of childhood into those encounters is an interesting one and one that people don't really talk about very much' (Thomas). In these interviews several interviewees mentioned their own experiences as children and young people as having been influential in their approaches to working with children (Alanen; Corsaro; Ennew; Frønes; Rizzini; Thorne; Woodhead). For some, particular events and transitions in their childhood and during their teenage years had made an impact. Alanen refers to her experience of moving country at the age of seven and how the challenges she encountered 'made me think that nothing in a child's life is necessarily simple'. Ennew shares her experience of teenage rebellion, leaving school early and being an unmarried teenage mother. She links her early experiences to her ability to relate to people 'of any age or gender who are scared, powerless, puzzled and don't know where the next meal is coming from'. Four interviewees mentioned insights gleaned from their 'working-class' backgrounds (Corsaro; Ennew; Frønes; Hart). The religious traditions within which they had grown up were significant for three interviewees (Rizzini; Thorne; Woodhead). In reflecting on influences in his career Woodhead recognises the power of his personal and family history, 'especially Quaker values about human rights and social justice, respect for the individual and for diversity, as well as international development work'. Thorne grew up in a Mormon community surrounded by lots of children and cross-age relationships and contact. This was significant not only in terms of preparation for research with children but also, 'because I had so many models of old people, I had so many in my world. It was much less age segregated.'

The disciplinary backgrounds of interviewees included anthropology, sociology, psychology, politics, philosophy, statistics, education, social work, communications, geography and history. Several of the interviewees were also professionally qualified: five were social workers (Frønes; Gilligan; Kellett; Mayall; Thomas); three were teachers (Alderson, Kellett, Mayall) (two were both social workers and teachers) and two were psychotherapists (Burman; Rogers). Without exception, practitioners saw their professional qualifications as enhancing their knowledge and communication skills with children in research. Thomas recalls the 'key moment' in his research career as being when he gave himself permission to 'start using some of the skills and techniques and tricks that I have used as a social worker' and stopped being 'a researcher in a suit'.

Routes into the field also varied with most engaging in research with children at postgraduate rather than undergraduate level. Some interviewees had come to work with children as a continuation of their research interests in topics related to children and childhood (Christensen; Cook; Corsaro; Hart; Hendrick; James; Prout); others had arrived through a more political or social activist route (Alanen; Ennew; Thorne; Rizzini) and/or had first been introduced to the area through campaigning and voluntary work (Alderson; Gilligan; Moss). Alderson refers to her first research project, aimed at changing the poor practices she had experienced as a new mother on a maternity ward, as 'probably the best piece of research I have ever done'. During his student years Moss became involved, as a volunteer, in a campaign to liberate children from the 'really appalling places' known at that time as 'sub-normality hospitals'. It was through 'that involvement and campaigning' that Moss met and began working with Jack Tizard who set up the Thomas Coram Research Unit in 1973 in London. Rizzini started work as a young psychologist in Brazil during a 'very violent military dictatorship from 1964 to 1984'. She recalls 'putting my life at risk' by informing journalists of the 'maltreatment of children in institutions', yet feeling compelled to do so because of what she had observed.

The academic backgrounds of interviewees were important in a number of respects not least because they provided the foundation for their research training. All interviewees had been introduced to quantitative methods as part of their undergraduate study, but there was considerable variation in terms of the emphasis, type and number of courses completed. Several interviewees described their training as highly quantitative (Alanen; Frønes; Rogers; Qvortrup). In terms of qualitative research, although a minority had undertaken qualitative courses as undergraduate and postgraduate students, the majority of interviewees described themselves as being 'self-taught'. The exception to this was the experience of Thorne who described her postgraduate qualitative training as 'fantastic'. The same pattern was evident in relation to research with children where none of the interviewees had attended specific training courses before starting in the field. Instead, interviewees reported transferring their research skills from working with adult groups to research with children (Alanen; Burman; Mayall; Rogers; Thorne; Qvortrup), drawing on their personal and professional practice experience of working with children (Alderson; Frønes; Gilligan; Kellett; Mayall; Thomas) and/or 'learning on the job' (Corsaro; Hart; James; Prout; Moss).

Different methodological approaches

Interviewees resisted drawing a sharp distinction between quantitative and qualitative methods or placing them in opposition to each other. Both quantitative and qualitative approaches were seen as important in contributing to topics within the field and building multi-layered perspectives. Differences in opinion among interviewees occurred in terms of the emphasis placed on quantitative or qualitative approaches, on preferences for multi-method and life course perspectives (Christensen; Frønes; Gilligan) and the extent to which children and young people should be involved in the research process (Ennew; Kellett; Thomas). A strong argument put forward for large-scale work and statistics is that these are seen as vital in gaining the attention of governments, power brokers and policy makers and thus potentially having a direct impact on children's lives (Alderson; Ennew; Qvortrup). For Qvortrup, accounting for children in statistical terms is one way of making children visible rather than children being 'hidden behind family or fathers and mothers and households and so on'. Other approaches were favoured depending on the topic of study. Frønes notes that although there have been a large number of smaller qualitative studies which 'brought to the surface knowledge of different groups' they provided scant information 'on the relationship between the situation when you are one, four, ten and twenty years old'. Frønes sees life course analysis as 'the most fruitful perspective' for his research which focuses on opportunity structures and inequality, because it offers 'the best way to understand children's lives, as related to family, social class, background, ethnicity, and yet at the same time, keep the perspective of childhood'. Gilligan notes his increasing scepticism about the value of one-off contact research with children and suggests that 'we need to think much more in longitudinal terms or life-course terms' rather than focusing on one point in time. Reflecting on current concern about research funding, Kellett argues that 'if you cut out the middle man you are going straight to the children and young people'. For Kellett, involving children and young people in the generation of knowledge and collection of data not only addresses funding and resource issues, but also provides 'a more authentic understanding' of children's lives. The need to involve children and young people is echoed by Ennew who aims to 'reach big enough samples' so as to produce high quality statistics and who also advocates teaching children how to interpret and analyse data.

Although almost all interviewees had conducted empirical research with children at some point in their careers some no longer did so. Several interviewees now concentrated on analysis of texts (Burman; Cook) or focused on theoretical development (Alanen; Hendrick; James; Prout).

Ethnography and qualitative research

Concern about quality, rigour and reflexivity in qualitative research was particularly evident in the interviews with three pioneering children's ethnographers (Christensen; Corsaro; Thorne). Christensen expresses concern about how even writing in an ethnographic style is now criticised by some colleagues in Childhood Studies as unnecessary and 'nonsense'. While she agrees that 'there has been too much qualitative work that has not gone into the necessary depth', Christensen is proud of her work and the reception it receives across a range of different disciplines and geographical boundaries. Christensen sets herself high standards, 'in order to get the necessary depth and insight because I truly want to understand children's perspectives as best as I can'. Corsaro emphasises that ethnography is a 'rigorous, long-term, intensive kind of research' and rejects the idea that qualitative research is 'soft' and that only hard sciences are rigorous – 'Wasn't Michelangelo pretty rigorous and he wasn't a physicist?' However, he is also concerned about the misuse of the term 'ethnography' in studies where 'people do ten interviews' or undertake observations for a very short period of time because 'that's not ethnography'. In terms of research paradigms, Corsaro does not see the need to 'constantly fight the battle between interpretive science and positivistic science' and instead sees them as making different assumptions rather than necessarily being in opposition. He argues, however, that qualitative researchers must stand up for what they believe in, even in multi-method research: 'That doesn't mean you can't do multi-method research, but you have to stay truthful to your assumptions.' Thorne defines herself as an 'ethnographic, qualitative sociologist'. She stresses the importance of qualitative researchers being systematic, 'careful about evidence and inference', and the need 'to understand epistemological variation and ways of knowing'. Thorne contends that 'all knowledge is situated and we need many tools' and suggests that a 'lot of energy is wasted in false debates'. She recognises the contribution of those who, for example, conduct surveys about the percentage of children living in poverty and acknowledges that her methods cannot produce such data, 'but I can tell you about how people cope with poverty, and live it'.

There was uniform agreement within the interviews that, following the 1990s paradigm and the focus on children as active participants in research, there had been a marked trend towards small-scale qualitative studies presenting children as social actors. However, interviewees, from across the continuum of quantitative and qualitative research, were unequivocal that such studies had now reached saturation point in terms of their contribution to the field (Alanen; Christensen; Cook; Frønes; James; Prout; Qvortrup). Several of the interviewees were past or present editors of high profile journals such as *Childhood* and *Children and Society* (Alanen; Cook; Frønes; Rizzini; Qvortrup; Thomas; Thorne; Woodhead). Strong comments were made about the boring, repetitive nature of many of the papers submitted, presenting small-scale studies of children as active participants and competent social actors. The lack of paradigmatic framing, theoretical context or critical thinking in many of the papers meant that data were often simply presented as 'children's voices' without interpretation or deeper analysis. Alanen, an editor of *Childhood*, commented that 'there is very little progress to be seen'. She questioned whether this was linked to the types of students working in the field which often attracts those from applied fields such as early childhood, education, child welfare and social work, who have an obligation towards children's best interests and are sometimes 'so over-interested that they are not critical anymore'. Hendrick also noted that Childhood Studies students tend to be young women from education and other applied courses. He was curious that this was the case 'even at Linkoping' during his many years of postgraduate teaching in Sweden, a country often associated with 'being so gender-friendly'. For Hendrick, Childhood Studies has a status issue in the academy similar to that of paediatrics and gerontology in medicine and this is one of the reasons why he is pessimistic about the viability of the field in the longer term. Thorne echoed his concern about the status of Childhood Studies in academia, noting that it does not have any natural advocates: unlike other oppressed groups, children aren't academics.

Several interviewees were sceptical about the idea that simply presenting what children say equates with giving children a 'voice'. This was on the basis that children, like adults, say different things to different people according to the context and that what children do not or cannot say is sometimes more significant than their verbal interactions (Cook; Corsaro; Ennew; Frønes; Rogers). Rizzini highlights 'giving children a voice' as an idea with which she struggles. She suggests that the issue is 'not about giving someone a voice' but rather asking 'why society does not listen and does not want to be disturbed by the way children question things'. The work of Rogers also highlights the complexities around the notion of the 'voice of a child'. From a Lacanian, psychoanalytic perspective, Rogers explains the 'interpretive poetics method' that she has developed over a period of years. She developed this method so as to 'really listen' for what Rogers calls 'the unsayable', the tacit knowledge that children have and how they find ways to express themselves, indirectly and often not in words. Ennew completely rejects the notion of children's 'voices' and argues: 'In today's mistaken political and academic context children have "voices" but only adults have opinions.' Ennew contends that until there is recognition that children 'are not just decorative additions to political life, their human rights will continue to be violated, often by the very people who think they are helping'. From his perspective as a current editor of the journal *Childhood*, Cook was clear that, 'we do not need any more work demonstrating to us that children have voice and agency'. Instead Cook, like several other interviewees, argued that we need to move to another level of analysis and to in-depth consideration of issues such as the conditions under which agency is produced, enhanced and constrained (Alderson; Christensen; James; Mayall; Prout, Thomas).

Children's agency

For Prout the contribution of the 1990s paradigm was that it brought the idea of children's agency to the fore. Prout acknowledges that, 'too much of the literature' has turned the idea that children might have agency into a statement 'children do have agency', rather than grasping that it is actually a way of looking – 'it is a question not a given answer'. He therefore stresses the need to 'move beyond noticing children's agency to unpacking how that agency comes into existence'. This theme arises in several interviews (Christensen, Cook, Hendrick, Kellett). Christensen offers a detailed example of agency in relation to a young child and differentiates between children's individual and collective agency. Kellett offers helpful distinctions between children as social actors, agency and children's voice – concepts that are sometimes fudged and confused within the Childhood Studies literature. Burman cautions that there is no single answer to questions about agency. For Burman, recognising who is asking questions about structure and agency and for what purposes is essential. Thomas believes that discussions about agency, 'sometimes cloak an ambiguity' about meaning. He suggests there are two kinds of questions about agency that work on 'different conceptual levels although they often resemble each other'. There is an 'ontological/epistemological question about how we understand agency and the relationship with social structure', and there are also 'practical/empirical questions about how much freedom of action children have in actuality'. For Thomas, until a clear distinction is drawn between these two types of questions, the debate about children's agency is 'unlikely to make much progress'.

There was wide agreement among interviewees that the concept of agency has to be understood within the structure–agency debate which has been at the heart of sociological theorising for many decades (Giddens, 1979). Mayall acknowledges that the issue of 'how do you inter-relate agency and structure' is 'not easy' but suggests that it is possible to examine what is meant by agency and 'how far does it include structure and just what are the interrelations between the large-scale and the small-scale?' From a critical realist perspective, Alderson presents a powerful case for how both agency and structure can be reconciled into an interdisciplinary model in Childhood Studies. Using feminism as an example, Alderson argues that, notwithstanding structural inequalities, 'feminism couldn't possibly be understood without knowing how women perceived and experienced it'. Similarly, while recognising how structural factors have an impact on children's lives, 'childhood cannot be understood without understanding how children perceive and experience it'. For Alderson, agency and structures cannot be 'split apart' and must be understood in relation to each other.

Parallels between Women's Studies and Childhood Studies

Feminist scholars, literature and debates had been very influential in the work of six interviewees (Alderson; Alanen; Burman; Mayall; Rogers; Thorne). Thorne had become involved as an activist in the anti-Vietnam War movement. This initially led to her work in Women's Studies and subsequently, to her interest in children's experiences of gender: 'I came at it very much through feminism and through the connection of women to children.' Rogers early work with Carol Gilligan and others at Harvard, 'certainly came from within feminism and the idea of listening to women's and girls' voices'. Mayall explains how insights from the 'writings by people like Ann Oakley and Dorothy Smith' have helped her 'understand what we are doing when we are carrying out research with children'. Other interviewees placed less emphasis on feminism, but did recognise it as having been one of the influential emancipatory movements that subsequently moved into the academy and paved the way for the new paradigm of the 1990s to be proclaimed (Frønes; Hendrick; Prout).

What is striking about these views is that, notwithstanding the links several interviewees made between Women's Studies and Childhood Studies, attempts to examine the parallels between the two fields have remained largely at the margins of Childhood Studies (Alanen; Mayall). Alanen recalls conversations during her student days with other 'socialist feminists' who saw class and gender as critical issues, but 'they did not see anything wrong with children and childhood'. Mayall specifically refers to Alanen's PhD in 1992 which 'drew on lessons from feminism to understand child–adult relations'. She also reflects on the feminist literature that indicates that 'women themselves are a bit wary of taking on children and childhood' and suggests that perhaps the initiative needs to come from childhood people 'who are willing to learn from feminism'. Mayall recognises some of the difficulties if the argument is made that 'childhood is oppressed by adulthood', because 'the notion of adults controlling childhood' is an uncomfortable message for adults to contemplate and may therefore encounter resistance. Alderson gives an insightful account of some of the reasons why the relationship between feminism and childhood is complex and thinks it is 'quite deeply psychological'. She notes that most 'childhood researchers are women' and most would see themselves as 'feminists' and perhaps 'feel a deep split between their feminism and their loyalty to themselves and childhood'. An added complication for Alderson is that, whereas feminism has a 'simple indisputable aim' that men and women should be equal, the aim of Childhood Studies is not so straightforward because the notion of equality between adults and children 'is enormously difficult, complicated and confusing – it is not a simple thing'.

While critical of feminism on a number of counts, Hendrick is 'impressed by the way it has moved politically and intellectually'. Hendrick argues that feminists 'recognised from the earliest days that they were involved in politics' and that this 'helped to direct feminism and kept it within a political framework'. He does not see this political awareness in Childhood Studies where those working in the field 'don't seem interested in politics' and there is no 'immediate connecting thread' with the outside world. Hendrick also notes that the interests between women and children are 'often intertwined' and that this 'clash between two sets of interests is something Childhood Studies should address'. Hendrick questions why Childhood Studies has not examined children's claims for recognition when the claims of other groups, such as 'women, gays and lesbians, ethnic groups, and disability groups are met, usually with consequences for children?'

Burman reflects on the demise of Women's Studies and the possible parallels with Childhood Studies. She recognises 'the good reasons' for the transition from women's studies into sexuality studies, gender studies and queer studies because of the 'danger of creating another kind of abstraction, ideal type, prototype, normalising orthodoxy that was exclusionary in its own way'. Burman notes the concern of some international childhood researchers about 'models of childhood that get re-inscribed as normative and prototypical' and the current 'quite lively debates' around this issue. Burman points out that, in the same way that the category of 'woman' 'came to be challenged for instituting or justifying certain normalisations and corresponding exclusions around who is qualified as the prototypical woman', this could also happen with 'child' and 'children' in Childhood Studies. Consequently, Burman argues that methodologically and conceptually the debates about intersectionality, 'that have come to preoccupy gender/feminist theory and research' are highly relevant to Childhood Studies.

From a US perspective, Thorne sees women's studies as having established a strong hold in academia. She notes that feminists have been well organised and, despite an 'anti-feminist' backlash, gender studies is 'huge' and 'still strong' in US sociology. Thorne points out that in gender and women's studies there was a 'political impetus to reach outside departments' and to link with and support other feminist scholars. She recalls that 'we knew where the feminists were and we got together and we created interdisciplinary ties and we created courses together'. Thorne observes that there is 'nothing quite like that for Childhood Studies and I don't think there ever will be'. Thorne sees this as significant in Childhood Studies because although 'we are advocating for a group that we care a lot about', the field does not have, 'that extra edge of a political movement' because it does not have members of the group 'in there fighting' in the same way as Women's Studies. 'We are all former children but we will never have 14-year-olds ganging up to force Berkeley to have a Childhood Studies programme!' (Thorne)

The current field and possible future directions

This third section reviews the current state of the field and possible future directions. A number of key questions were raised in Chapter One about whether there are agreed definitions and boundaries in the field of Childhood Studies. What emerges from these interviews is that no clear definitions or boundaries presently exist and that Childhood Studies can best be understood as an umbrella term for a multiplicity of theoretical and methodological approaches.

For some interviewees, children and childhood are their central focus and disciplinary interests are secondary. Disciplinary boundaries are seen to limit and constrain the collaboration required to comprehensively address issues relevant to children and childhood in an increasingly complex global environment. Other interviewees, while dissatisfied with how their disciplines have approached children and childhood, remain firmly embedded in their disciplinary base. Childhood Studies is seen as an important field to which they wish to contribute, but it does not define or boundary their work.

In terms of the future, the priority for some interviewees is the need to build a coherent field that can contain the multiplicity of interests and approaches and yet be sufficiently unified to face current and future threats and challenges. Conversely, some interviewees do not have a strong attachment to the field of Childhood Studies either in terms of their own professional identity or their investment in the future of the field. Children and childhood are uniformly seen as important topics for research, but some interviewees are not overly concerned about whether such research remains within the field of Childhood Studies or evolves in different ways and under other headings.

Multiplicity of approaches

The theoretical and research interests of interviewees in this book demonstrate that Childhood Studies comprises a complex and diverse grouping with significant variations in emphasis among experienced high profile academics working in the field. What is important is that fundamental differences between interviewees were apparent as to: 1) whether the research focus should be on children, childhood or both; 2) the perceived importance of disciplinary boundaries; 3) whether the field should now prioritise paradigmatic and theoretical issues; or, conversely, 4) whether it is time for the field to gravitate towards less theoretical strands such as applied practice and children's rights.

The strength of their disciplinary identity, their theoretical and research interests and practitioner agendas all influenced the ways in which interviewees situated themselves within the current field. There was a continuum ranging from those who positioned themselves very firmly within Childhood Studies (Christensen, James, Kellett; Mayall) to others who described themselves as being on the borders of Childhood Studies (Burman; Ennew; Hendrick; Rizzini; Rogers), most of whom drew or identified with other cognate fields such as psychoanalytic studies. One exception was Moss who prefers to think in philosophical rather than disciplinary terms and therefore finds it difficult to locate his work within the parameters of any one discipline or any single field.

The difference in disciplinary emphasis was particularly apparent in discussions about the role of sociology vis-à-vis Childhood Studies. Some sociologists feared that the loss of a clear sociological base underpinning Childhood Studies will lead the field away from what is seen as its original mission – to develop a sociology of childhood which can make inroads and gain mainstream recognition in the wider discipline of sociology. This view was particularly strong among sociologists whose pioneering work is macro-oriented and who consider intergenerational relations to be fundamental to the field (Alanen; Qvortrup).

In contrast, those interviewees particularly associated with the 'new sociology of childhood' in the UK placed less emphasis on the centrality of sociology as the core discipline. While acknowledging the development of a sociology of childhood as important, Prout has 'moved away' from seeing it as a 'discipline bound task' towards an 'openness to multidisciplinary and interdisciplinary thinking around childhood'. Prout explains what he sees as some of the limitations of modernist sociology and argues that twentieth-century sociology cannot simply be recycled into Childhood Studies. James sees Childhood Studies as an 'interchange' where the conceptual focus is children and childhood and disciplinary interests are secondary. James states that she contributes what she can as an anthropologist to a particular topic but also acknowledges that 'in order to answer the whole question' she needs to include people from other backgrounds. She is concerned about what she sees happening in some cases, whereby children 'have become a vehicle for disciplinary objectives' so that disciplinary considerations are primary and the focus on children and childhood is secondary. A further issue for James is that 'the applied children's rights side has become very powerful and very strong'. While acknowledging the value of practitioner based work, James sees it as a 'particular kind of job' and questions whether it should be included in the 'same bundle of activities as a more academic Childhood Studies'.

Those from disciplines and backgrounds other than sociology represented a diverse grouping who positioned themselves in a number of ways. Childhood Studies, while recognised as important, was just one aspect of their work. Rogers considers her work to be at the 'edge of Childhood Studies and psychoanalysis' and sees 'some of the most exciting work' being undertaken by people 'who are pushing the field outside of sociology and into very new directions'. Rogers does not see Childhood Studies as a 'settled field'. Instead she sees it as a 'field of the future' that will allow different disciplines 'to take up a common enquiry about children's experiences, or children's subjectivity, or children's experiences in cultural contexts' in ways that cannot be imagined by many working in the field. Burman also considers herself to be at the borders of Childhood Studies. She believes it would be unhelpful to have a grand narrative about children and childhood because 'it would immediately become oppressive and coercive and normalising'. Burman believes that Childhood Studies is 'necessarily going to be quite patchy and disparate' and is interested in how this can lead to 'helpful and inspiring conversations with people who work in massively different areas'.

Gilligan is clear that the focus of the field, 'isn't just the intellectual pursuit of ideas', but rather is about gaining knowledge that will 'benefit and have an impact on the reality of children's lives' not just in minority countries, but globally. For Gilligan there is a danger 'that the club of scholars is far too exclusive' and may not be 'sufficiently related to real world issues' or to the everyday experiences of children, parents, teachers and other practitioners who 'play out the realities of children's lives in so many ways, day in and day out'. He suggests that there 'are a lot of unacknowledged vacant spaces at the table of Childhood Studies' and that more scholars from different linguistic, cultural and economic backgrounds need to be included. Kellett, one of the key advocates for applied children's rights, highlights the important work being undertaken by NGOs and fieldworkers who are embedded in the contexts in which they research and are best placed to bridge language difficulties. Kellett argues that the strengths of applied practice projects are their evidence base and 'on the ground' accounts of majority world contexts. From this perspective, a shift away from the focus on debating the theoretical nature of children and childhood towards applied practice and children's rights is seen as important in order to access and disseminate majority world findings (Kellett).

The main threats currently facing the field were seen to be economic and political. It was noted that the economic, political and public mood prevailing at the time of the 1990s paradigm has shifted (Corsaro; James; Kellett; Moss). Crises in terms of world debt, ecology, energy and food shortages are now to the fore and the ongoing economic crisis has immediately seen a drastic change in the availability of research funding (Corsaro; James; Mayall; Moss; Prout; Rizzini). Against this backdrop and given a generally more conservative climate, some interviewees questioned whether there might be a backlash against the children's rights movement (Kellett; Prout). Moss identifies a major challenge to all disciplines in all fields, including Childhood Studies, in terms of how to 'nurture a resistance movement' to the 'rampant and powerful neo-liberal political and economic regime into which everything is being sucked' and which he sees as 'extraordinarily damaging and catastrophic to us and our planet'. Moss highlights the dual nature of the task in terms of both sustaining a resistance movement and moving towards 'a much more plural and democratic politics of education and childhood'. He also argues the need for Childhood Studies, on a larger scale, to 'engage with the magnitude of the crises facing us as a species' and he is adamant 'that survival and flourishing is the challenge facing children today and children tomorrow'.

Disciplinary, multidisciplinary, interdisciplinary

The question of whether Childhood Studies is a distinct field, a multidisciplinary field or an interdisciplinary field of inquiry has been examined in the literature over the course of the last decade (Woodhead, 2003; Prout, 2005; James, 2010). As noted in Chapter One, the terms 'multidisciplinary' and 'interdisciplinary' are not clearly defined within academia, but, rather, are terms that are used in various ways both within and across disciplines, sometimes interchangeably. Prout (2005, 145) notes that the 'potential advantages of interdisciplinarity are widely accepted in contemporary academic circles not least because the 'cross-disciplinary gaze is more likely to detect and correct the naive assumptions to which monodisciplinary work is vulnerable'. However, Prout also notes that, 'even if there is agreement that Childhood Studies should move towards interdisciplinarity, it is far from clear how this should be accomplished (Prout, 2005, 145).

A clear message from these interviews is that rather than being a new discipline or sub-discipline, Childhood Studies is viewed as a broad multidisciplinary field in that the conceptual focus and centre of analysis is children and childhood (Corsaro; Gilligan; James; Kellett; Prout; Rogers; Thomas; Thorne). The multi-disciplinary nature of Childhood Studies, in terms of contributions from a range of disciplines, is seen by some interviewees both as a defining feature of the field and as one of its strengths in comparison to single disciplinary approaches (Corsaro; James; Prout; Kellett).

Kellett views Childhood Studies as a 'distinct field' but prefers to think of 'Childhood and Youth Studies'. She describes it in this way because 'no other single discipline can authentically convey what it is to be a child because childhood itself is multi-faceted'. Kellet argues that it is multidisciplinary because 'discrete disciplines' which have their own 'discrete methods and approaches' combine to 'create new understandings' which are far more powerful than individual disciplinary perspectives. Gilligan believes that he has been 'enriched by international contact' and also by taking a multidisciplinary approach and not being 'too narrowly focused on my own discipline'. He likes to 'look over the hedge to see what is going on elsewhere' and sees limitations in 'staying too much inside your own paradigms or your own frameworks'. For Gilligan the ultimate test of what is important is how ideas, theories, and approaches have had an 'impact on the experience of children's lives, or the experiences children have in their lives and on the contexts in which children live their lives'.

Corsaro views the field as 'multidisciplinary' in that it attracts people 'from different fields and different angles' but 'I don't see much interdisciplinarity in childhood.' Similarly, Rogers suggest that at the moment Childhood Studies is 'more multidisciplinary than truly interdisciplinary', largely because 'fields have not learned terribly well yet to speak to one another'. Her hope for the field in the future is that it will allow different disciplines to work in ways 'that we don't even imagine right now because most of us have been trained within a similar field'. Frønes sees the 'new paradigm' as having been 'a sociological endeavour' rather than offering an 'interdisciplinary perspective' and suggests that what is now needed is 'interdisciplinarity; that is, the coming of different perspectives and methods'. Moss considers interdisciplinarity 'extraordinarily important' to the extent that he finds it 'very difficult' to locate himself within a particular discipline. Being aware that different paradigms see things very differently is crucial for Moss so that people are conscious of choosing their paradigmatic positioning rather than 'pretending that they are just adopting the only way possible to think about a subject'.

While recognising the strengths of interdisciplinary work, Alanen sees detachment from core disciplines as a potential problem for the field and emphasises that 'you can't be interdisciplinary without a strong base in a discipline'. Her concern is that Childhood Studies is moving towards a situation where 'we all form our own circles and work only with other childhood researchers' which she sees as limiting both theoretically and methodologically. Similarly, Qvortrup cautions that 'interdisciplinary cannot simply mean a melting pot for anything; it must have an agreement of approach'.

Drawing on her personal experience, Thorne acknowledges some of the difficulties in 'cross-disciplinary collaboration'. She also, however, attests to some of the 'meaningful cross-disciplinary collaborations that happen as people find one another', as it is in these interdisciplinary spaces that some of the most 'creative breakthroughs' in knowledge take place. She comments on the 'intellectual policing' she has experienced in her own career and her dislike of what she sees as 'disciplinary chauvinism'. While identifying herself as a sociologist, Thorne enjoys being in 'interdisciplinary spaces and having legitimacy for singing whatever song feels like the right song'.

The importance of interdisciplinary work was stressed by most of the interviewees both as a way of developing the field and engaging with the increasingly complex issues relevant to children and childhood. However, it was acknowledged that existing institutional structures are not conducive to interdisciplinary collaboration and that the development of interdisciplinary work therefore often requires individuals to find ways of working across disciplinary borders despite institutional and budgetary constraints. Rizzini agrees that the 'idea of interdisciplinarity is a good one', but points out that 'the structures and grants for research continue to be fragmented and absolutely connected to certain interests'. She argues that structural and budgetary constraints often mean that it is not possible to 'do things together in a real way'. There was some evidence of creative and pioneering work beyond the humanities and social sciences with colleagues from fields such as medicine, architecture and chemistry (Alderson; Christensen; Rizzini). Overall, however, there was still limited evidence of interdisciplinary work within Childhood Studies and this was widely seen as an area in need of prioritisation and development (Corsaro; Frønes; James; Moss; Prout; Rogers; Thomas; Thorne).

The future of the field

There was a wide spectrum of opinions about the viability of the field of Childhood Studies and possible future directions. Hendrick is pessimistic about the future of Childhood Studies due to the failure of the field to address fundamental political questions, to create a 'political agenda' and to establish a 'political presence'. Alanen asserts that the field has become stagnant, theoretically and methodologically. Like Hendrick, she advocates that Childhood Studies should be engaging with the major debates within social science and bringing those issues into Childhood Studies as well as taking Childhood Studies into those debates. For Qvortrup, 'fragmentation is the really big danger' if the field continues with the current emphasis on the plurality and diversity of childhoods and small-scale studies. He sees this as the 'crux of the matter' and believes that if the focus of the field is not 'intergenerational' then 'Childhood Studies does not have a future.' Thomas believes that 'the move to intergenerationality as a focus of study' is important and, 'may even prefigure a fundamental shift in the field'. James is concerned about what she sees as the current trend towards 'less theoretical work' and also highlights the lack of research funding as a crucial issue.

The need to link empirical work and theory, as in the natural sciences, is a strong theme in the interviews with Alanen, Corsaro, Frønes and Hendrick. Science, 'must not be remote from real lives' according to Frønes, who sees the challenges for the field as 'interdisciplinarity, reflexivity and being useful for children, families and practitioners'. Relevance and the imperative to address the reality of children's lives globally are echoed in the interviews with Ennew, Gilligan, Hart, Kellett, Rizzini. All argue for a broadening of the community of childhood scholars, not just in the minority world, by recognising the important work being undertaken in the majority world by activists and practitioners.

Hart is confident that regardless of the structure adopted for Childhood Studies in universities, the field will 'survive as a significant interdisciplinary field of study because it has shown its worth'. Rizzini describes herself as 'optimistic and realistic' in that changes do not 'happen overnight' and 'persistence and continuity' are essential. She is open to a new field emerging and stresses that because 'new paradigms' cannot remain 'fixed for ever', it is important to 'allow new waves, new movements' which allow for 'fresh or refreshed' ideas to be considered. Christensen similarly rejects the idea that the 'field is dying' and emphasises the importance of interdisciplinary collaboration and research to enable the field to develop in new directions. Mayall predicts that the development of children as researchers will be a continuing trend. She argues that, paradoxically, it may be in countries where children are recognised as 'productive workers' that children constructing and undertaking research projects will be more accepted than in minority world contexts. The development of children as researchers was also a strong theme for Ennew, Kellett and Thomas. Kellett notes the range of different perspectives in the current field and cautions that if people 'start to disagree too much' and go into 'silos and camps', they run the risk of ultimately destroying the field. She is positive about the future of the field and believes it should be concentrating on 'children's lives and experiences' and furthering their 'well-being'. Rogers believes that 'the field of the future is something that is very difficult for us and even our generation to imagine'. Rather than encouraging upcoming young scholars to 'follow in a path we have already made', Rogers emphasises the importance of allowing the next generation of scholars 'to make their own way in a way that is truly original and will meet the sense and the needs of the future'.

Global childhoods

Without exception interviewees acknowledged the need to address the current imbalance between minority world and majority world research. Finding and improving strategies for supporting and collaborating with majority world scholars was also seen as essential. According to Gilligan 'we are much too preoccupied with the realities of children in the minority world'. He argues that the vast majority of children live in majority world countries 'and the realities, experiences and the positive and negative aspects of those lives' are not sufficiently reflected in Childhood Studies. The focus and location of minority world researchers means that 'it is difficult to cultivate' local research expertise in majority world contexts (Gilligan, Chapter 10 in this volume). Woodhead, who has experience of undertaking research in Ethiopia, Bangladesh, Philippines and countries of Central America, also highlights the development of scholarship in the majority world as a major concern. In terms of progress he notes that 'we are still a drop in the ocean' in terms of building capacity in 'any area to do with expertise around children'. Prout raises questions about Asia, China, Australasia, South America and other areas where childhood scholars have 'not been included as much as they should have been'. He urges the next generation of western scholars to be international in their thinking, to make contacts, to engage with perspectives 'from these newly emerging parts of the world' and to publish in their journals.

A particular difficulty highlighted is that majority world scholars are rarely encouraged or trained to undertake work that builds indigenous theories of childhoods in their own countries (Hart; Rizzini). In Hart's experience students often attend a minority world university, immerse themselves in the theories and methods from western contexts and apply them when they return to their own country. For Hart 'this is a dangerous intellectual hegemony in the study of childhood that needs to be corrected'. Minority world researchers 'need to get their hands dirty in the Global South' according to Ennew. Having worked in almost one hundred countries as an activist and an academic, Ennew believes that the best scholars she ever met were in Africa – people from the South who had trained in the North but were dedicated to their work in the South. She explains that is why she is 'cosied up in the South' in terms of her own research, because she is committed to developing models that work for children in the Global South rather than using models that are 'imposed from the North'. In terms of positive models Kellett points to the 'good research and fieldwork' that emanates from NGOs who are 'very close to the action in the native language', yet are able to disseminate their findings through English-speaking staff. She points to the work of Shier (2010) in Nicaragua as one such example. Kellett suggests that applied research has not always been sufficiently valued by some academics and argues that this needs to change so as to provide a sufficient 'dissemination platform' for majority world findings. For Kellett a move towards less theoretical and more applied research 'in terms of the overall balance' may well be part of the future direction of the field, if the deficit of majority world research studies is to be significantly addressed.

Rizzini as a minority world scholar based in Brazil is very clear that she cannot speak for 'the South'. She points out that there are multiple ways of thinking and that although she can, 'to some extent', speak about 'this continent' her views are always partial. Rizzini highlights the difficulties posed by the increasing trend towards English as the global language and the fact that most academic work, including journals, is published in English. This issue was raised by several interviewees and was seen to inevitably limit or prevent broader access to work from important contributors in the majority world who either cannot write in English, cannot afford to pay to have their work translated, or do not have access for financial reasons to significant journals (Christensen; Hart; James; Mayall; Prout; Rizzini; Woodhead). Consequently, a vast body of knowledge from other non-English speaking countries is overlooked. This was particularly evident for Rizzini when she was an editor for the journal *Childhood* where, for example, a lot of the submissions were 'papers about Africa but written by a UK citizen' Thomas identifies 'inequalities of access to knowledge' as an area where support of majority world scholars could be offered by 'persuading our institutions to share their library resources with universities in money-poor countries'.

In terms of the future direction of childhood research, interviewees were very clear about the need to take a more expansive view of children and childhood and move beyond the confines of North American and European research contexts. Rogers hopes that 'the digital age will open up education to people around the world' so that adults will become 'intrigued with their own culture, their own version of childhood and their own children'. She foresees this leading to a 'proliferation of new scholarship' and approaches to research that 'the field can't even imagine right now' and where the 'primarily white, western American/ European world view will come to be seen as one of many views'. In a similar vein, Kellett predicts that because of the possibilities offered by modern communications 'the extent of global content in Childhood Studies is set to increase significantly over the next decade'. A consistent theme throughout the interviews was the need to further develop and strengthen approaches to research which resonate with majority world children and childhoods, and to include and support the work of majority world scholars and contribute to the building of a robust body of knowledge about global childhoods.

In conclusion

This book prioritised high profile pioneers whose careers spanned the decades before and after the birth of Childhood Studies. In documenting the recollections, reflections, hopes and predictions of these opinion leaders there was no expectation that a single shared story of the past, an agreed assessment of the present or a single vision for the future would emerge. Rather, the aim of this volume was to capture important knowledge about this period and provide an informed base for discussions about the evolution of Childhood Studies, where it is now and the possible directions for the field in the future. Undoubtedly there are still many unresolved issues and the need for rigorous and critical analysis of childhood and children's lives will continue. A clear message to emerge from these interviews is that there are huge challenges facing children and childhood globally in the coming decades. In moving forward therefore, it will be important to both reflect upon and learn from the work of this pioneering generation of key thinkers while also trusting young scholars from around the world to find their own ways of creatively responding to the issues of their time.

References

Corsaro, W, 1985, *Friendship and peer culture in the early years,* Norwood, NJ: Ablex

Giddens, A, 1979, *Central problems in social theory, structure and contradiction in social analysis*, London: Macmillan

Hart, R, 1978, *Children's experience of place: A developmental study*, New York: Irvington Publishers (distributed by Halstead/Wiley Press)

James, A, 2010, Interdisciplinarity – for better or worse, *Children's Geographies* 8, 215–16

James, A, Prout, A (eds), [1990] 1997, *Constructing and reconstructing childhood*, London: Falmer Press

Jenks, C (ed), 1982, *The sociology of childhood: Essential readings*, London: Batsford

Jenks, C, 1990, *Childhood*, London: Routledge

Oakley, A, 2005, *The Ann Oakley reader: Gender, women and social science*, Bristol: Policy Press

Prout, A, 2005, *The future of childhood: Toward the interdisciplinary study of children* London: Routledge Falmer

Qvortrup, J, 1990, Childhood as a social phenomenon: Introduction to a series of national reports, *Eurosocial Report 36*, Vienna: European Centre

Qvortrup, J, Bardy, M, Sgritta, G, Wintersberger, H, 1994, *Childhood matters: Social theory, practice and politics*, Aldershot: Avebury Press

Qvortrup, J, Corsaro, WA, Honig, M-S (eds), 2009, *The Palgrave handbook of Childhood Studies*, London: Palgrave Macmillan

Shier, H, 2010, 'Pathways to participation' revisited: Learning from Nicaragua's child coffee-workers, in B Percy-Smith, N Thomas (eds) *A handbook of children and young people's participation*, pp 215–30, Abingdon: Routledge

Smith, DE, 1988, *The everyday world as problematic,* Milton Keynes: Open University Press

Woodhead, M, 2003, *The case for childhood studies,* Dublin: Children's Research Centre, Trinity College Dublin

Index

Page references for notes are followed by n